Traditional Korean Theatre

Studies in Korean Religions and Culture

General Editors:
> Lewis R. Lancaster
> Chai-shin Yu

TRADITIONAL KOREAN THEATRE

Translated with the Introductions
by
Oh-kon Cho

State University of New York—Brockport

ASIAN HUMANITIES PRESS
Berkeley, California

ASIAN HUMANITIES PRESS

Asian Humanities Press offers to the specialist and the general reader alike the best in new translations of major works and significant original contributions to enhance our understanding of Asian religions, cultures and thought.

UNESCO COLLECTION OF REPRESENTATIVE WORKS

Published with the agreement of the Republic of Korea. This book, translated from the Korean has been accepted in the translations collection of the United Nations Educational, Scientific and Cultural Organization (UNESCO).

1988

Asian Humanities Press
Berkeley, California

ISBN 0-89581-876-0
Library of Congress Catalog Card Number 87-71272

To my mother

Printed Korean text credits

Yangju *Pyŏlsandae:* Oral transmission by Pak Jun-sŏp and Kim Sŏng-t'ae; Recording by Yi Tu-hyŏn. Published in Han'guk kamyŏngŭk, pp. 248-274.

Hahoe *Pyŏlsin-kut:* Oral transmission by Yu Han-sang. Published in *In'gan munwhaje,* pp. 112-116.

T'ongyŏng *Ogwangdae:* Oral transmission by Jang Jae-pong and O Chŏng-tu; Recording by Yi Tu-hyŏn. Published in Han'guk kamyŏngŭk, pp. 372-377.

Suyŏng *Yayu:* Recording by Institute of the Traditional Arts, Pusan University. Published in *Han'guk ŭi minsokgŭk,* pp. 111-135.

Pongsan *T'alch'um:* Oral transmission by Kim Jin-ok and Min Ch'ŏn-sik; Recording by Yi Tu-hyŏn. Published in Han'guk kamyŏngŭk, pp. 301-325.

Kkoktu Kaksi: Published in *Chosŏn yŏngŭksa,* pp. 199-230.

Illustration credits

Figure 1, 2, 3, 4, and 5: Ministry of Culture and Information, The Republic of Korea
Figure 6: Tim Keefe

Contents

Preface

T he traditional theatre which includes various forms of mask-dance drama and puppet plays is an important cultural asset of Korea. It has a long history which stretches back several hundred years; during this time it served religious, enlightenment, and amusement purposes.

Despite its long history and early popularity, this theatre suffered a number of setbacks—almost to the point of extinction—especially from the beginning of the twentieth century to the end of World War II. These were mainly the result of poor economic conditions, the oppressive measures taken by the occupying Japanese military, and a prejudice against the native arts as the influx of foreign influence became overwhelming.

For the past fifty years, however, some notable changes have taken place for the preservation of the rapidly disappearing forms of this theatre. Since the beginning of the second quarter of the twentieth century some scholars have begun to record theatrical activities and various play scripts which had been preserved by the oral tradition. Since the end of World War II, productions of some plays have taken place. Perhaps most important of all, the government of the Republic of Korea, recognizing their importance, sanctioned the various traditional forms of theatre, and designated them as "Important Intangible Cultural Properties of the Nation."

Today no one can doubt that this theatre will be perpetuated. But, at the same time, no one expects that the traditional Korean theatre will suddenly burgeon overnight and regain its former popularity. The publication of this book will not only reinforce efforts for the preservation of this theatre but will also take it one step further by introducing it to the English-speaking world.

Recently, in addition to performances for the native audience, some groups have made presentations in the United States, Japan, and the Western European nations. The non-native spectators who had the rare opportunity of seeing these performances of Korean plays were especially tantalized by their brilliant theatricality. It is hoped that the translations included in this volume will recapture some of that vitality.

Solving the problem of choosing the plays to be included in this book was not easy. Each play exists in a variety of versions, for all had been orally preserved. In addition, there were a number of plays—some of them with few variations—from the same region. Therefore, it was decided that one representative play from each region should be included. Scripts were then selected from the different versions of the same play using readability as the main criteria. However, some degree of subjectivity was unavoidable. Considering the limitation of space, it was impossible to include all the plays which deserve to be contained in the book.

The task of translating the plays was a difficult one. Although all the translations are based on recently published texts, they were by no means in the fashion of orderly western scripts. They were loaded with difficult and rarely used poetic expressions, colloquial discourses, regional dialects, local folk songs, and obscure puns. In addition, included in the plays were many incomplete sentences as well as overly long passages. These problems necessitated some degree of editing.

Another difficult problem to be resolved was how faithful the translations should be to the originals. This was a particular challenge. Spoken dialogue in a play might be obvious to some people, but its true meaning would be hidden in the subtext. Especially, the vast range of idiosyncratic language included in the plays made an extraordinary demand on the the translator.

The translations in this volume have not adopted the extremes of colloquial dialogue often found in other translations. Although the traditional players of these plays were mostly regarded as uneducated pariahs of the time, it is important to note that—however incomplete it might be—the dialogue of the plays contained a good deal of poetry. It is also a common understanding among the students of dramatic literature that the characters in a play usually speak a more sophisticated language than that used by people of similar social standings in real life.

Most characters in the plays retain their Korean proper names, except those whose names clearly delineate their characters such as Shoe Peddler, Lion, Shaman, and Blind Man. If necessary, the literal meanings of the characters are included in the NOTES. Also provided in the NOTES are the basic movement patterns of the dances which are employed in the performance of the plays. Some unique musical instruments like *kŏmun'go, pip'a,* and *haegŭm* remain in Korean. General descriptions of the masks and costumes worn by each character are also provided in the NOTES. Whenever it is necessary to decipher the unique meanings of puns and certain terminologies, explanations are made available in the NOTES. Almost all names of the people— whether they are Koreans or Chinese—remain in Korean pronunciations as they are always pronounced in Korean when these plays are performed. Such commonly accepted names as Buddha, Confucius, and Mencius take their western pronunciations.

Because each theatre has its own history and degree of uniqueness, it is impossible to provide a general introduction. Therefore, a short introduction is provided for each theatre prior to the play.

I am deeply grateful for the general help and encouragement I have received from various institutions and individuals in the preparation of this book. The libraries of University of California at Berkeley [East Asiatic Section], Michigan State University, University of Michigan, and Ohio State University have gracefully allowed me the free use of their collections. Especially, the librarians at California have given me invaluable assistance in locating materials in my reserach from 1972 to 1973 and in the summer of 1979. My thanks also goes to Mrs. Patricia Goodlin and Professor Kenneth L. Jones who have undertaken the painful responsibility of reading the original manuscript. My gratitude is also extended to Professor Yi Tu-hyŏn, Seoul National University, who has pointed out incorrect translations of certain lines in the plays. The book is more lucid and readable because of their help. I am also thankful to Dr. Cho Yong-kyun, my nephew, who has helped me in defining some of the medical terminology in the book.

I also wish to extend my thanks to Mr. Park Bong-shik, Secretary-general of the Korean National Commission for UNESCO and Mr. Paik Syeung-gil, the editor of *Korea Journal,* who not only printed the earlier versions of the manuscript in their publications, but also initiated the idea of issuing my works in this book form. My thanks are also due to the Korean National Commission for UNESCO which offered me a grant to complete the manuscript and has undertaken the publication of the book.

I wish to express gratitude to Professors William Ross and Farley Richmond, my mentors, who have always offered me their encouragement. I also wish to express my thanks to some of my colleagues at State University of New York at Brockport who have given me their support. Lastly, I want to thank Jasoon Koo, my wife, who has offered me constant inspiration to complete the final stage of the manuscript.

Brockport, N.Y   .O.K.C.

Yangju *Pyŏlsandae*

Introduction

Origins

Like theatre in many primitive societies, Korean mask-dance drama may have originated in dance which was performed as a part of religious ceremonies in ancient times. In the context of heaven worship and reverence to the gods, the people in the ancient society of Korea performed sacrificial rites at certain times during the year. To placate the supernatural forces, people sang and danced as part of these rituals.

The "master of ceremonies" for the ritual was a male shaman. One of his functions for the occasion was to perform a dance inducing the god to descend from heaven. The shaman's simple dance gradually developed into a more complicated one until eventually it became a form of dance drama.

Among the important early ceremonial rites were *ch'ŏngun* [a ceremony for heaven worship] of Mahan,[1] *much'ŏn* [another kind of heaven worship ceremony] of Yae,[2] and *yŏnggo* [a festival which was held in the twelfth month according to the lunar calendar] of Puyŏ.[3] For these special ceremonial rites, it is presumed that some participants may have worn masks when they sang and danced.

If it is true that masks were worn by the participants in these ceremonies—although the literary documents to support this conjecture have yet to be found—the early form of mask-dance drama may have already been in existence in Korea before the period of the Three Kingdoms [18 B.C.-935 A.D.].[4] By the time of the period of Silla [57 B.C.-935 A.D.], it is believed that such dances as *kŏmmu*, a sword dance based on the story of the legendary seventh son of King Tonghaeyong, Ch'ŏyong, which contained the rude elements of drama, had definitely emerged.

These mask-dance dramas of Silla were frequently performed during the Koryŏ period [918 A.D.-1392 A.D.]. When the Koryŏ dynasty was succeeded by the Chosŏn dynasty [1392 A.D.-1910 A.D.], this new court also accepted them as important cultural assets of Korea. It was during the later period of the Koryŏ dynasty when these many different forms of dance drama finally began to coalesce into a new kind of mask-dance drama which is today commonly referred to as *sandaegŭk* [or *sandae*].[5] It is this broad category to which Yangju *pyŏlsandae* belongs.

Sandaegŭk not only contained the vestiges of many dance dramas of previous times, but it was also apparently influenced by another ceremonial ritual, *narae*, a ceremony which was performed to rid the palace of evil spirits. Although it could be performed at any time, except during summer, *narae* was generally presented on New Year's Eve in order to expel the demons and the misfortunes of the old year while welcoming the arrival of the new one. For this ceremony, the participants also wore hideous-looking masks.

Regardless of its origins, *sandaegŭk* was probably the first important form of Korean mask-dance drama. Eventually this theatre was no longer just a form of simple primitive entertainment. This development took place mainly toward the end of the Koryŏ dynasty. But it was the Chosŏn court which finally took full advantage of this theatrical form. From the beginning the rulers of the Chosŏn dynasty employed performances of this drama for the entertainment of foreign envoys, especially those from China. To oversee as well as control this theatre and other performing arts, the Chosŏn court transformed Narae-togam into the Office of Sandae-togam, the Master of Revels, requiring the players of this theatre to register.

Registration with the government did not mean that the players presented themselves to the office regularly. Rather they were allowed to form their performing groups and travel all over the country during the season when the farmers were not busy. Only when they were notified by the Office of Sandae-togam to appear at court events were they ordered to rush to perform. It appears that these performances were quite frequent and commanded a great deal of interest among the general populace until the seventeenth century.

In 1634, however, the Chosŏn court abolished the Office of Sandae-togam. As a result, the players began to settle down in various areas near the capital. Now their livelihood depended entirely upon their income from performing, although the government subsidy had never been large. In the three hundred and fifty years since then this drama gradually became a folk theatre.

When the players of *sandaegŭk* settled down in the area outside the great gates of Seoul—probably their social standing was not high enough for them to take up residence within the city walls—they started organizing their own companies independent of the government. Then they began to travel both to the capital and to the countryside. Of these early groups, the Rokpŏnni Sandae, the T'oegaewŏn Sandae, the Aeogae [or the Ahyŏn] Sandae, the Noryangjin Sandae, the Sajikkol Ttakttagip'ae were the best-known companies.

As far as the origins of the Yangju Pyŏlsandae Company are concerned, an interesting legend exists. Approximately two hundred years ago, the townspeople of Yangju—located roughly fifteen miles northeast of Seoul—began to invite the Sajikkol Ttakttagip'ae to perform *sandaegŭk* on the eighth day of the fourth month, Buddha's birthday, and the fifth day of the fifth month, the Tano Festival, according to the lunar calendar. But this group frequently missed their engagement with Yangju due to their heavy travel schedule, an indication of their popularity at that time. Disturbed when no players appeared for the scheduled performance, some petty town officials and villagers got together and began to make their own masks, imitating those of the Sajikkol Ttakttagip'ae. Then they tried performing their own *sandaegŭk*. The result was an unexpected success. Ever since then, the townspeople have performed this mask-dance drama, which is now called Yangju *pyŏlsandae*. [6]

All of the original groups have long since disappeared. When we talk about *sandaegŭk*, therefore, it is generally identified with the which is performed at Yangju today. For convenience's sake, however, the theatre at Yangju has been differentiated by giving it a new name; this theatre is commonly called Yangju *pyŏlsandae*, a different *sandae*, while the theatre of the original groups is referred to as *ponsandae*, the original *sandae*.

Today it is difficult to determine the differences and similarities between *ponsandae* and *pyŏlsandae* because, as has been mentioned, all the groups which performed the former have long since vanished without leaving any literary documents. But it is assumed that they were substantially similar, since Yangju *pyŏlsandae* was subsequently modeled on one of the original groups.

Players and Stage

Historically the players of *sandaegŭk*, who were often referred to as *p'yŏnnom*, or pariahs, lived and worked on the outskirts of the capital city. A record suggests that they were called upon to perform by the court for such occasions as the arrival of foreign envoys, the ceremony to rid the palace of evil spirits, the return of rulers to the palace, a shamanistic service to pray for rain, and other courtly events. For this service, the players were provided with cloth and grain by the government.

Even after the Office of Sandae-togam was abolished, the players were still frequently called upon to perform at the palace until the beginning of the eighteenth century. To increase their meager livelihood, the government issued them certificates enabling them to solicit for contributions. For this purpose, they were given two types of authorization by the court according to the seasons; in the spring the document was sealed with the picture of a cicada, while in the autumn the seal of a tiger was used. With these certificates, the players of *sandaegŭk* could solicit money and grain usually at a ferry, a market, or a temple.

Traditionally the players of *sandaegŭk* organized a guild, *tojung,* which was usually made up of eleven male members. In the group there were three types of memberships: *yŏngwi, chusŏk,* and *osang.* In the category of *yŏngwi,* there were four members who generally played the roles of Nojang, Somu, Sinharabi, and Saennim. Two *chusŏk* played the roles of Yŏnip and Nunkkŭmjŏki, while five *osang* performed the roles of Wanpo, Om, Mŏkchung, and others. In the group, the eldest, who generally played the role of Wanpo, took the leadership of the company.[7] But the role assignments were never permanently fixed; they rotated frequently according to one's acting, dancing, and singing ability.

In the instance of Yangju *pyŏlsandae*, the players were originally unpaid petty town officials whose professions were hereditary. They belonged to a low social strata. Generally these people engaged in farming, but undertook the responsibilities of lowly government offices or the performance of this drama whenever it was necessary.

Prior to the performance, the players of Yangju *pyŏlsandae* were required to offer a sacrificial rite to the spirits. This was performed by the entire group in the costume hall, *kaepokch'ŏng*. The offerings included the wine used in propitiatory service, three kinds of rice cake, three kinds of fruit, dried pollacks, cooked pig's feet, and a cooked cow head. All the masks were arranged behind the sacrificial table. Then the representative of the group would pour a bowl of the wine and bow. After this, he recited the following ode to the masks: "*Yusaech'a*[8] . . . [year] . . . [month] . . . [day].[9] With the preparation of all sorts of offerings, we have invited everyone to the place of the guardian deities to perform a sacrificial ceremony . . ." The main purpose of this sacrificial rite was two-fold: first, to ensure the safety of the performers and the audience; second, to expel the evil spirits from the village.

As soon as the sacrificial offerings were over, all of the players began to eat the food and drink the wine which had been offered to the spirits. When they began to feel tipsy from the effects of wine, the players would begin to perform.

Every year a number of performances took place at Yangju: on Buddha's birthday, the Tano Festival, and the Autumn Harvest Festival. Of these, the one which was performed on Buddha's birthday, which was called *kwandŭngnori*, the lantern festival, was the most splendid. For this performance, the entire village was lit with colorful lanterns of every size and shape. Then the performance of this drama, by the illumination of a bonfire, took place about ten o'clock in the evening, and lasted until dawn. However, performances of this drama have taken place during the daytime recently.

Probably until the time when the Office of Sandae-togam was

abolished there was a tall stage, whose exact dimensions and structure are unknown today, where *sandaegŭk* was performed. When the official sanction was rescinded, however, this drama began to be performed on an open area stage. The open area stage, used for performances at Yangju, could be set up in the following simple manner. The costume hall, for instance, was installed on one side of an open field—usually at the foot of a hill—while the musicians took their positions at one end of the circular playground. Then the audience either stood or sat, facing the musicians, across the playground. The dimensions of the stage area had to be large enough to accommodate a variety of dances since the performance of this drama depended heavily upon them. The size of the costume hall was approximately sixteen by sixteen feet and was enclosed with muslin. There were generally two doors, facing the stage, through which the players frequently made their entrances and exits, but not always. Sometimes they entered onto the playing area from the musicians' side. Neither a curtain nor an artificial scenic background was necessary for the performance. To indicate a change of scene a break in the action of a few minutes was all that was required.

Masks

P resently all the masks of Yangju *pyŏlsandae* are made from dried gourds with the addition of other materials such as paper, wood, and pine bark. Records suggest that wooden and paper masks were also used during the Chosŏn dynasty. It is said that none of the original Yangju *pyŏlsandae* masks survived from which new masks could be modeled. Rather these were created out of the mask maker's memory of earlier masks.

The masks were usually made by a skilled player or by a cabinet maker. First, a dried gourd was selected. Second, the holes for eyes and mouth were carved out of the gourd with a sharp knife. This procedure was followed by the addition of a nose and eyebrows which were glued onto the face of the mask. Then several layers of paper were glued onto it. When the paper dried, the mask was painted the appropriate color with the addition of a beard when necessary.

Around the edge of the mask a cloth called *t'alpo* was attached, this covered the back of the head, and tied the mask around the wearer's neck. Before putting on the mask, the player had to place a towel around his forehead to leave a space between the mask and face, thus making it easy for him to breath, speak, and sing. Otherwise, the mask could easily hurt the player's face.

All masks of Yangju *pyŏlsandae* had a static expression with the exception of Nunkkŭmjŏki. The eyes of this mask could blink by means of the player pushing a wire looped to the brass eyelids with his tongue. Whenever a new mask was made, a sacrificial offering had to be performed. In addition, we are told that when the company was invited to play at another village, a similar prayer, with the display of the masks, was performed in front of the village's guardian deity tree before they embarked on their tour. Of all the masks of Yangju *pyŏlsandae,* those of Yŏnip and Nunkkŭmjŏki are supposed to be the oldest. For this reason, they are regarded as the most sacred by the players. Probably for this reason, these two masks are usually placed in the center during the sacrificial offerings. Furthermore, these two roles are generally played by the experienced players who belong to the rank of *chusŏk* [which literally means the main seat].

There are thirty-two roles in Yangju *pyŏlsandae.* But only twenty-two masks are used for its performance. Consequently, the beginning student of this drama might be confused by the double and even triple casting. A mask which the audience has identified with a particular character in a previous scene may appear in a different role in the next scene. For instance, there is no mask for Shoettugi in Act VII, Scene 3. Therefore this character must make his entrance wearing the Ch'wipali mask. Another example is the case of Shoe Peddler in Act VI, Scene 2, and Toki in Act VIII. Both players of these roles must play in the Malttugi mask, the servant of Saennim, thus creating further confusion for the uninitiated audience. [10]

Dance, Music, and Musical Instruments

Like many other traditional forms of Korean mask-dance drama, dance which is more elegant and beautiful than that of Pongsan *t'alch'um*[11] or T'ongyŏng *ogwangdae*[12] is one of the important elements of this drama. Frequently, a scene employs only dance, without a single line of dialogue. Such roles as Sangjwa, Waejangnyŏ, Monkey, Yŏnip, and Nunkkŭmjŏki do not have spoken lines, only dance and mime gestures. The other roles which do require dialogue also demand a great deal of dancing. The performance of this drama, therefore, varies depending upon the dancing skills and interpretative abilities of the performers. For example, *hapchang-chaebae*, clasping of hands accompanied by a double bow, by Sangjwa could take as long as fifteen minutes.[13]

In Yangju *pyŏlsandae*, almost all the basic Korean mask-dance forms can be found. Of these, some dances which are frequently employed are *yŏdaji*-dance, *kopsawi*-dance, *kkaeki*-dance, *mŏngsŏk-mari*-dance, and *samjin-samt'oe*-dance.[14]

The accompanying music or rhythmic pattern for the performance of Yangju *pyŏlsandae* is a slow *yŏmbul*, a rhythmic *t'aryŏng,* or a flowing tune of *kutkŏri.*

The songs which are included in Yangju *pyŏlsandae* are mostly derived from the folk songs and the shamanistic ravings of the Chosŏn period. For example, "The Moon Song" and "The Song of the White Sea Gull" are folk songs, while the one chanted by Tokki's Sister in Act VIII is derived from a shamanistic raving for the deceased soul. The songs, which frequently serve as cues to the musicians to beat out a particular rhythmic pattern, are often intermixed with dance and dialogue. Probably due to the fact that this drama has been preserved orally, the lyrics of these songs are frequently altered in a subsequent scene or never sung completely to the end. Often the contents of the song, curiously enough, have no bearing on the plot or subject of the scene at all.

For the music, six instruments are employed. These are referred to as *samhyŏn-yukkak.* They are: one *chŏtdae* [transverse flute], two *p'iri*

[fife], one *haegŭm* [two-stringed Korean fiddle], one *changgo* [hour-glass-shaped drum], and one *puk* [barrel drum]. In addition, one *kkwaenggwari* [small gong] and other instruments may be added.

The Play

Originally there was no written play script from which the player could perform *sandaegŭk*. Hence we neither know who created the script, nor the exact time of its inception. It is assumed that at the beginning a rough synopsis of plots depended heavily upon the intuitive spontaneity of the players not only in terms of the dialogue but also for the songs and dances. Presumably throughout its history, more dramatic stories, dialogue, songs, and dances were added until it developed into what it is today. This drama was finally written down during the second quarter of the twentieth century.

The dramatic structure of Yangju *pyŏlsandae* is totally devoid of organic structure. Nowhere is there a strong plot line. The play consists of a series of episodes which can be disjoined and rearranged without damaging the play as a whole. For example, Act I is concerned with Sangjwa, a monk, while Act II is an exchange of nonsensical dialogue betwee Om and Mŏkchung. The transgression of the Buddhist monk is the subject of Act V, Scene I. Any of these could be transposed.

Another intriguing characteristic of Yangju *pyŏlsandae* is the appearance and disappearance of characters. Some characters are introduced in certain scenes and never appear again. Yŏnip and Nunkkŭmjŏki, for instance, whose masks have been regarded as quite important by some scholars, appear only in Act V.

The play appears to be unconcerned with organic plot development, careful preparation, logical cause and effect, suspense, or climax; instead, the displaying of many different topical subjects and ideas is the main concern in each scene. But the play achieves its appeals through humor, ideas, and spectacle.

The language of Yangju *pyŏlsandae* can be somewhat differentiated from that of Pongsan *t'alch'um* which is full of poetry and songs.
This drama contains more crude words which are typically colloquial. It
appears that this type of anti-literary, prosaic language easily persuades
an audience to look squarely at something and observe it for what it
really is. With the use of very descriptive language, the anonymous
playwright attempts to unmask someone; in this case, people of the
corrupt privileged class. Despite the fact that the literary value of this
drama may not be very highly regarded, the language appears to serve
its purpose, that is to entertain, communicate, and satirize.

In the play, descriptive and down-to-earth language is abundant.
For example, "he had died of love sickness after extreme masturbation
with a thousand clams" or "I must make you lie down on your stomach
to perform sodomy with you." The language of this type also appears
to be perfectly spontaneous without a logical structure; it is marked by
a constant variety of tone and shift of subject matter. If one of the
important aims of this drama is to stimulate pleasure derived from the
shocking quality of the language, the dialogue precisely serves this
purpose with the utilization of callous and crude slang and taboo
expressions.

The use of puns in this play is also abundant. In Act III, for
example, when the hungry Mŏkchung asks Om what he is wearing on
his head, the latter answers that he does not owe anything to anyone.
The word "wear" [*tsuda*] has the same sound as the word "use" in
Korean. Hence, he means that he has not borrowed anything from
Mŏkchung.

In Yangju *pyŏlsandae*, three types of privileged class people
become the major targets of satire: The corrupt local official, the
apostate Buddhist monks, and the degenerate aristocrats. The elements
of satire in the play may have offered the audience an opportunity to
witness the humiliation of the privileged class people. In addition,
this drama may also have provided a fresh perspective on the life style
of a certain group of people. For example, in Act VII, Scene 2, the
moral turpitude of a local police chief is exposed when, mesmerized by
Somu, a sorceress-concubine of Saennim, he steals her from her old,

weak bedmate. The scene vividly illustrates the despotic character that was typical of many contemporary local officials of the time during which this drama was popular.

Another important subject of comic satire in this drama concerns the corruption of Buddhist monks. During the Koryŏ period, the corruption of Buddhism, the national religion, was wide spread. Some corrupt monks participated in national politics, *e.g.,* Myoch'ŏng and Sin Ton,[15] and, contrary to Buddhist tenets, some monks engaged in carnal pleasures. Under the circumstances, it is little wonder that the moral failings of the monks became the object of mockery in this play.

Nojang, a high monk who exposes his own corrupt side, becomes the subject of ridicule in Act VI, Scene 1. He not only dances as he runs between the two young sorceresses, but he also pantomimes plucking and eating the girls' mouths and underarms. In Act VI, Scene 3, he is again an object of ridicule. This time for his epicurism. He has engaged in lascivious intemperance with the girls. He is further mocked when he sticks his head out from under the girl's skirt, implying an act of copulation. The high monk who is expected to dedicate himself to spiritual enlightenment has exposed himself to profanity. Worst of all, he has indulged his sexual desires.

The aristocrats, *yangban,* are another popular target of derision in this drama. During the time when this drama was taking shape, the monopoly of power and privilege enjoyed by the *yangban* was almost absolute. The doors of education and the civil service examinations, for example, were open only to the children of this privileged class. The result was the creation of an elite class above the vast majority of the populace. Consequently, the lives and destiny of the nation's population were determined by this small group of nobles.

In Act VII, Scene 1, the three members of a *yangban* family have become somewhat infatuated with the idea of sight-seeing on their way to take their civil service examination. When the day is almost over, their servant finds them temporary lodging in a pigpen, an obvious reference to his opinion of the aristocrats and an attempt to literally reduce them to the level of pigs. The *yangban* are further ridiculed when one of them resorts to low language and proves to be no different from his servant in terms of choice of language or personal behavior. It is further revealed by the servant that the aristocrat's mother had behaved like any common woman, having had an affair with her servant. Thus the scene suggests that the aristocrats, too, talk and behave like ordinary people.

Notes

1. Mahan. A tribal state which ruled the southwestern portion of the Korean peninsula roughly from the fourth or third century B.C. to the third century A.D.

2. Yae. A tribal state which dominated the people on the eastern coast of the Korean peninsula for approximately the same period as Mahan.

3. Puyŏ. An ancient tribal state which ruled present-day Manchuria from roughly the thirteenth century B.C. to the third century A.D.

4. This includes the kingdoms of Koguryŏ [37 B.C.-668 A.D.], Paekje [18 B.C.-660 A.D.], and Silla [57 B.C.-935 A.D.].

5. Yangju *pyŏlsandae* belongs to the general category of *sandaegŭk*, although the exact form of the latter is unknown. These two terms, however, are to some degree interchangeable.

6. Quoted in Yi Tu-hyŏn's *Han'guk kamyŏngŭk*, p. 205.

7. Ch'oe Sang-su, "Sandae kamyŏngŭk ŭi yŏngu," *Haksulji*, Vol. V. [1964], pp. 4-5.

8. The beginning of the first sentence of an ode in Korean.

9. The day, month, and year when this play is performed.

10. For detailed descriptions of each mask, see the Notes of the translation of the play.

11. A form of mask-dance drama from Pongsan, Hwanghae-do Province, presently a part of North Korea.

12. Another form of mask-dance drama from T'ongyŏng, South Kyŏngsang-do Province.

13. Yi Tu-hyŏn, p. 212.

14. The basic movement patterns of each dance in this drama are provided in the Notes of the translation of the play.

15. During the reign of Inchong [1123 A.D.-1146 A.D.] of Koryŏ, Myoch'ŏng, a monk, resorted to outright rebellion when he found that his attempt at intrigue as to the transfer of the capital to P'yŏngyang from Kaesŏng was unsuccessful, proclaiming a new kingdom called Taewi in 1135.

When Sin Ton, whose original name was P'yŏncho, an obscure monk, was selected and elevated to the highest clerical post, *kuksa,* by King Kongmin [1351 A.D.-1374 A.D.] of Koryŏ to carry out an important land reform he not only furthered his private fortune, but also managed to have carnal relationships with numerous women against the Buddhist tenets.

The Play

Procession

[For the performance, the villagers take out the properties and other necessary things from the Sajik-tang.[1]

The procession takes place from the village square to the playground where this play is performed.

Wanpo[2] and Omchung[3] with a long rectangular flag (*yŏnggi*) stand in front of the procession.

Then one of the Mŏkchung[4] and Malttugi[5] with a club stand behind them.

The musicians, playing their instruments, follow them. The small orchestra is made up of six musical instruments,[6] plus a *hojŏk* (Korean oboe), a *kkwaenggwari* (small gong), and a *ching* (large gong).

Nojang,[7] two Somu,[8] and Ch'wipali[9] stand behind them.

Next come the villagers who help with the performance of the play, as well as with other village affairs, and the spectators follow last.

When they pass by the houses of patrons they let the flag stand and stop the procession to collect either money or rice for the performance.

To defray expenses, rent is also taken from the merchants who set up stands in the area for this special occasion.

The other performers and sponsors, who are already at the playground, prepare the costumes in the *kaepokch'ŏng* (costume hall), as well as offerings for the deities.

When the procession arrives at the playground, Nojang and Somu enter into the costume hall, while the rest of the players dance.

Now the rest of the players go to the costume hall and change their costumes before participating in the sacrificial offerings.]

The Offerings

[Prior to the offerings, all masks are arranged behind the sacrificial table.

Of the twenty-two masks, the Sinharabi mask and the Miyalhalmi mask must be placed at the seat of honor along with Yŏnip, Nojang, and Nunkkŭmjŏki. The rest of them are arranged according to the order of appearance.

On the sacrificial table, there are a jar of propitiatory wine, an ox head (or a pig's head), pig feet (or a whole pig), rice cakes, egg-coated shish kebabs, pears, apples, chestnuts, cakes seasoned with sesame seeds, pine nuts, beans, a shad, slices of dried beef, and dried pollack. A sheet of sacrificial paper to be burned completes the list.]

The Recitation of Sacrificial Offerings

"*Yusaech'a.*[10] . . year . . . month . . . day.[11] With the preparation of all sorts of offerings, we have invited everyone to the place of the guardian deities in order to perform a sacrificial ceremony. Please eat and drink before you return to your home. We are offering you a chalice of humble wine with a dried pollack. We pray for the safe return of Teacher Ko, Teacher Yu, and Teacher Chang."

[Now in a singsong tone.]

Every different individual,
And every person with a different name,
Including grown-ups, children, and old people,
Please return to their homes safely
After the performance of this play.
So please help us!

Act I
The Sangjwa Dance

[Sangjwa I [12] walks to the center of the playground from the costume hall. He wears white full-dress over armour, red belt, and peaked monk's cowl. He now walks in quick short steps toward the musicians, who generally face south, and stops about ten feet from them.

The musicians play the tune of *yŏmbul.* [13] Now Sangjwa I bows twice putting his hands together as he dances *kŭtŭrŭm*-dance [14] to the tune of the music.

He now dances *sapangch'igi*-dance [15] turning around to face the four directions, lifting his full-dress over his head. When he faces each direction he bows twice.

He then goes in front of the musicians and takes off his full-dress. When he claps his hands as if signaling, the musicians play the tune of *t'aryŏng.* [16] To the music, he dances *kkaeki*-dance. [17] Then he stops in front of the musicians to rest.

(Sangjwa II also dances *kŭtŭrŭm*-dance and *p'alttukchapi*-dance [18] to the tune of *t'aryŏng.* He finally dances *kkaeki*-dance. But recently the role of Sangjwa II has been eliminated from this scene.)]

Act II
Omchung and Sangjwa

Om [19]: [He runs onto the playground from the costume hall. Then he stands defiantly, his hands on his hips.] I haven't been to this damn place for many years. Now everything makes my legs shake. The world has also become so chaotic and topsy-turvy. [He beats the ground with his stick.]

Sangjwa: [He jumps up in front of the costume hall where he has been resting. Then he snatches the stick away from Om.]

Om: [Surprised. As he whirls his sleeves.] Thief! You thief with a pale skeletal face! You've always been talented in stealing. If I could find an iron stick when you snatch away my wooden stick, things could go pretty bad with you. Just like when a mystical creature[20] appeared during the last year of Songto era.[21] [He walks around as he plays his small cymbals.] Oh, . . . You damn fellow. Look! You behave as if you've done the right thing. You've been stealing. Besides, you've beaten me. You fool! Have you finished your hysterical rampage?

Sangjwa: [He claps his hand to signal the musicians to play a tune of *t'aryŏng*. Then he begins to dance to induce Om to join him.]

Om: Hey! You have extra *ch'a, p'o,* and *ojol.*[22] You devilish fool. [He begins to dance with Sangjwa. One loud strike of an hourglass-shaped drum.] You aren't an ordinary fellow. [He strikes Sangjwa with his sleeve. Sangjwa retreats to his original place.]

    Chŏlsu chŏlsu chihwaja chalulu.[23]

    . . .

[He dances *kŭtŭrŭm*-dance. Then he signals the musicians to play a tune of *t'aryŏng* to which he dances *kkaeki*-dance. Now he goes to Sangjwa to rest.]

Act III
Mŏkchung and Omchung

Mŏkchung: [He strides about five or six steps towards the center of the playground. Then he stands, his legs wide, and his hands on his hips.] Hey, hey, you! I haven't been out here many months. So I feel both the upper and lower parts of my body shaky. I feel rather droopy. Well. That isn't right. Let me practice my old pestering. [He spreads the end of his full-dress over his head. Then he makes the sound of a cow mooing.] *O-o-u! O-o-u-! O-!*

Om: [He stands up quickly and strikes Mŏkchung's face.]

Mŏkchung: [Shocked. He turns around whirling his wide sleeves in an expression of pain.] Ouch! What is it? Who is this fellow who beats me like a thunderbolt? I haven't even seen him.

Om: You didn't even see me. Damn fool! Why do you have to come to someone else's playground, crying "*O-o-u-a-a*" like a mooing calf on the green pasture during the summer months? What kind of noise is that?

Mŏkchung: What kind of talk is that? I didn't say I just made my entrance into the world out of my mother's womb. I said I just now made my first entrance onto the playground. I mean this is my first time here.

Om: I . . . see. This couldn't be your first time out of your mother's womb. You mean this is the first time you've come to the playground. Isn't that right?

Mŏkchung: That's right.

Om: That's nice.

Mŏkchung: My goodness. It's someone else's. . .

Om: [He strikes Mŏkchung and runs away.]

Mŏkchung: Damn fool! He has beaten me and suddenly disappeared, . . . They say "even a grub worm wiggles when it is stepped over." He has beaten me. I haven't committed any crime. I must catch him. Otherwise, I will be indignant. I wonder in which cave he is hiding. [He finds Om among the audience. As he holds Om's old hat, he turns him now this way, now that way.] You son of a bitch! I'm glad I've found you.

Om: Why is that so?

Mŏkchung: What? "Why is that so?" Don't you remember what you did to me? You son of a bitch! *Anaiyaae*.[24]

Om: *Anayayi!*

Mŏkchung: What are you wearing on your head?

Om: You fool. I didn't borrow anything from you to use.²⁵ Did I use a daily loan? Or a monthly loan?

Mŏkchung: Wait a minute. What are you talking about? What are you wearing on your head?

Om: [As he feels Mŏkchung's head.] Let me see your skull. Oh my goodness. I don't think you've ever been to the city gate where laborers gather daily to do all kinds of miscellaneous work. Had you ever been to the gate, you must have had at least a felt hat.²⁶ Even a palanquin driver wears a felt hat. You're running around with a bare topknot. You must be a woodcutter.

Mŏkchung: What is that which is fluttering on your head?

Om: When you find out, you'll be swooned.

Mŏkchung: It doesn't matter whether or not I'm swooned. I want to know.

Om: Really?

Mŏkchung: Yes, I must.

Om: Really? Well, . . . U-o—.

Mŏkchung: You fool. Only the calf during the summer months moos while she grazes on the river bank. Why do you have to moo like a calf in front of so many people? . . . What is that which flutters on your head?

Om: The thing which flutters? That's a flower given to an envoy from a great country by the emperor.

Mŏkchung: Ha, ha, ha! A flower given by an emperor? You must be an absurd fool. Because you're wearing it, it must be an absurd thing. Hey! Is it a flower given to you by the emperor? You fool! Couldn't he find anyone else's skull to put it on?

Om: This is an imperial gift. An imperial gift!

Mŏkchung: An imperial gift?

Om: Well, let me tell you . . .

Mŏkchung: What do you call that round thing on your head?

Om: It's a brooch for the hair. It's called *o'knu*.

Mŏkchung: A white heron?[27] Do you mean the white heron which eats cranes?

Om: No, that's an *o'kno*, not *o'knu*.

Mŏkchung: *Yo! Ch'ul!*[28]

Om: *Yu!*

Mŏkchung: Oh! You're praising yourself as high as the sky. Anyway, what's that which you're wearing on your head? I want to know everything.

Om: Well, if you find out, you'll be swooned.

Mŏkchung: It doesn't matter whether or not I'm swooned. I want to know.

Om: When you find it out, you'll get mad and lose your head.

Mŏkchung: It doesn't matter whether I get mad and lose my head. I want to find out.

Om: Do you really want to find out?

Mŏkchung: Yes, exactly.

Om: It has many names.

Mŏkchung: If it has many names, there must be many different kinds of it.

Om: Of course.

Mŏkchung: Well, tell me.

Om: This is called a broomcorn cake made with roughly ground milo by an old granny who lives by the bell house. This is also called a lentil pancake with roughly chopped outer leaves of cabbage. Or this is called an old felt hat, too.

Mŏkchung: It has many names. . . three. But I don't need one of them at all. I only need two. I haven't had my breakfast for many days. I'm very hungry. I must eat a lentil pancake and a broomcorn cake. *Ututuk!* [He pantomimes eating Om's headgear as he holds it.]

Om: You son of a bitch. You must be crazy. How on earth can you eat my hat?

Mŏkchung: Did you say it was your hat? I thought you said it was a lentil pancake or broomcorn cake. So I ate it. I was hungry.

Om: I see. You tried to eat it thinking it was a broomcorn cake or a lentil pancake.

Mŏkchung: Exactly! *Ot! Chung!*

Om: You stupid imbecile. The width of your face is a foot and a half. But its height is a foot and six inches. I'm not sure whether your face is upside down or made wrong. I must measure it. He tries to measure Mŏkchung's face with his palm.]

Mŏkchung: You devilish fool! Do you have to measure my face? Were you born of the yardstick-worms' wedlock?

Om: The yardstick-worm? It isn't the only one who measures things. I think your face is extremely strange. So I want to measure it.

Mŏkchung: [He feels Om's face. In a singsong tone.]

> *Anyway,*
> *Why is your face so bumpy, rotten,*
> *And yellowish as well as bluish?*

Om: My face is yellowish, bluish, and whitish? Is that a question?

Mŏkchung: That's right.

Om: Well, . . . *Ua——*. When the Goddess of Smallpox[29] from the south was looking for a manly man, she sat on the throne on my face.

Mŏkchung: [Strikes Om's face.] You fool! What absurd talk! Did you say the Goddess of Smallpox sat on your face?

Om: Hey. What kind of talk is that? You don't know the reason. The Goddess of Smallpox doesn't discriminate between an aristocrat and a plebeian.

Mŏkchung: I see. You're saying she sits on everyone's face in every street and corner throughout the country. But how was it possible that she sat on your cow-dung-like face?

Om: Well, . . . Let me tell you. . .

Mŏkchung: Well, . . . monk!

Om: Yes?

Mŏkchung: [Feeling Om's face with his hand.] My goodness. You fool. You have a severe case of scabies. But you're saying that it was the Goddess of Smallpox paid a visit to your face, or it was an imperial gift, or it was a jade hair brooch. What nonsense! You have a real sticky case of scabies. [He scratches his body up and down.] Oh, I'm itching! I'm itching!

Om: You imbecile. You're saying nonsense about my face. It's nothing more than a foolish thing like a pig which tries to stop a gushing spring with a stick while pushing it up and down. Are you saying I've a case of scabies? Hey, monk. Look!

Mŏkchung: Yes.

Om: [Exasperated. He rolls up his sleeves. He is ready to fight.] I have what? What did you say?

Mŏkchung: A case of scabies.

Om: What? A case of scabies?

Mŏkchung: Oh, my. . . Let's stop it. You're going to eat me alive, are you? You don't have scabies. Not only that, your face looks as smooth and glossy as though it were planed. Let's stop fighting.

Om: How about that? You fool. The scabies on my face are as rough as silica sand. But you're now saying that it is smooth and glossy as if planed. Besides, . . .

Mŏkchung: Well, I've never seen a wicked fellow like you. I feel like I've met a most vicious thief today. What bad luck! You haven't finished your hysterical rampage, have you?

Om: Who the hell is it who does an hysterical rampage? [In a singsong tone.]

I've heard about
The beauty of Kŭmkang-san Mountain
. . .

Ttŏngkitŭk kkungkitŭk.

[He now begins to dance *p'alttukchapi*-dance, *kkaeki*-dance, *yŏdaji*-dance,[30] *kopsawi*-dance,[31] and *mŏngsŏkmari*-dance[32] to the tune of *t'aryŏng.*]

Mŏkchung: [Elated. At the beginning, he only sways his hips while moving his shoulders. Then he starts to dance with Om.]

Om: [He teases Mŏkchung as he dances *hŏrijapi*-dance,[33] swaying his hips and shaking his head. Mŏkchung strikes him. Om runs away into the costume hall.]

Mŏkchung: Ah, . . . Ha! What an absurd fellow! He has terrible scabies on his face. But he babbles on about me saying I was totally nonsensical. Oh, my. What bad luck! Now shall I do my customary epileptic fit? Here I come. . .

[Two strikes of an hourglass-shaped drum.]

Damn you! You aren't a simple fool.

[In a *pullim.*[34]]

Chŏlsu chŏlsu chihwachocha.
Chŏruru ttŏng ttŏng.
Kkung ttŏng kkung.
[To the tune of *yŏmbul,* he begins to dance *sapangch'igi*-dance,

p'alttukchapi-dance, *samjin-samt'oe*-dance,[35] *nalgaep'yŏgi*-dance.[36] Now he dances *kkaeki*-dance, *kopsawi*-dance, and *mŏngsŏkmari*-dance to the tune of *t'aryŏng*. Then he walks to the musicians, takes off his full-dress, and rests.]

[Now Mŏkchung II, III, and IV also dance *kkaeki*-dance in order. Then they go to the musician to rest.]

Act IV
Yŏnip and Nunkkŭmjŏki

[Yŏnip[37] enters, covering his face with his fan, followed by Nunkkŭmjŏki[38] who shields his face with his wide sleeve. When they enter onto the playground a few steps from the musicians, all the Mŏkchung, who also make their entrance in front of the orchestra, form a semi-circle, except Om who stands alone.]

Om: [He turns and looks at Yŏnip. Then he signals the musicians to play accompanying music. He sings.]

Oh, the moon, the moon, the moon,
Where Yi T'ae-paek had great fun.

Ttŏng ttŏng ttŏngkitŏk.
Ttŏng ttŏng ttŏngtŏk.

[As he dances to the tune, he slowly approaches Yŏnip and peeps into his face.] Ah. Dear me! He looks horrible. [Horrified. He runs away to the spot in front of the musicians where he was before and sits down.]

Mŏkchung: Look! He has not only swooned, but is almost dead. I wonder what is up there? A manly man like me shouldn't be afraid of anything. They say "injustice cannot win justice." So I'm afraid. He is a fool who can have a fit while he is dreaming. See how I, a *yangban*,[39] can go and see that fellow. I won't be frightened at all.

[In a singsong tone.]

The mottled bamboo stick
With twelve joints from Sosang,[40]
I clasp it...
And...

Ttŏngtŏkttŏk kkungtŏk ttŏngttŏng.
Ttŏngkutŏk nilriri nilriri nilriri.

[When he sees Nunkkŭmjŏki, he is frightened. He begins to dance to the tune of *t'aryŏng* as he retreats in front of the musicians. He sits down. All the Mŏkchung go and look at Yŏnip and Nunkkŭmjŏki in order. They all retreat in front of the musicians and sit down.]

Yŏnip: [To the tune of *yŏmbul,* he dances a fan-dance at center stage.]

Nunkkŭmjŏki: [He chases all the Mŏkchung. As he dances, he circles Yŏnip twice. He exits to the costume hall.]

Yŏnip: [To the tune of *t'aryŏng,* he dances *p'alttukchapi*-dance, *kkaeki*-dance, and *mŏngsŏkmari*-dance. He exits to the costume hall.]

Act V
Scene 1: Buddhist Invocation

[Wanpo enters from the costume hall as he dances *kkaeki*-dance, and goes to all the Mŏkchung who stand in front of the musicians. There are supposed to be eight monks: they include two Sangjwa, four Mŏkchung, Om, and Wanpo. (There is a theory that the monk with a hat is included among the four Mŏkchung, while another theory says Wanpo and the monk with a hat are identical characters.) Regardless, they are generally called Eight Mŏks.[41]]

Wanpo: [He slings a small gong on his hip. He goes toward all the Mŏkchung.] What are all of you?

Mŏkchung I: We're all monks. [All the Mŏkchung form a semi-circle as they stand, facing the musicians.]

Wanpo: If you're monks, you should be praying for Buddha. What are you doing in the mundane world?

Mŏkchung I: That isn't right. Outwardly, we look like monks. But deep in our minds, we're nothing more than libertines. We frequent the whorehouse, too. Didn't you know that?

Wanpo: I see. You look like monks. But naturally you're libertines.

Mŏkchung I: That's right.

Wanpo: If so, you must know how to sing a song.

Mŏkchung I: Of course, we do.

Wanpo: Because you're monks, you must start with a Buddhist invocation.

Mŏkchung I: Let's pray to Buddha.

All: [In a chorus.]

> *Namuamit'abul.*[42]
> *Namuhalmit'abul.*[43]
> *Namuŏmit'abul.*[44]

Mŏkchung I: *Namuhalmit'abul.*

Wanpo: Yes, yes, yes!

Mŏkchung I: Why? What is it?

Wanpo: What the hell are you saying?

Mŏkchung I: I just repeated what you said.

Wanpo: Because I was a monk, I said *namuŏmit'abul.*[45] But you were saying *namuhalmit'abul.*[46] Aren't you trying to contradict Buddhism.

Mŏkchung I: You don't know what you're saying. Because you're one generation lower than me, you've said *namuŏmit'abul.* But I've said *namuhalmit'abul.*[47]

Wanpo: I see. You're one generation higher than me.

Mŏkchung I: You fool. That's right.

Wanpo: Am I one generation lower than you?

Mŏkchung I: Right.

Wanpo: Hey. You shouldn't say that. We're all monks. We must do the same thing. Join us when we say *namuŏmit'abul?*

Mŏkchung I: Should I join you?

Wanpo: Well, let me tell you something. . .

Mŏkchung I: No, I don't want to join you. I don't want to lower myself.

Wanpo: No, that isn't right. That shouldn't be said in that way.

Mŏkchung I: Then let me hear it.

All:

> *Namuŏmit'abul.*
> *Namuabit'abul.*
> *Namuŏmit'abul.*
> *Namuabit'abul.*

Mŏkchung I: Hey. It sounds good.

Wanpo: Of course. There is no question about it. It should be said in this way. Because we pretend to be monks, we've prayed to Buddha. But we're all libertines. Let's sing a song! What do you think?

Mŏkchung I: Well, we've learned them all. Let's try it.

All Mŏkchung: [In a singsong tone.]

> *When half of the maple leaves*
> *Change their color*
> *Then blue is the stream and the river.*
>
> *In every valley,*
> *There're maples.*

In every field,
There're wild chrysanthemums.

Mŏkchung I: Hey. What do you think? Isn't it fantastic?

Wanpo: That's good. Outwardly, we look like monks. But we're all libertines.

Mŏkchung I: Yes, that's right.

Wanpo: *Yae, yae, yae.*

Mŏkchung I: *Kuryae.*[48]

Wanpo: That isn't right for us. We also know the old song about the sea gull. Let's sing it.

Mŏkchung I: Of course, you're right.

All: [Wanpo plays his small gong. They sing.]

> *You, the white sea gull,*
> *Don't fly away,*
> *Flapping your wings.*
> *I'm not here to catch you.*
>
> *His Majesty has deserted me.*
> *So, to keep you company,*
> *I've come.*
>
> *In the bright spring sun in the wind,*
> *When the five slender willows sway,*
> *Shall we ride a white pony*
> *To visit*
> *The gay quarter of blossoms and willows?*[49]

Mŏkchung I: Who is the fucking fellow who wants to go only for one day?[50] I want to go for two or three days.

All Mŏkchung: [In a singsong tone.]

> *In rumor,*
> *The beauty of Kŭmkang-san Mountain,*

We heard. . .
[The elated monks dance to the tune of *t'aryŏng*. But one of them walks away from the group.]

Wanpo: Hey, you! What the hell are you doing? You're leaving us, are you? Don't go away! Sing a song with us.

All Mŏkchung: [In a singsong tone.]

At the end of Samch'ŏng-tong,[51]
There starts Tohwa-tong.

When I journey down to Kyŏngsang-do Province,
I get five tongs[52] *of ramie fabric*
And five tongs[53] *of plain cloth.*

When I journey up to Ch'ungch'ŏng-do Province,
I get five tongs of white cotton broadcloth
And five tongs of unbleached cotton weaving.

Four times five makes twenty.
Then I roll up all twenty tongs.

When I pass the Sae Pass[54] *in Munkyŏng*
With all twenty tongs on my shoulder,
There suddenly appears a highwayman.

Wanpo: [He sings.]

It's an invocation.
It can be for a scripture reading.

Let's pray to the deities
For the prosperity of our families.

Whose family will prosper?
Here is our master
While there's our bachelor student.

Throughout the year
We raise our precious boys
And cute babies.

One year is twelve months.
But for a girl of sixteen
There can be thirteen months in a year.[55]

Throughout a year
Let's pray for peace and safety.

Yi. . . ae.

[In chorus.]

Ahuhae ae. . . rokuna.

Mŏkchung I: All monks are behaving foolishly. That means something bad is going to happen in the temple. They say when the temple is not peaceful, the Buddha begins to eat chicken and birds.[56] We must maintain peace in our temple. But we're going in all different directions. Let's say some well-wishing remarks for our temple.

Wanpo: You're right.

Mŏkchung I: [He sings.]

Haetong[57] *is the country of Chosŏn.*[58]
Thirty-seven officials are what she has.

In Hanyang[59] *to the throne*
When the Yi family[60] *was ascended,*
Quietly hung was a male phoenix.

Let's build a royal palace
For the Six Boards of the Government.[61]
Then there also will be
The Five Military Divisions.[62]

When every province
And city are established,
There also must be a blue dragon
In the Wangsim-sa Temple.

On the Eastern Pass
And the Ten Thousand Pass
There're white tigers.

Madam Yi is taking a journey.
I wonder which boat she is taking.

If she boards the wooden boat,
It will be rotten.

If she boards the stone boat,
Into the sea, it will plunge.

If she boards the earthen boat,
In the water, it will dissolve.

If she boards the paper boat,
In the sea, it will melt.

If she boards the iron boat,
The male phoenix will arise.

Climb up the back mountain
And let's strip off
The leaves of lotus and bamboos.

With red silk, frame the sails
And hoist them to the golden star.

The front boatman on the bow.
The rear boatman on the stern.

The extra boatman on either side
And the admiral on the center.

In this way
Let's go sight-seeing in Uiju[63]
Sailing up the streams
Of the Yalu River.[64]

Her Highness of Uiju
With her prayer
Makes the posterities cherish.

Whose posterities are they?

In the upper hall,
There sits our master.
In the middle hall,
There's our bachelor student.
In the lower hall,
There is our precious baby.

The snow-white baby,
Like tree branches and cucumbers,
Grows fast.

Grows bigger and bigger.
Now he is seven.

He has mastered Ch'ŏnja, [65]
Yuhak, [66] Tongmongsŏnsup, [67]
The Book of Ode, [68]
The Canon of History, [69]
The Works of Mencius, [70]
And the Analects of Confucius. [71]

[In chorus.]

In rumor, we hear faintly,
The young gentleman is taking
His civil service examinations.

Look!
His servant.
He runs into the stable.

Brings out his pony,
Brushing him up and down busily.

With sparkling decorations and make-up
Splendid is the young gentleman.

His fine flute
The full-dress
With blue and black.

The hair, black-cloud-like,
Combed with a crescent comb
Braided[72] like a narrow wooden board.[73]

The handsome hair,
Adorned with ornaments.
His elegant figure, we see.

For him,
A flare skirt with twelve stripes of cloth.

For a young Buddhist disciple,
A seven stripe skirt.[74]

Three or four stripes,
For a dish cloth.
And the remnants,
For a thimble, too.

Tucking a white paper under his arm
Holding the examination paper in his bosom.

Ride on the carriage
Drawn by a trotting pony.

Arriving proudly
At the threshold of the Kwanghwa-mun Gate
In Seoul, the capital of the nation.

From the Chinese ink water-well
On the inkstone,
Drops a drop of lotus water, runs down.

Until the weasel-tail brush[75] wears out
In this and that way,
Writes non-punctured Chinese writings and tales.

When his writing wins the First Prize
The grown-up plays a flute
While boys dance.

When they round and round
The street corners,
Playing and dancing,
The childhood friend,
Sticking his head out of the window,
Shouts for the happy event.

[All exit except Sangjwa, Om, Mŏkchung I, and Wanpo.]

Act V
Scene 2: Acupuncture

[Sangjwa, Om, and Mŏkchung I dance *kkaeki*-dance in order one by one as they go before the musicians. They stand. Mŏkchung I, wearing the Malttugi mask,[76] goes to his children played by Sangjwa, Om, and Mŏkchung II. He finds Wanpo whom he has apparently been looking for. Then he again goes back to his children.]

Mŏkchung I: Hey! I'm glad to see you.

Wanpo: Why?

Mŏkchung I: It is none other than. . .

Wanpo: What?

Mŏkchung I: Including my son, grandson, great-grandson, and myself. . . four generations are here. . .

Wanpo: Four generations, including yourself?

Mŏkchung I: Well, since I heard the sound of an hourglass-shaped drum and gongs, we came out to see the play. My children told me they were hungry. So I gave them a couple of *yang*s.[77] With that money they bought something to eat. Since then, either they have become quiet spectators of the play or they are dead suddenly. I heard you knew so much about so many things. I thought you could cure them. That's why I was looking for you. Can you cure them? Can you come quickly to examine them?

Wanpo: Ha, ha, ha! I'm quite lost. As you know, I'm neither a doctor
nor do I know anything about medicine. You must be desperate. Is
it urgent?

Mŏkchung I: Urgent.

Wanpo: Because of our friendship and my sense of moral duty, I can't
reject your request. Anyway, let's go. Are they dead yet?

Mŏkchung I: I don't know whether they're at the moment of death or
not. You must examine them.

Wanpo: Hey. Don't you know what the moment of death is? Let's go!
[After he has examined the patients.] Hey. They already give off a
smell.

Mŏkchung I: Are they already rotten?

Wanpo: Well, . . . I don't know whether they're dead or alive.

Mŏkchung I: Please, examine them, will you?

Wanpo: Hey, hey, hey! [Pointing to Mŏkchung I.] Do you like the
drink?

Mŏkchung I: I'd never regret even being drowned in wine.

Wanpo: You like wine, don't you?

Mŏkchung I: Of course.

Wanpo: There must be a winery in your village.

Mŏkchung I: There's a winery.

Wanpo: He is a sot who is drowned upside down in the wine jug. Even
after death, he is still drunk. It'll take him many days before he gets
sober. [Pointing to Mŏkchung I.] You're troubled by the Goddess of
Anti-marriage. Your ears are dead. You look like you're rotting in
the hot sun and the sultry weather of "the dog days" in the months
of May and June. Hey. Is there a house of feasting in the village?

Mŏkchung I: There's a house of feasting.

Wanpo: Is there a family of mourning in the village?

Mŏkchung I: There should be a house of feasting and a family in mourning in such a large village as ours.

Wanpo: He is stricken by the Goddess of Anti-marriage at the house of feasting. He's also stricken by the evil influence emitting from the house where someone has died. He is dead by both diseases. His body has already been stiff for a long time. Hey. Well, . . . [Pointing to Sangjwa.] How old is he?

Mŏkchung I: About fifteen.

Wanpo: Fifteen? He must have had his initial sexual intercourse.

Mŏkchung I: I don't know about that.

Wanpo: I see. He must have died of a sexual disease. He has been dead for many hundred years. His face is pale like the gray ceiling, . . . his bones are snow white.

Mŏkchung I: That's the reason I asked you to come.

Wanpo: I'm in serious trouble. Didn't they die when they were getting into divinity?

Mŏkchung I: That's why I asked you to come! Why don't you perform some exorcism? If they recover themselves, they'd be lucky. If they die, no one can help them.

Wanpo: I'm in serious trouble. Unexpectedly, I've got myself into trouble. Hey. Since they might have been exorcised when there was a sudden striking sound of an hourglass-shaped drum, I might have to quietly sing a line from "The Song of the White Sea Gull." If there's a possibility of recovery, I'll sing a little more. If they don't recover themselves, I don't know what else to do. We may have to try something different.

Mŏkchung I: If the children die, you'll be responsible.

Wanpo: [He begins to play a small gong as he sings.]

You, the white sea gull,
Don't fly away,
Flapping your wings.
I'm not here to catch you.

His Majesty has deserted me.
So, to keep you company,
I've come.

In the bright sun in the wind
When the five slender willows sway,
Shall we ride a white pony
To visit
The gay quarter of blossoms and willows?

Mŏkchung I: Who is the fucking fellow who wants to go for only one day? I want to go two or three days. [He sings.]

In the deep stream
By the green mountain
The blue and yellow dragons
Wiggle their bodies.

[He tries to dance.]

Wanpo: Hey. Hey!

Mŏkchung I: What? What is it?

Wanpo: I don't care about them. I no longer care about them. You fool. You've lived this long for nothing. Listen! You've brought your first generation, the second generation, the third generation, and the fourth generation to the playground. Then you heard the striking sound of an hourglass-shaped drum. But you let all of them die. After that, you were desperate, asking me to help you to revive them. But when I started to sing a few lines from "The Song of the White Sea Gull," you danced. You fool. What kind of nonsense is that?

Mŏkchung I: You don't know what you're talking about. There should be a share for the old mourner. That's the reason why I've danced. Also I became elated. Anyway, they were already dead. No one can help them.

Wanpo: Elated?

Mŏkchung I: That's right.

Wanpo: It is clear that they were exorcized. Look. They are now moving. I don't think they are dead. I don't know what to do.

Mŏkchung I: What can we do? You have to somehow revive them.

Wanpo: I have to revive them again? You damn fool. I. . . Well, I have an excellent idea.

Mŏkchung I: What is that?

Wanpo: I don't know what to do any more. Well. This village is now called Chaetkol. There's a man whose name is Sinjupu who used to live here. But sometime ago he moved to a faraway place. He is not called Sinjupu because his name is Sin,[78] but because he is a newly born man. I often hear he is well-known for his profession as a doctor. His reputation has spread as far as Seoul. I'm not sure whether he is at this time free or not. We must go and find out. If you can bring Sinjupu, I'll discuss the matter with him to revive the children. Go and bring him here.

Mŏkchung I: I should go?

Wanpo: Yes, of course. You should.

Mŏkchung I: What shall I do if I can't find him?

Wanpo: Damn you. I've never seen a man like you. You must go and find him.

Mŏkchung I: Don't you think it will be a fruitless journey?

Wanpo: Well, you have to go.

Mŏkchung I: I'll go.

Wanpo: Go!

Mŏkchung I: [He goes to find Sinjupu. He circles around the playground several times.] Where is Sinjupu's house? I'm looking for Sinjupu. He moved to Monjitkol from Chaetkol. Where is Sinjupu's house?

Musician: [This role is played by one of the accompanying musicians. He speaks in the voice of a boy woodcutter.] Go in that direction.

Mŏkchung I: No, I don't want to go in that direction.

Wanpo: Why not?

Mŏkchung I: After I passed by Chaetkol and Monjitkol, I happened to meet a boy woodcutter on the mountain cliff. When I asked him about Sinjupu's house, he told me I should inquire about him in the lower hamlet. Since he was talking down to me, I didn't want to go any more, . . . no matter whether my children would die or not.

Wanpo: Well. Well. You flatfooted fellow. You didn't go because the boy talked down to you. Well. Even if the boy had slapped you in your face while directing you, you should have gone. You ought to think about how to cure your children. Let me look at you. You beggar. You're running around with a bare topknot without a hat. No wonder the boy didn't know whether you were a grown-up or a boy. Don't you think he thought you were one of his friends? That was why he talked down to you. Can you look at me?

Mŏkchung I: Why can't you go?

Wanpo: [He circles around the playground several times.] Hey! Do you know where Sinjupu's house is? He moved to Monjitkol. He is called Sinjupu because he is a newly born man.

Musician: [In a boy's voice.] Go in that direction.

Wanpo: [To Mŏkchung I.] What do you think? Look. Obviously I'm an adult with a hat. . .

Mŏkchung I: Should I go again?

Mŏkchung I: The mortuary. You went to bed with your mother. You must cure them. I don't care whether you went to bed with her or not. I don't care!

Sinjupu: Look. I'm in trouble. I. . . *yae yae yae.*

Mŏkchung I: What are you doing?

Sinjupu: Look. Oh my. He is completely dead. He is about fifteen years old. He has died of love sickness after extreme masturbation with three thousand clams. No doctor, no matter how talented in medicine, can cure him. This fellow is handsome with high cheekbones. He must know how to drink. Oh my goodness. He is red. He is in trouble. His face looks like an iron stick in the fireplace. He must have been killed by the Killer God of Wine of Mourning Dress at the house of mourning. There's no way of curing him. I'm going.

Mŏkchung I: You stupid imbecile. You killed the people. You can't go. I don't care whether you bury them or not. It is now up to you.

Sinjupu: I'm in serious trouble.

Mŏkchung I: Check their pulse.

Sinjupu: There's no use of checking it. [He finally checks Sangjwa's pulse by holding his little finger. Sangjwa plays the role of Mŏkchung I's great-grandfather.] Shall I give him an acupuncture? Where?

Mŏkchung I: You imbecile. Had I known it, I could have pricked him. I heard that acupuncture should be on the thumb or on the middle finger. But I've never seen anyone pricking the little finger. How is he going to be cured?

Sinjupu: You don't know what you're talking about. He has been dead for many decades. So I have to collect all his blood on a small part of his body before I prick all over his body with needles.

Mŏkchung I: I see. Medicine must be practiced differently by a different

Wanpo: Go!

Mŏkchung I: [As he returns to Wanpo.] I hope it won't be a fruitless journey.

Wanpo: You have to go and find out.

Mŏkchung I: Well, I'm going. [He walks for a while.] Sinjupu!

Sinjupu: Who the hell is Sinjupu? He must go to bed with his mother.

Mŏkchung I: Why are you saying that? He is Sinjupu not because his family name is Sin, but because he is a newly born man.

Sinjupu: Why are you calling me?

Mŏkchung I: I came to look for you. Four generations of my family came to see the play. But I don't know whether they're dead or alive. I heard you have a distinguished talent in acupuncture. You must come and cure them.

Sinjupu: Well. If you have four generations here, it is obvious that I'm your great-great-grandfather. Without my needle you'll cease to have your sons and grandsons. Let's go. Go! [Sinjupu and Mŏkchung I come to the patients.] Well. Where are they lying?

Mŏkchung I: This is the mortuary.

Sinjupu: What?

Mŏkchung I: The mortuary. You went to bed with your mother. You must cure them. I don't care whether you went to bed with her or not. I don't care!

Sinjupu: Look. I'm in trouble. I. . . *yae yae yae.*

Mŏkchung I: What are you doing?

Sinjupu: Look. Oh my. He is completely dead. He is about fifteen years old. He has died of love sickness after extreme masturbation with three thousand clams. No doctor, no matter how talented in medicine, can cure him. This fellow is handsome with high cheekbones. He must know how to drink. Oh my goodness. He is red. He is in trouble. His face looks like an iron stick in the fireplace. He must have been killed by the Killer God of Wine of Mourning Dress at the house of mourning. There's no way of curing him. I'm going.

Mŏkchung I: You stupid imbecile. You killed the people. You can't go. I don't care whether you bury them or not. It is now up to you.

Sinjupu: I'm in serious trouble.

Mŏkchung I: Check their pulse.

Sinjupu: There's no use of checking it. [He finally checks Sangjwa's pulse by holding his little finger. Sangjwa plays the role of Mŏkchung I's great-grandfather.] Shall I give him an acupuncture? Where?

Mŏkchung I: You imbecile. Had I known it, I could have pricked him. I heard that acupuncture should be on the thumb or on the middle finger. But I've never seen anyone pricking the little finger. How is he going to be cured?

Sinjupu: You don't know what you're talking about. He has been dead for many decades. So I have to collect all his blood on a small part of his body before I prick all over his body with needles.

Mŏkchung I: I see. Medicine must be practiced differently by a different doctor. As long as you cure them, it is fine with me.

[Sinjupu starts to prick each one of the patients with his needles. The first patient stands up and makes his exit as he dances *palrim*.[79] while the second one exits as he sings "The Song of Kŭmkang-san Mountain." The third one exits as he dances *kkaeki*-dance. Mŏkchung I and Wanpo exit, dancing, facing each other.]

Act V
Scene 3: The Playing of a Drum by Aesatang

[All Mŏkchung (two Sangjwa, four Mŏkchung, Om, and Wanpo) enter from the costume hall and stand in a row facing the musicians.

When Wanpo strikes his small gong, Mŏkchung I plays his small drum. Then Waejangnyŏ[80] enters with Aesatang[81] dancing wildly like a madwoman as she carries a black coat worn by a Buddhist monk. Aesatang goes south, while Waejangnyŏ goes to the monks and strikes their faces.]

Mŏkchung I: [To Waejangnyŏ.] What the hell are you doing?

Waejangnyŏ: [She nods as though they have been acquaintances. She points to Aesatang suggesting that she is her daughter.]

Mŏkchung I: Damn you! Do you have another daughter like her at home?

Waejangnyŏ: [She pantomimes as though she is saying that she has a few more daughters like her.]

Mŏkchung I: My goodness. You must be a bitch and want to sell the house. Go quickly and bring her here. I'll give you some money in brass coins.

Waejangnyŏ: [She nods as if she agrees to Mŏkchung I's suggestion. Then she goes to Aesatang and pantomimes suggesting that she should go to him since he will give her some money.]

Aesatang: [She shakes her head, indicating she refuses to do her mother's bidding.]

Mŏkchung I: Isn't five *yang*s in brass coins enough? I'll give her ten *yang*s. Bring her quickly.

Waejangnyŏ: [She gives Aesatang ten *yang*s.]

Mŏkchung I: [To Waejangnyŏ.] Go and prepare a table of side dishes for drinking. [To Aesatang.] Don't you go even an inch away from here.

[In a singsong tone.]

Olsiku chŏlsiku.

[In chorus.]

Things are going well.
Ah—ha. . . chok'una. [82]

Waejangnyŏ: [For the drinking table a small drum is used, while a small gong is employed for the drinking bowl. She brings out the small drum and the gong. She pantomimes as if she pours the wine. Then she drinks it first.]

Mŏkchung I: You bitch! Did you drink it first? You bitch. Drop dead!

Waejangnyŏ: [While she takes the wine table away, two Sangjwa and two Mŏkchung exit. She now dances *kkaeki*-dance to the music. Then she exits.]

Aesatang: [She dances for a while as she plays the drum held by Om and Mŏkchung I.]

Mŏkchung I: [He suddenly jumps on Aesatang and snatches the drumstick from her.] Look. You bitch! You should have been stricken to death by lightning. You've never held the drumstick before in your life. You shouldn't play it. You also shouldn't play it while you're wearing a jacket, a skirt, a slip, and a petticoat, including underpants. [He chases Aesatang.] Look, she is being chased. Her footsteps sound like: "*cchwak cchwak*" as if a tobacco pouch made with strings is being torn. You bitch. Look how I play the drum. The drum must be played with full gusto and with two sticks in both hands. You also must be completely naked. What the hell kind of drum beating is that? [A strike of a drum.] Don't you think I play it according to the rhythmical motion? [Another strike of a drum.] Then in that way. What do you think? Isn't it fascinating? Look. You fucking bitch. You beggar. What the hell are you doing making such funny sounds as "*k'ong, k'ong,* [83] *k'wang, k'wang,* and *noktu, noktu.*" [84] What kind of coquettish behavior is that? You bitch!

Wanpo: [He suddenly takes away the drum which is held by Mŏkchung I. As a result, Mŏkchung I paws the air missing the drum. The other Mŏkchung and Om exit.] Look. You idiot. What kind of playing is that? You've criticized her. Why do you have to paw the air? Did you skip your breakfast?

Mŏkchung I: Hey. What the hell are you doing?

Wanpo: What? What are you saying?

Mŏkchung I: When you come you must inform me about your coming.

Wanpo: You fool. Because you've criticized her, I thought you were a fantastic drummer.

Mŏkchung I: Stop it. Why don't you hold it right? So I can beat out a tune.

Wanpo: Is that right?

Mŏkchung I: [He plays the drum. But when Wanpo lowers the drum, he again paws the air.]

Wanpo: [He keeps lowering the drum.]

Mŏkchung I: How am I supposed to play it?

Wanpo: How in the hell is that the way to play a drum? Hey. You fool. Can't you play it?

Mŏkchung I: No, I can't play it.

Wanpo: Can you play it while you stand on your hands?

Mŏkchung I: Oh, I see. Do you want me to play it while I stand on my hands?

Wanpo: Can you play it?

Mŏkchung I: Hey. Stop it. Hold it right. [Wanpo holds the drum high in the air.] Hey! It's too high. How am I going to play it?

Wanpo: Can't you bring a ladder and play it?

Mŏkchung I: Stop it. Please hold it right. Let's try it right. [He puts the strap on the drum and makes Wanpo carry it on his back.]

Wanpo: I see.

[In a singsong tone.]

Ho---hon.
I've an eastern gourd
In my cauldron.

Ho---hon.
I've an eastern gourd
In my cauldron.

[Mŏkchung I goes to Wanpo and strikes the drum hard.] Hey!
You fucker. Everything has its owner. Why do you have to strike
someone else's possession without permission?

Mŏkchung I: You dissolute fellow. What is it called?

Wanpo: It has many names.

Mŏkchung I: It has many names?

Wanpo: That's right.

Mŏkchung I: I want to know them.

Wanpo: If you hear them you'll lose your head and have a fit.

Mŏkchung I: It doesn't matter. I want to hear them.

Wanpo: Well. Its family name is the big drum; but its given name is
the small drum.

Mŏkchung I: I see.

Wanpo: If I strike hard, heaven and earth will tremble. When you hear
that sound, you'll become mad and jump up and down. So I can't
play it.

Mŏkchung I: That's good. Let me play it just once.

Wanpo: Do you really want to play it?

Mŏkchung I: Yes, I want to play it.

Wanpo: Even if you get mad and lose your head?

Mŏkchung I: That's fine. Even if I get mad and lose my head I want to play it.

Wanpo: Really? [He suddenly strikes the drum.] How is it?

Mŏkchung I: It sounds good.

Wanpo: [When Mŏkchung I tries to play the drum, he walks east with the drum on his back.]

Mŏkchung I: [He paws the air by missing the drum.] You fucker! What the hell are you doing? Why do you have to go in that direction?

Wanpo: I should have gone to bed with your mother. I was becoming elated. So I went in that direction.

Mŏkchung I: Hey, hey, hey! If you walk east, you'll become so and so.

Wanpo: If I walk east, why will I become so and so?

Mŏkchung I: If you walk east, you and your mother's backside will greet each other.

Wanpo: Did you say that my backside will greet your mother's if I walk east?

Mŏkchung I: That's right.

Wanpo: If so, I'll be all right as long as I don't walk east.

Mŏkchung I: [He paws the air.] Hey! What are you doing?

Wanpo: What? Why are you saying that?

Mŏkchung I: You told me that you'd swear before you walked east.

Wanpo: That's the reason why I went west.

Mŏkchung I: Oh, I see. You went west because you swore that you wouldn't go east. Is that correct?

Wanpo: Correct.

Mŏkchung I: Hey. You're the fellow who would have ankle belts while wearing a pair of short pants. [85] You're quite stubborn. Now if you go east you'll give me your mother. But if you go west you have to force me to have your mother.

Wanpo: Well. You say if I go east and west, you'll force me to keep your mother. That means it is all right as long as I don't go east or west.

Mŏkchung I: Right.

Wanpo: Is that so? [He returns south as he carries the drum on his back.]

Mŏkchung I: What are you doing?

Wanpo: You stupid imbecile. What are you talking about? You told me I shouldn't go east or west. So I went south.

Mŏkchung I: I see. I made you swear not to go east or west. So you went south?

Wanpo: Right.

Mŏkchung I: What a clever fellow. Now if you go east, south, or west, you have to give me your family.

Wanpo: If I go east, west, or south, you'll give me your mother. Did you say that?

Mŏkchung I: Yes.

Wanpo: Well, so be it. As long as I don't go east, west, or south, I'll be fine.

Mŏkchung I: Oh, yes. [When he tries to play the drum, Wanpo goes north.] Where are you going again?

Wanpo: You told me I shouldn't go east, west, or south. There was nowhere left to go except north.

Mŏkchung I: Oh, I see. You've sworn not to go in three directions except one. So you went in that direction.

Wanpo: Right.

Mŏkchung I: I don't think it's going to work out for you. If you go east, west, south, or north, this time such and such a thing is going to happen. Do you understand?

Wanpo: Such and such a thing is going to happen? Isn't that what you're saying?

Mŏkchung I: That's right.

Wanpo: [He whirls around carrying the drum on his back.]

Mŏkchung I: What kind of nonsensical thing are you doing?

Wanpo: You imbecile. What did you say? Since I swore that I wouldn't go east, west, south, or north, I didn't have anywhere else left to go. So I had to whirl around.

Mŏkchung I: I see. You couldn't go east, west, south, or north because you swore that you won't go in those directions. So you whirled.

Wanpo: Right.

Mŏkchung I: It doesn't matter whether you whirl or not. You're the one who'll go to bed with your mother.

Wanpo: Even if I've whirled and whirled?

Mŏkchung I: Yes.

Wanpo: Yes. [When Mŏkchung I tries to play the drum he takes it off his back and puts it down.]

Mŏkchung I: Now what kind of fit are you practicing?

Wanpo: You told me I would go to bed with your mother even if I whirled. So I had no choice but to put it down. Because I'm not carrying it on my back any longer, it's all right, isn't it?

Mŏkchung I: Do you mean you've put it down permanently?

Wanpo: That's right.

Mŏkchung I: I don't think it's going to work. You rascal. You stand up with your feet together. I'm going to make you stand straight right here. [He holds Wanpo so that he can't move. Then he draws a circle around him.] You must stand straight like a pair of shoes on the ground. You only can move around within this circle. If you happen to step over the line, you'll go to bed with your mother.

Wanpo: Hello, everybody! Look at us! This fellow is the one who has stepped out of the line. Who do you think has stepped out of the line?

Mŏkchung I: Ha, ha, ha! Well, I don't know what to do with you. You're quite a smart fellow.

[In a singsong tone.]

In the deep blue water
By the green mountain
The blue dragon
Wiggles up and down.

. . .

[Mŏkchung I and Wanpo dance to the tune of *t'aryŏng* as they exit.]

Act VI
Scene 1: The Scene of the Apostate Monks

[All Mŏkchung enter one by one as they dance *kkaeki*-dance. They stand in a row in front of the musicians, facing the entrance. Nojang, led by Sangjwa II, enters. He walks leaning on his stick as he hides his face with his fan.

When all the Mŏkchung see Nojang, they are surprised. All the Mŏkchung dance one by one and go to Nojang who nods while he keeps his face hidden with his fan.

Om is the first one who goes to Nojang. He is frightened by him and returns to his place. Another Mŏkchung goes to Nojang. He is also frightened by him and runs back to his place. All of the Mŏkchung repeat the same.]

Wanpo: You stupid fellows. His face is all rotten. Why do you have to be frightened by him? Hey, you! A manly man ought to know that injustice cannot win justice. Why are you in such a commotion? I must go and look at him. [He goes to Nojang as he dances to the tune of *t'aryŏng* and looks at him. As he roars with laughter.] Master! Please go away!

Nojang: [He nods as though he is pleased and fans himself slowly.]

Wanpo: [As he scolds the rest of the monks.] The old master from the temple is absolutely unshakable. You senseless fellows. Don't you know what is going to happen to you when he says something? Why are you jumping up and down happily? [He goes to Nojang.] Well. Would you be pleased if I stuff both your ears with the gentle tune of "The Song of the White Sea Gull?"

Nojang: [He nods as if he is pleased.]

Wanpo: I see. Because he likes what I've said, he is nodding. Don't you worry. We'll sing a part of the song.

All Mŏkchung: [They sing.]

> *You, the white sea gull,*
> *Don't fly away,*
> *Flapping your wings.*
> *I'm not here to catch you.*
>
> *In the bright spring sun in the wind*
> *When the five slender willows sway,*
> *Shall we ride a white pony*
> *To visit*
> *The gay quarter of blossoms and willows?*

Om: [Elated and singing, he comes out dancing.] Who is the stupid fellow who wants to go only one day? I want to go for two, three, or four days.

> [In a *pullim*.]

In rumor,
We've heard
The beauty of Kŭmkang-san Mountain.

[Becoming elated while he sings, he begins to dance.]

Wanpo: Hey! You crazy, senseless fellows. No matter what I say or do to try to persuade the master to return to the temple, he is absolutely unshakable. But why are you so elated, jumping up and down? Please control yourself despite your elation!

Om: It doesn't matter whether the master is angry or not. I'm becoming elated.

All Mŏkchung: [In a singsong tone.]

Samch'ŏng-tong,
Hwagae-tong,
Tohwa-tong.
They're all tongs.

Outside Tongsŏ Gate
There's Anam-tong
Which is also a tong.

When I journey down to Kyŏngsang-do Province
I get five tongs of ramie fabric
And five tongs of plain cloth.

When I journey up to Ch'ungch'ŏng-do Province
I get five tongs of white cotton broadcloth
And five tongs of unbleached cotton weave.

Four times five makes twenty tongs.
I roll, roll them
And sling them on my shoulder.

When I pass the Sae Pass in Munkyŏng
There appears an unexpected highwayman.

Om: [Elated. In a *pullim*.]

An unexpected highwayman.

In the deep blue water
By the green mountain
The blue and yellow dragon
. . .

[He dances.]

Wanpo: You crazy fellow. I told you not to do that. You're doing it again.

Om: I'm getting excited. It doesn't matter whether or not the old master is angry.

Wanpo: Hey. There's no other way. We must escort him.

Nojang: [He strikes Wanpo's face with his fan. Then he points to Om.]

Wanpo: Listen.

All Mŏkchung: Ye---s.

Wanpo: Arrest the fellow whose face is black and red. He wears an old felt hat.

All Mŏkchung: Yes! We have arrested him. [They arrest Om.]

Wanpo: Make him face down on the ground.

All Mŏkchung: Yes. We've made him face down.

Wanpo: Make a show of flogging him and put him to death.

Mŏkchung I: [Makes Om face down on the ground and flogs him a few times.] I gave him a single harsh flogging and now he's dead.

Wanpo: Now let's go fishing for yellow fish near Yŏnp'yŏng-do Island.

All Mŏkchung: That's a great idea.

[They sing as they play their small gongs.]

Hey, we're now near Kanghwa. [86]
Hohyyo houya.
This is Kanghwa.

Yuhal, yuhal, yuhal, yuhal!
Let's moor the boat.

To beg for barley
Let's moor the boat.

Should we beg for barley?
Or for wheat?

[They carry Nojang to the center of the playground as they sing a song. The carrying of Nojang by the monks is used as a parable for the catching of a large yellow fish from the Yŏnp'yŏng Sea. They now put Nojang in front of the musicians. Then they circle around him.]

Wanpo: Hey, hey, hey! A great thing has happened. A huge fish has been caught. When we went fishing for yellow fish, the King of the Dragon Palace gave us a fish to eat. Now there's no other way but for all of us to eat it. Who is going to eat the head?

Sangjwa: [He feels Nojang's head as he pantomimes that he wants to eat the head.]

Wanpo: You damn fellow. You've heard that the head of a fish has the best taste, while in birds and animals the tail has the most exquisite flavor. You little aggressive fellow. You want to eat the head? [Om pantomimes eating the middle part of Nojang, while Wanpo eats the lower part of his body. Now they circle around Nojang as they dance. Headed by Sangjwa, they exit to the costume hall.]

Nojang: [After all the Mŏkchung have made their exit, he regains consciousness. He pantomimes as if cleaning his eyes and brushing his teeth. His cloth is tattered and dirty. Leaning on his cane heavily with both hands, he tries to stand up. But he falls down. He tries again, making it almost half way. The third time, he finally stands up with great difficulty. He whirls around slowly, faltering

several times. Casting away his cane, he begins to dance *kŭtŭrŭm*-
dance to the tune of *yŏmbul* as he holds his fan. Then he changes
his dance to *mŏngsŏkmari*-dance, *kopsawi*-dance, and *hwajang*-
dance to the tune of *t'aryŏng*.

Somu: [At this time two Somu[87] enter and dance *chara*-dance,[88]
circling around Nojang. Nojang dances *kalchija*-dance[89] as he goes
between the Somu, nodding to one of them as if he is pleased with
what is happening. He does the same to the other girl.]

Nojang: [He pantomimes that he is plucking a girl's mouth and
underarm and eating them. The girl expresses her dislike in
pantomime. When he goes to the other girl she pushes him away
with her hand on his chest. He is angry and takes off his hat
adorned with pine branches. Then he rips off his robe. Now he
pantomimes as though he is gambling with money. Losing money,
he gets angry. He does this and that. The two Somu pick up
Nojang's robe and wave their hands suggesting that he come to
them. Nojang refuses. Once more, the two Somu signal him to
come. Now he goes to them. Then he puts his robe back on and
dances with the girls. Then he takes off his belt tying it to one of
the girls, as though he is trying to fly her like a kite. Now he circles
the two girls' necks with his rosary and, dancing together, they
circle the playground. Finally they go to the left in front of the
musicians. They sit down.]

Act VI
Scene 2: Shoe Peddler

Shoe Peddler[90]: [He enters carrying a monkey, who is wrapped in a
cloth, on his back. He shouts out in the manner of a peddler.]
Please buy genuine cowhide shoes for women!

Nojang: [He crosses to Shoe Peddler and suddenly opens his fan. With
his fan, he strikes Shoe Peddler's face. Then he retreats a few
steps.]

Shoe Peddler: Ouch! [Shocked.] Oh my goodness. What is that? I've had three bowls of wine for breakfast. As a result, my face is bright red. The eagle from Nam-san Mountain[91] must have thought I was a morsel of meat and tried to snatch me away. I almost lost my face. [He again shouts his wares.] Please buy genuine leather shoes decorated with flowers for women.

Nojang: [Again he goes to Shoe Peddler and suddenly opens his fan.]

Shoe Peddler: I see. They say "The wild goose must seek out the sea: but not be sought by the sea." So the butterfly must fly to the flowers, but not the flowers to the butterfly. The crab must find out the hole, but the hole must not find out the crab. The male dog must find a female dog, but the female dog must not find the male dog. Now I understand. He wants me to come to him to sell the shoes. [He takes the monkey off his back. Then he goes to Nojang and strikes the ground with his whip.] Why did you call me?

Nojang: [He raises his fan swiftly.]

Shoe Peddler: Do you want to buy shoes? What size?

Nojang: [He points to the two Somu.]

Shoe Peddler: Do you want your grandmother to wear size six? And size five for your mother?

Nojang: [He shakes his head and fan.]

Shoe Peddler: Let me try again. Do you want size six for your wife and size five for your concubine?

Nojang: [Nods.]

Shoe Peddler: You damn fellow. When you're pleased, you shake your head like a pig. What size, sir?

Nojang: [He pantomimes with his finger as if indicating the size of shoe on his fan.]

Shoe Peddler: You stupid imbecile. What are you? Are you the son of a yardstick worm? Why do you have to measure the fan? I understand. When are you going to pay me?

Nojang: [He swiftly raises his fan and points at Shoe Peddler with his finger.]

Shoe Peddler: I see. On the twenty-first of the Eleventh Month of next leap year. [He strikes the ground with his whip. Then he roars with laughter. He jumps up. To the audience.] I want to ask all of you, the old and the young. Is there a twenty-first of the eleventh month in the leap year? Look. I must have met a robber. I expected to do well with my business today. But I'm afraid that I might be badly robbed by this fellow. First, I must unwrap my merchandise. [He beats the monkey.]

Monkey[92]: [He suddenly emerges out of the wrapping cloth.]

Shoe Peddler: Listen. To sell the shoes, I went to the back yard of a house with a tile roof. Through the collapsed part of the hedge, I happened to see two girls sitting in the yard doing something. One looked so so. But the other one looked extremely beautiful with her gently curved shoulders and her round, flat bottom. You and I are both bachelors. Why don't you go and bring her to me? Then I can have her at night or at meal time, or whenever I feel like having her. In addition, we can have her during the condolence visit by our friends when our parents die. We can also have clean clothes everyday. But you're not going to be able to have her at meal time. You look like a stinking tramp without clean clothes. Why don't you try to lure her out for me? Use whatever method you know. First, I must teach you something. So study whatever I teach you. [He makes Monkey stand, his legs apart, hands on his hips.] Do whatever I tell you.

Monkey: [Nods. Then he begins to tremble.]

Shoe Peddler: Stop trembling! It isn't winter. Why are you trembling? Don't tremble. Just study whatever I teach you.

[In a singsong tone.]

Konch konch konch.
Chuiam chuiam chuichchuiam.
Chilraraebi hwŏl hwŏl.[93]

In the large brass bowl
The steamed short-ribs.
In the small brass bowl
The steamed spring chicken.

The dragon chicken,
The sunlight chicken,
And the mountain pheasant.

In the large brass bowl
The steamed short-ribs.
In the small brass bowl
The steamed spring chicken.

[As he looks at the trembling Monkey.] Hey! Stop trembling.
Why are you trembling so hard? You know the reason. You're
smart. You have good brains.

[In a singsong tone.]

Pongchi[94] *pongchi pongchiyo.*
The bag for the roast sesame
Is also a bag.

The bag for the black pepper
Is also a bag.

The bag for the hot pepper
Is also a bag.

Between the cinnamon trees
The grinding of your mother's vagina
. . .

Hey, you! It's good to grind with your mother. You fool.
There're so many good things in the world. Anyway you look
smart. It seems to me you have good brains and clear eyes.

Monkey: [When he signals the musicians with his hand, they play the tune of *t'aryŏng.* He begins to dance *mŏngsŏkmari*-dance and goes to Somu to seduce her. As he whirls the end of his red armour, he circles around her. Now he feels Somu's cheeks with one hand as he lets his other hand rest on her shoulder. He again dances an obscene dance. Finally he goes to Shoe Peddler and suddenly strikes his face.]

Shoe Peddler: Well. How did things go? Did everything go well?

Monkey: [He dances *kopsa*-dance[95] as he pantomimes that he has had sexual intercourse with her.]

Shoe Peddler: [Beating Monkey.] You had sexual intercourse with her? What am I supposed to do? Since I don't know what else to do, I must make you lie down on your stomach! [He makes Monkey lie down and pantomimes as though he is having pederasty with him. Then he swiftly strikes Monkey's buttocks.]

Monkey: [Shocked. He exits to the costume hall as he dances *mŏngsŏkmari*-dance.]

Shoe Peddler: [As he dances to the tune of *t'aryŏng,* he also exits to the costume hall. Nojang and the two Somu remain in front of the musicians.]

Act VI
Scene 3: Ch'wipali

Ch'wipali[96]: [He enters the playground five or six steps from the musicians and stands. He has a branch of the flowering cherry.] Damn it. It smells strange here. Why on earth is the smell of incense so intense? It disturbs my nose. *Woryo yiyiyiki!*

Nojang: [He walks to Ch'wipali and swiftly opens his fan.]

Ch'wipali: [Surprised. Retreats.] Damn it. Because I've had a few bowls of wine, my face is quite flushed. So the eagle from the mountain peak, thinking my face is a tasty fish, is flying around me. If I'm not careful, my face will be snatched away. [He goes around as though chasing the eagle away. Then he goes to Nojang.] I see.

Nojang: [He again swiftly opens his fan.]

Ch'wipali: If it was a black-eared kite, it would have already gone away. But since it's still here, a strange thing has definitely happened. [He goes to Nojang as he places his hand in front of his forehead. Then he looks at him.] Ha, ha, ha! You stupid imbecile. You hedge monk. Even though the world has become so corrupt, a monk like you shouldn't join mundane society. Much less with two women. What an absurd world! You! What the hell are you doing here?

Nojang: [He swiftly opens his fan and places it between Ch'wipali and Somu.]

Ch'wipali: Damn you. Are you trying to make me keep my distance from the girls?

Nojang: [He makes one of the Somu run her hand across his stomach.]

Ch'wipali: Hey. Do you have a stomach-ache? Why do you have to let her smooth your god damn stomach? What preposterous behavior! Even if the monks have become so corrupt and strange, you should stay in the temple to chant *kwanchachaeposal*[97] or any Buddhist invocation. You shouldn't have come to the mundane world to fool around with girls. What absurd behavior! I don't know what to do with you.

[In a singsong tone.]

The butterfly.
Let's fly to the green mountain!
You, the tiger butterfly,
Should come, too.

The fallen new red leaves
Under the heavy frost
In September and October.
. . .

No matter what you are. You're not a match for me. Let's go
into a deep cave in the steep green mountain and spend our lives
there and fight each other until our eyeballs protrude.

Nojang: [He gestures as though he does not agree to Ch'wipali's
proposal.]

Ch'wipali: You don't want to do it. You flippant fellow. Should I
ridicule you with "The Song of Kŭmkang-san Mountain" or with
"The Song of the Mottled Bamboo Stick?"

[In a *pullim.*]

The mottled bamboo stick
With twelve joints from Sosang,
I clasp...

[He dances.]

Nojang: [He dances with Ch'wipali to the tune of *t'aryŏng*. When
Ch'wipali begins to dance *hŏrijapi*-dance, Nojang strikes him with
his fan.]

Ch'wipali: Hey, you! Despite the fact that you're only a monk, you're
strong. No wonder you can keep two women. If you weren't
strong, you wouldn't even be able to keep one woman. You're
tough. You have beaten me. They say even a sparrow squeaks
when it is killed. Let's fight!

Nojang: [He takes off his robe and ties it to his belt.]

Ch'wipali: Look. You're going to eat me up, aren't you? After you've
beaten me, you've taken off your robe. You damn fellow. Since
you've taken off your robe, why shouldn't I take off mine? [He also
takes off his jacket and casts it on the ground.] Let's fight and see
whether Masan[98] will collapse or P'yŏngt'aek[99] will split into two
pieces. They say even a sparrow squeaks when it's killed. If so, how
is it possible for me to run away from you? [To the audience.]
Hello, ladies and gentlemen! If there's anyone who is concerned
with their safety, please stay away from here. It is entirely possible
that there'll be murder.

[In a *pullim*.]

In the deep stream
By the green mountain
The blue and yellow dragons
Wiggle their bodies.

[He dances]

Nojang: [He dances *kkaeki*-dance with Ch'wipali.]

Ch'wipali: [He goes to Nojang and strikes his back.]

Nojang: [He crawls in between the legs of a Somu.]

Ch'wipali: Look! Since he's beaten by me, he has become a coward. Now these two girls are mine. [He sings and dances as he places one of his hands on a Somu's shoulder.]

Chŏlsu chŏlsu

. . .

Nojang: [He sticks out his head from underneath a Somu's skirt.]

Ch'wipali: [He is surprised and turns around.] What are you doing? Why does a dignified animal like you have to come to this mundane society? Please return to your place. *Shee-e, shee-e, shee-e!* [100]

Nojang: [He hides himself under a Somu's skirt. Then he again sticks his head out.]

Ch'wipali: Do you want to play with me? Look. You son of a bitch. *Shee-e, shee-e, shee-e!*

Nojang: [He finally exits with one of the Somu.]

Ch'wipali: [To the Somu who is going with Nojang.] She got a monk husband. [He begins to dance with the other Somu.]

[In a *pullim*.]

In the deep stream

By the green mountain
The blue and yellow dragons
Wiggle their bodies.

[He dances *kkach'igŏlŭm*-dance,[101] while Somu dances *chara*-dance. As he puts his hands on Somu's shoulder.] Grandmother. What the hell am I saying? I called her grandmother. What absurd talk! I have to get rid of this type of absurd talk. Even a dignified man can behave silly when he is mesmerized by a woman. Even a hero or a patriot can't help himself. [He dances. Then as he raises his hand.] Mother! My goodness. What absurd talk!

[In a *pullim*.]

In rumor
We've heard
The beauty of Kŭmkang-san Mountain.

[He dances. As he embraces the Somu.] Wife! That's right. You stupid bitch. This time I called you right. [He lies down in front of the Somu.] Even if you've had a nap with a monk in the temple, I don't think you've heard a song from a libertine. Would you like to hear a song?

[He sings.]

When heaven and earth
Maintain their eternal youth
And immortality,
The solitude of the mountain
Will last a century.

How did you like it? [He stands up and dances. He realizes that his topknot has come loose.] Damn it. What is happening to me? Since I've been mesmerized by a girl, I didn't realize my topknot has tumbled loose. Had the people seen me, they might have thought my parents were dead.[102] What a disgrace! [He ties up his topknot.] I have to turn my hair ninety-nine times to make a topknot. But I still have my hair left. What beautiful hair I have.

[In a singsong tone.]

The topknot.
The boxing. [103]

This and that bitches.
You all must dance chara-dance.
Chŏl chŏl chŏl.
Chŏlsikuna.

[He finishes his dance. Then he lifts the back of the Somu's skirt and crawls between her legs.] Up to now, I've never had a chance to look at a woman's rear garden. I must take a look. What a beautiful rear garden! It is wide enough for a man of six tons to sit and do it on her. Oh my goodness. What a fucking bitch you are! Since you've taken naps so often with the monks, you haven't cleaned your rear garden yet. It stinks! Like three-year-old pickled fish. *Ullululu!* [He vomits a little. Then he comes to the front of the Somu.] I've looked at the rear garden. Now let me see the front yard. [He lifts the front of the Somu's skirt and looks at the lower part of her stomach.] Look! It is better than the pine bushes. If I can pull one of them and give it to the string player, he can use it well. You bitch. [He pulls a hair from her and holds it in his hand.] Look! How long it is? I'm going to give it to the string player to make a string to play a tune. But he must play it in this way.

[In a singsong tone.]

Kkang-kkang kkang-kkang.
Kkikak-kkang-kkang.
Kkong-kkong kkong-kkong.
Kkang-kkang

[He pantomimes as though he puts his hand under the Somu's skirts and screws it in her vulva. As if he feels her clitoris.] What is this? It has teeth like a crab. It is pulling my finger. What a great feeling! [He sticks his head under the Somu's skirt. Then he pulls his head out.] *Ullululu!* [He vomits. Then he dances.] Now let me mill it. Look. This damn mill is well located.

[In a singsong tone.]

The spotted mill.
The mackerel mill.
The shad fish mill.

Oh, the legs for the pants.
Oh, the silk for the jacket.

[The Somu lies down quietly.] You disappointing bitch. No wonder. I didn't feel anything at all. What unreliable behavior. [He holds the branch of the flowering cherry between his legs and goes behind the Somu. Then he pantomimes as though a dog is having sexual intercourse.] The white dog in the village is having sexual intercourse. *Kkying kkying kkying.*

Somu: [She is having the labor of childbirth. Ch'wipali calls for the Midwife.]

Midwife [104]: [She enters as she dances *kkaeki*-dance, carrying a bundle of wrapping which holds the childbirth instruments and a baby doll. She caresses Somu's abdomen. She cuts the birth cord and gives the baby a bath. Then she exits to the costume hall as she dances *kkaeki*-dance.]

Ch'wipali: [He circles around the playground as he dances *kkaeki*-dance.] You bitch! Make her have a quick childbirth. Hold her temple. Massage her stomach! [As he suddenly sees the baby.] Oh, look! The Three Gods of Childbirth knew I was very poor. So they sent me the baby fully clothed. That was so. They had no choice but to do that.

[In a singsong tone.]

The beggar.
The beggar.
The beggar.

The silk cap, the jacket,
The pants, the leggings,
The wristlets, and the rubber shoes.

He's wearing all of them.

That's right. What should I name him? Since the baby was born on the ground, he must be called Playground.

Baby [105]: [This role is played by Ch'wipali. In baby talk.] Papa!

Ch'wipali: Yes.

Baby: [In baby talk.] Give me a piggyback ride.

Ch'wipali: Yes. Since the baby is born head first from his mother's womb, I must give him a piggyback ride upside down to prevent him from having stomach trouble. [He carries Baby upside down on his back.]

[In a singsong tone.]

Please, don't you cry.
When your mother goes to a play
She'll get a rice cake for you.

Please, don't you cry.
When your father goes to the fair
He'll buy you a rice candy.

Please, don't you cry.
You're a baby
As big as a green mountain
With ten thousand peaks.

I can neither buy you with silver
Nor can I get you with gold.

To the relatives, you're harmonious.
To the brothers, you're fraternal.
To the country, you're patriotic.
To the parents, you're filial.

Baby: [In baby talk.] Papa.

Ch'wipali: Yes?

Baby: [In baby talk.] I have to study a little.

Ch'wipali: Yes, of course. Yes. To succeed and rise to fame you must study.

Baby: [In baby talk.] Please teach me.

Ch'wipali: [He puts Baby on the ground.]

[In a singsong tone.]

Hanulch'ŏn ttarachi. [106]
In a cauldron
There's burned rice.

Dip a dog dishful of rice
For the teacher.
But two bowls for me.

You flippant fellow. Did you say that you'll have two bowls of rice, but I can eat only one dog dishful of it? You deserve to be whipped. [He beats Baby.]

Baby: [In baby talk.] Papa.

Ch'wipali: Yes.

Baby: I have to study about P'yŏngan-do Province.

Ch'wipali: Oh yes. That's right. You must study it. [He teaches him *Hangŭl.* [107]]

[In a singsong tone.]

Kiŏk niŭn
Tikŭt riŭl. [108]

When I build a house with kiŏk [109]
I had a miserable life with tikŭt. [110]

The wretched life of mine
Has now become so woeful.

What pitiful talk!

Baby: [In baby talk.] I want to drink some milk.

Ch'wipali: Yes. Hey. The baby's mother, let him have some milk. [Somu does not let Baby drink her milk. Instead she strikes Baby. As Ch'wipali holds Baby in his arm.] You frivolous bitch. The baby isn't made either by you or by myself. He is born only out of our mutual pleasure. Why aren't you going to give him milk? Because you've beaten him, why shouldn't I also mistreat him? [He throws Baby on the ground.]

[In a singsong tone.]

The green mountain.

. . .

[He exits as he dances *kkaeki*-dance, while the Somu dances *chara*-dance as she exits.]

Act VII
Scene 1: *The Servant at a Temporary Abode*

Malttugi[111]: [He enters accompanying Saennim,[112] Sŏpangnim,[113] and Toryŏngnim.[114] They stand on the south side of the musicians. Shoettugi[115] and his wife are already sitting in front of the musicians.] The servant of a temporary lodging! The servant of a temporary lodging!

Shoettugi: Who are you? Why are you shouting for "the servant of a temporary lodging?" I'm on inside duty.

Malttugi: Imbecile. Why do you have to be on inside duty? There're as many people as ten thousand mountains and plains.

Shoettugi: You fool. What kind of talk is that? It doesn't matter whether or not there're as many people as ten thousand mountains and plains. I am on inside duty because I am sitting with my wife.

Malttugi: I see. You're sitting with your wife. You call it inside duty.

Shoettugi: Exactly.

Malttugi: You fucker. I'm glad to hear your voice.

Shoettugi: [He abruptly stands up and bows to Malttugi.] *Anayayi.*

Malttugi: *Anayi!* I've seen you so many times. As many times as I see chopped straw in the gruel for cattle. Don't you have a pain in your foot?

Shoettugi: My goodness.

Malttugi: Hey. By the way, I'm in trouble.

Shoettugi: What's the matter?

Malttugi: My masters—Saennim, Sŏpangnim, and Toryŏngnim—are on their way to take civil service examinations. But they've become so crazy about sight-seeing. So they've forgotten the examination day. Now they're asking me to find a temporary lodging for them. But as you know, I don't have a single close relative or friend here. It is already night. I'm in such a hurry. I'm in trouble. But I'm glad to meet you here unexpectedly. Please find a temporary lodging for them.

Shoettugi: Why are those mother fuckers crazy about sight-seeing? Why are they asking you to find a temporary lodging? I understand your trouble. I'll try. [He circles around the playground several times. Then he stops in front of Malttugi.] I've found a temporary lodging.

Malttugi: How did you find it?

Shoettugi: I drove a few stakes for horses into the ground. Then I enclosed them with belts. After that, I made a door.

Malttugi: The house must look like a western-style house.

Shoettugi: Exactly.

Malttugi: If they want to get into the house, they must walk on their hands.

Shoettugi: Exactly.

Malttugi: If so, they must look like piglets. Hey, hey! Saennim is outside. You must go and bring him here.

Shoettugi: Why should I bring those mother fuckers?

Malttugi: But there's no other way. Considering our good relationship, you're the one who has to go and bring them here.

Shoettugi: I see. Considering our good friendship. . . I understand your situation. I'll do it.

Malttugi: Are you sure?

Shoettugi: Yes. [He stands in front of Saennim, Sŏpangnim, and Toryŏngnim. They are followed by Malttugi. Then they march into pigpen saying.]

Oink, oink, oink.

Saennim: Malttugi.

Malttugi: Yes, sir.

Saennim: Who has found this temporary lodging?

Malttugi: I didn't find it. I don't have a single close relative or a friend here. So I had to ask Shoettugi to find one. He found it for me.

Saennim: I see. It is very tidy and clean. I like it.

Malttugi: You're all *yangban*. So we've decided to find a two story lodging, the one on the top and the other down. You don't have to smoke together in the same room.[116]

Saennim: I see.

Shoettugi: [To Malttugi.] What is your position in the house?

Malttugi: I am a steward.

Shoettugi: I see. But how can a steward wear a felt hat?

Malttugi: No, that isn't correct. I'm an adopted heir of the family.

Shoettugi: I see. You're an adopted heir. [It is said that this means he is an illegitimate child of the family.]

Malttugi: If so, you go and greet Saennim.

Shoettugi: Why should I greet that mother fucker?

Malttugi: That isn't right. When he passes the examination, he'll be promoted as though he climbs up to the top of a ladder. Then you'll benefit from him, too.

Shoettugi: I imagine so. When I hear his voice, it sounds like he is a great dead monk or a bundle of hemp yarn.

Malttugi: A government office. . . I'm sure he will secure one. Go and greet him.

Shoettugi: [He circles around the three *yangban* as he dances to the tune of *t'aryŏng*. To Saennim.] My goodness. I thought you were the son of a *yangban*. But you're nothing more than a mongrel. You're wearing a cloth wrapping for bean curd. [He is referring to the Confucian ceremonial hood which is worn by Saennim.] You're wearing a full-dress and carrying a flower-decorated fan. But you also have a knapsack on your back. So you must be the son of a *hwarang*. [117] [To Sŏpangnim.] You wear a four-cornered horse-hair hat and a full-dress, and carry a fan. But you also have a knapsack on your back. So you too must be the son of a *hwarang*. You are all bad fellows. [To Toryŏngnim.] You, too, are wearing a cloth wrapping for scoundrels [He is referring to Toryŏngnim's Taoist hat] and armour. But you have a knapsack. [He comes to Malttugi.] Hey. I looked at them and found they were all sons of a *hwarang*, not sons of a *yangban*.

Malttugi: You may be right. Their family is poor. So they had to rent their clothing. As a result, the assortment of colors for their attire do not match.

Shoettugi: I see. That might be true. But I don't think they're children of a *yangban*.

Saennim: Malttugi.

Malttugi: Yes, sir.

Saennim: You damn fellow. Where have you been?

Malttugi: I've been looking for you.

Saennim: Where?

Malttugi: Yes. After I brushed the pony, I fitted him with a tiger skin saddle. Then I rode him to the outskirts of Nam-san Mountain, Ssanggye-tong, and Pyŏkgye-tong. Then I trotted quietly through Tongjak-tong. After that, I came through the Namtae-mun Great Gate [118] and went to Ilkan-chang, Yimok-kol, Samch'ŏng-tong, Sajik-kol, and Okung-t'ŏ. [119] After I passed by the Six Boards of the Government, I went to Ch'ilkwan-an, P'alkak-chae, Kuri-gye, Sipcha-kak, Tabang-kol, [120] which is also called a child's head, and Kamt'ujŏn-kol, which is often referred to as a man's head. Now I crossed at the top of a boat as I went through the side streets, searching for you. But I never found you. Not even a single offspring of yours. Then I happened to meet one of my acquaintances who told me that you went to the playground. So I came here quickly and found you—who is also my only grandson.

Shoettugi: [After hearing what Malttugi has said.] Hey, hey, hey! I thought about not letting him into the house. But when I think about the help which I would like to get from him in the future, I have no choice but to greet him.

Malttugi: You should do that.

Shoettugi: Saennim. I, Shoettugi, a servant, will greet you. Be careful. If you don't receive my greeting properly, you will not only be beheaded but also your bones will splinter into a million pieces. [He walks frivolously toward Saennim as he holds his hands together while keeping his right foot upward.] Ah, Saennim. I. . . [Saennim does not respond to him. He bows to Saennim and returns to Malttugi.] Hey. I think he must be a real *yangban*. He was very grave and dignified.

Malttugi: Of course, he is very dignified.

Shoettugi: What kind of family does he come from?

Malttugi: His family is like this. On moving day they have to open the shrine gate. They also must make a wick with a piece of straw rope and pull one end of it. Then they come out in a row. After that, they put one of their legs in the dog dish while keeping their other leg out. Then they make "cchŏk cchŏk" sounds. That is their family.

Shoettugi: If so, they must be pigs.

Malttugi: Exactly. Go and greet Sŏpangnim.

Shoettugi: [As he goes to Sŏpangnim.] Ah, Sŏpangnim! Ah, Sŏpangnim! I. . . [As he turns to Maltuggi.] He was a real yangban.

Malttugi: Whether you greeted him or not, Saennim looks like a dog's bottom. . . while Sŏpangnim appears to be a dog's buttocks. There's Toryŏngnim. He is from the main family. Go and greet him cordially. Otherwise, you'll not only be beheaded but also your bones will splinter into a million pieces. Go and greet him.

Shoettugi: Hey. What kind of long fucking greeting is that? That's all right. [To Saennim.] Hell, Saennim! Malttugi, a servant, is asking me to tell you that he is going to greet you. Please be careful. He is asking me to tell you that he is the one who cleans both the upper and lower parts of the village when he can't get a bowl of wine. But when his face gets flushed after his first, second, and third drink, he goes between the houses on the lower and upper parts of the village to eat all the clams, both old and new, the mackerels, shad fish, yellowtail fish, and conches from the sea. Not only that, he also beats up the children. He wants to greet you.

Saennim: [As he suddenly opens his fan.] You. Look!

Malttugi: Yes, sir.

Saennim: You've spoken to the yangban who is aged and noble in such an extremely absurd way. You mother fucker! You must be one of those. . . [In a dignified tone.] Malttugi.

Malttugi: Yes, sir.

Saennim: Arrest Shoettugi and bring him here.

Malttugi: [He carries the struggling Shoettugi upside down.] I've arrested him.

Saennim: What has happened to that fellow's fucking face? Did he participate in the Chŏngju Campaign?[121]

Malttugi: No, sir. I am bringing him upside down so that your mother won't swoon and die when she sees him.

Saennim: Pull out his head and insert it hard into. . .[122]

Malttugi: Yes, I've inserted it hard. . . [He turns Shoettugi quickly.]

Saennim: What is the thing which wiggles under his body?

Malttugi: Yes, sir. That is the thing with which your mother plays in the night.

Saennim: You. Damn you!

Malttugi: You mother fucking. . . I definitely have a name. But why do you have to call me "Damn you?"

Saennim: Look. If you have a name, what is it?

Shoettugi: You should call me by my name. It consists of F for fruit and A for apple.

Saennim: F for fruit and A for apple? F for fruit? A for apple?

Shoettugi: No! You shouldn't say it in that way. You are a *yangban* and studied *Hanulch'ŏn ttaji*.[123] You should know that they should be read *ch'ŏn-ji-hyŏn-hwang*.[124] Likewise, you also have to read my name together.

Saennim: Af. . .?

Shoettugi: Why do you have to read the last letter first?

Saennim: You mother fucker. Your name is quite difficult. F. . . a. . .

Shoettugi: What a crazy thing you're saying? You have to read them together. Otherwise, it is useless even if you were to read it for ten years and three months.

Saennim: [Finally.] Fa. . . [ther]!

Malttugi: Yes.

Saennim: [Being insulted by his own servant, he is indignant.] Shoettugi must be pardoned and acquitted. Now arrest Malttugi, my servant, and bring him here!

Shoettugi: Yes, sir. That's quite a smart idea. [He snatches Malttugi's felt hat and puts it on his head. Then he takes the horse whip away from Malttugi.] You damn fellow. Look! Since you've started to frequent a *yangban*'s house, you've been wielding power. Now you've not only lost your power for ten years, but also you have to live without food for ten days. I'll make you suffer.

Malttugi: Are you drunk?

Shoettugi: Am I drunk? Let's go. Let's go! [He leads Malttugi.] Saennim, according to your order, I've arrested him and brought him here.

Saennim: Make him lie down on his stomach and strike him. Give him a single hard exuberant strike. Then kill the criminal with another hard strike.

Shoettugi: Yes, sir. That's quite right. [To himself.] I think he must be a fellow who can even take money from a child. What kind of crime did he commit to make him lie down on his stomach? [When he is ready to strike him, Malttugi pantomimes that he is willing to give him money if he strikes him lightly. Shoettugi nods.]

Saennim: Damn you. Look!

Shoettugi: Yes, sir.

Saennim: Are you plotting to go to a wenching house?

Shoettugi: No, sir. If I strike him hard, he thinks he will die in front of you. So he is asking me to give him a pretend strike.

Saennim: No! That's wrong.

Shoettugi: Then what is it? What shall I do? I'm in trouble.

Saennim: No!

Shoettugi: He says he'll give you ten *yang*s if you make me give him a pretend strike. Ten *yang*s.

Saennim: No!

Shoettugi: He now tells me he'll give you twenty *yang*s. Twenty *yang*s! Twenty *yang*s!

Saennim: No!

Shoettugi: What shall I do? I'll add ten more *yang*s to that twenty *yang*s to make thirty *yang*s.

Saennim: Thirty *yang*s?

Shoettugi: Is it good enough?

Saennim: Damn you!

Shoettugi: Yes, sir.

Saennim: The man who is standing there is Toryŏngnim. He is from the main family. It has been nineteen years since he has received the wedding gifts from his future bride's family. Send twenty-nine *yang*s and ninety pennies to my home. With the remaining ten pennies, buy a bowl of wine for yourself and mix it with cold water and drink it. Then you'll have diarrhea, like you often have after eating a lot of turnips in November and December. After that, drop dead!

Shoettugi: Yes, Saennim. That's quite right. [Saennim and his fellow *yangban* exit to the costume hall.]

Malttugi: [Stands up.]

[In a *pullim.*]

In the deep stream
By the green mountain
The blue and yellow dragons
Wiggle their bodies.

[Malttugi and Shoettugi dance, facing each other, and exit.]

Act VII
Scene 2: P'odobujang

[P'odobujang [125] enters and sits down on the left side of the musicians. Saennim enters with Somu, his concubine. P'odobujang goes to the right of the musicians and sits down.]

Saennim: [He lives with the young Somu enjoying her as a conversational companion, although he is a peachy-faced old man with gray hair. Naturally, he is uneasy about his age. So he tries to placate Somu.] We live happily and interestingly. But I often wonder whether or not there is a young village tramp who tries to make me a cuckold? Beat out a tune! [He circles as he dances *kkaeki*-dance to the tune of *saemachi.* [126] Then he goes behind Somu and sits down.]

Somu: [While Saennim dances, she dances *chara*-dance on the same spot.]

P'odobujang: [He suddenly goes to Saennim and separates him from Somu.]

Saennim: [Surprised.] How about that? I felt strange and became suspicious. Damn you! You wicked fellow. You rascal! [He puts his head under Somu's underarm. Now he sticks his head out.] I've been suspicious about this. I have been living with a young woman. So I've always been worried about this kind of thing. No wonder. [To Somu.] You must trust me like you trust the sky. Everything will be all right. This tall and spacious tile-roofed house is all yours.

I don't think I can live too many years. So please don't change your mind. Trust me like you trust the sky. The young woman who lives with an old man is always well treated. Please, don't change your mind. I won't change mine. You, too, shouldn't change your mind. Beat out a tune! [He dances *kkach'igŏlŭm*-dance to the tune of *saemachi.*]

P'odobujang: [He joins them, dancing in excitement. Then he holds Somu's hand as he puts his legs between those of hers, first the right one and then the left one, alternately.]

Saennim: [Indignant. He calls his concubine as he jumps up and down. He now pushes P'odobujang's back with his fan.]

P'odobujang: [He runs to his original place for the time being when he is chased by Saennim.]

Saennim: [He stands as he embraces Somu.] What kind of flippant behavior was that? What have I been telling you all these days? Yes? Didn't I tell you that you shouldn't behave in such a way? Well. A young woman must like a young man. I've been telling you this all these days. Please, don't behave like that. The conjugal affection and the loyalty between you and I are even larger than Samkak-san Mountain. [127] When I find even a single bean in the street, I pick it up and blow on it, puffing and puffing, with my mouth to clean it. Then I split it into two pieces to toss the worm-eaten part into your mouth, while I eat the best part. This way of life has been our love. But why on earth have you changed your mind? [While he dances with Somu, P'odobujang comes and pushes him away.] That fellow has come back again. He deserves to be tortured on the rack. [He signals the musicians to stop playing. To Somu.] These things are not right. He looks like a man from a reputable family. He has a handsome round face. He must be a son of a dignified man. I must go and persuade him not to come back again. As long as an old man like me tells him, he won't do it again. I must go to his house. Meanwhile, take good care of yourself even if you get a bit lonely at home. Beat out a tune! [He goes as he dances *kkach'igŏlŭm*-dance to the tune of *saemachi.*

Now he stops.] It isn't right to leave a young woman alone in a large house. This worries me. Since I've already told her, however, I must go. Although I can't walk well, I must go by myself. [He goes toward P'odobujang as he dances. He suddenly strikes his face with his fan.] You son of a bitch! Why do you have to mesmerize my concubine? Can't you find any other woman? Since I'm old, I have to have a concubine for company in the long nights during the months of winter. When I can't sleep well in the night, I chat with her or ask her to scratch my back. As you see, I keep her to make my lonely hours shorter. But whenever you don't find my shoes on the step stone in front of my house, you jump over my hedge, thinking I'm not in the house, to make me a cuckold. You wicked fellow. I am telling you again. If you come back, I am going to go to bed with your mother. [As he dances, he goes to Somu, casting an amorous glance at her. Now he holds her by her underarm.] How have you been? Did you go somewhere?

Somu: [She points at the sky with her finger.]

Saennim: Oh, I see. You went to the sky with a star. Our conjugal affection and loyalty are as good as if I collect fifty percent interest from you in the fall after giving you a loan in the spring. I'll loan you three tin canfuls of frozen dog dung in the winter to collect fifty percent interest from them in the spring when the ground thaws to sow the melon seeds. These have been our conjugal affection and loyalty. Now you understand why I collect fifty percent interest from you, don't you? Such are the terms of our close relationship. Last night you put your hand on my stomach and let it glide downward, searching for something. Then you held it—squeezing and squeezing it—saying "Let's do it! Let's do it!" But I was old and weak without virility. That's the reason why you've been unfaithful to me. Isn't that right?

Somu: [She grabs Saennim by the collar and slaps his face. Then she signals P'odobujang to come to her. She kicks Saennim.]

P'odobujang: [Thinking that she has now become completely his woman, he is in splendid spirits. He pulls his hat down to make sure that it won't fly off. Then he dances vivaciously as he goes toward Somu while he lets his coat ends open like swallows' wings. He holds Somu's hands alternately as he dances with her.]

Saennim: [Thinking he is losing his concubine to P'odobujang, he calls her as he jumps up and down in great confusion. He goes to P'odobujang to regain Somu from him. But he is overpowered by P'odobujang. He finally chases P'odobujang away. Then he stands by Somu and breathes deeply.] I can't help it. I don't know what to do. Even when a tree gets old, the birds stop coming to it. Since I am old while you're young, you must like a young man. So I have to let you make yourself happy. But let me hold your hand once for the last time. [Somu does not offer her hand to him. P'odobujang offers his hand to him. He holds his hand and weeps. Then he suddenly realizes that he is holding P'odobujang's hand.] Damn it! You deserve to be slaughtered. You've quickly extended your hand to me while you're standing by her. You're my enemy. How is it possible for me to cry while holding your hand? [He pushes him away.]

P'odobujang: [He is pushed away by Saennim.]

Saennim: That is the way it should be. Even though we've been living for many decades as man and wife, it is impossible for you to extend your hand lightly when I ask you. That's the reason why we call ourselves man and wife who embrace each other to enjoy. But a manly man's talk is as heavy as one thousand golden nuggets. Since I have already withdrawn my sword, I can't put it back into the sheath. It is right for a young woman like you to enjoy a young man. I can't stop your life. So you should live with the young man happily. But let me hold your hand once for the last time.

Somu: [She offers her hand to Saennim.]

Saennim: This is really a woman's hand. Oh, yes. This is really your hand. Well. [He weeps.] When I, a manly man, once say something, I should take my action accordingly. I shouldn't do anything else. A young woman like you should marry a young man and have many sons and grandsons. They'll bring prosperity,

happiness, wealth, and fame to your family, including the joy of
their weddings. I wish you a very happy and easy life. *T'uwae!* [He
spits on the ground. Now he attaches the decree of divorce from
him to the front end of her jacket. Then he sends her off as he
swears to the decree. Now he requests the musicians to play the
tune of *saemachi* to which he dances *kkach'igŏlŭm*-dance for a
while. He exits to the costume hall.]

Somu: [She dances with P'odobujang who dances *kŏmmu*-dance [128] for
a while. She exits.]

Act VIII
Sinharabi and Miyalhalmi

[Sinharabi [129] enters to the middle of the playground. Miyalhalmi [130]
also makes her entrance. Sinharabi sings as he circles around the
playground. Tokki [131] and Tokki's Sister [132] are already in front of the
musicians.]

Sinharabi: [He sings.]

> *Children, my children.*
> *Have you seen a sandae mask-dance play?*
> *I, an old man of eighty,*
> *Have seen it, too.*

> *When I look up*
> *I see many deep valleys*
> *And mountain peaks.*

> *When I look down*
> *I see a wide white sandy beach.*

> *Oh, you, the sixteen-year-olds,*
> *Don't scoff at old age!*

> *Yesterday I also was a youth.*
> *But today I am peachy-faced*
> *With gray hair.*

[Miyalhalmi makes some rustling sounds. He looks at her.]
Hello, wife! Why did you have to follow me? Why did you have to
follow me, leaning on your cane, while dropping tears and letting
your nose run? You followed me like a small thin snake which
chases a green frog. By the way, what did you do with our old
cauldron with holes and with the broken spoons?

Miyalhalmi: [She swiftly lifts her skirt and points to her stomach.]

Sinharabi: That's right. You are very scrupulous. Anyway, you're eighty
years old while I am ninety. Why don't we separate from each
other?

Miyalhalmi: [She nods as though she agrees to his proposal.]

Sinharabi: [He sings.]

> *Scratch hard your yellow hair,*
> *Clasp your hands,*
> *Leave your cane on your stomach,*
> *Then drop dead!*

Even a famous beauty in Tang China had to die. But what is the
use of living for a life as fleeting as the dew on the grass?

Miyalhalmi: [As she hears Sinharabi's song, she dies.]

Sinharabi: [Without knowing that she is dead, he goes to look for her.]
They say we should search even for a missing dog which has been
eating rice out of the same cauldron. How is it possible for me not
to look for my wife who has lived with me for the past thirty
years?

[He sings.]

> *Wife, have you gone to the Pine Village*
> *Over Mansu-san Mountain?*
>
> *Did you go to Yi T'ae-paek,*
> *The prince of drinking,*
> *To ask him to drink with you?*

Did you go to see
The four old hermits in Sang-san Mountain [133]
To help their checker game?

Or did you go to the Yŏngch'ŏn-kang River
To wash your feet in the water?

[He finds a dead body. He is shocked.] My goodness! An unclean event happened in the street. [He examines the dead body and finds that it is his wife.] Hello, wife! Stand up! Such a temperament you have. I told you that story only because I loved you so much. Your temper is as sharp as a dried leaf which easily catches fire. Why are you playing dead? I am not going to be deceived. Stand up, wife! My goodness. Look. She really put her cane on her stomach and died. Her body is already stiff. She is dead. What shall I do? I am an eighty-year-old man and wear a cloth full of patches. I have happened to experience this unfortunate incident on the road. [He covers her body.] What shall I do? I have a prodigal son. But it has been many years since he went to Manchuria to work with a railroad construction company. There are so many people out there. He might have come back and hidden in the crowd. I have no choice but to call him.

[In a singsong tone.]

Tokki---!
Tokki---!

Tokki: Why are you calling me? [He jumps out from the front section of the musicians.]

Sinharabi: Are you Tokki?

Tokki: I am Kkakkwi. [134]

Sinharabi: Tokki?

Tokki: Yes, I am Tokki.

Sinharabi: If you're Tokki, where have you been all these years?

Tokki: I was shitting.

Sinharabi: Were you caught by a diarrhea? Hey! Why did you have to shit for so many years?

Tokki: Well. That isn't the reason. Let me tell you the story. Do you remember that you asked me to take six *yang*s, the monthly payment, to Comrade Kim in the other village after you sold the calf?

Sinharabi: Yes.

Tokki: Well, . . . On my way to Comrade Kim's house, I happened to see a few old people—about eighty or ninety years old—who were playing dominoes under the willow tree. I felt I should play, too. There was a lot of money. Have you ever heard of someone who doesn't like money? So I decided to win some money by loaning those six *yang*s to an old man. Of course, I couldn't participate as a regular player in the game. So I asked him to bet my money for me. But I lost all of it just over his shoulder. After that, I couldn't come home because I was afraid that you might beat me until my bones splintered or until my death. So, after that, I ran away.

Sinharabi: What was I supposed to do when you ran away? It doesn't matter. Well. Your mother had a cold fart.

Tokki: She had a cold fart?

Sinharabi: She made the air stink.

Tokki: You mean she has already gone up?

Sinharabi: She gave up her spoon. Do you understand?

Tokki: I always worried about her. I felt sorry for mother because she had to endure all your small talk ever since she married you. It is fortunate for her that she finally died. I also felt sorry to learn that she had to die on the road. Since you have such inturned teeth, like a difficult man, I think you could easily eat up the whole family. Now what shall we do?

Sinharabi: There is no need to talk about this or that. Her death has already occurred. Your sister who used to live in Chaetkkol moved to Monjitkkol. Bring her home, so we can have the funeral.

Tokki: Ha, ha, ha! What kind of fucking fortune do I have to endure? Look. You're asking the chief mourner whose hair has tumbled loose to carry the obituary. Isn't there anyone else in the village? Well, . . . If there's no one else, I will go.

Sinharabi: Go!

Tokki: Do you think she is at home?

Sinharabi: You have to go and find out.

Tokki: I'm not sure whether or not she is at home. That damn woman used to run around committing adultery.

Sinharabi: Well. Go and find out.

Tokki: I'm going.

Sinharabi: Go! Come back quickly.

Tokki: Does she live as well as she used to?

Sinharabi: I haven't heard from her for the last three years.

Tokki: Well, father. . .

Sinharabi: What is it?

Tokki: Have you written to her during this time?

Sinharabi: You! How can you possibly ask your father whether he has written to her or not?

Tokki: Well. What else can be asked in our house?

Sinharabi: You mongrel. Stop talking like that!

Tokki: Well, I'm going.

Sinharabi: Go! Haven't you gone yet? You!

Tokki: [He goes before the musicians and calls his sister.] Sister! Sis---ter!

Tokki's Sister: Who are you?

Tokki: I am Tokki.

Tokki's Sister: Kkakkwi?

Tokki: Tokki is here.

Tokki's Sister: A plane? [135]

Tokki: You have become deaf. Tokki is here.

Tokki's Sister: Oh, a chisel.

Tokki: My goodness. Tokki is here.

Tokki's Sister: Oh, Tokki.

Tokki: Yes.

Tokki's Sister: You came back again? But there's no use your coming
here again. I've mortgaged everything already to the pawn shop.
Now I'm barely managing to keep myself alive by doing day labor
at Comrade Kim's house. Even if I were to run around in a short
skirt, I still couldn't make ends meet. In the old days you used to
sponge on me by tricking me out of a couple of hundred *yangs*. So
you came back again? But there's no use your coming to me this
time. I don't have any money. Go back to your home.

Tokki: Oh, sister. It's natural for you to talk to me in that way because
you've been deceived again and again by me. But what I'm going to
tell you now is not a lie. It is the truth. It's easy for you to talk that
way because I often lost money which I tricked out of you in the
rice candy peddling business. But that isn't what I want to tell you
now. Our mother is gone to *Saep'yŏng-ri*. [136]

Tokki's Sister: Did you say mother had a cold fart?

Tokki: Mother has already gone up completely.

Tokki's Sister: I don't believe you even if you say that you can steam
soybeans for making soybean paste or sauce.

Tokki: No! That isn't what I am saying. When father went to the playground to see a *sandae* mask-dance play, mother followed him. Father mistreated her a little, I assume. So mother felt sad about her mistreatment by him. Then she died suddenly, stiffening her body. As you know, father is a difficult man and doesn't have anything. . . neither money nor friends. Of course, I have been a prodigal son. But I believe there must be something which is called the natural relationship of man. When father was in such a sad state and called me, I recognized his voice at once. So I ran to him and asked him what was happening. Then he told me mother died. What should we have done at that moment? Father asked me to take the obituary note to you and bring you home. Even though I can be a prodigal son and trick some money out of you, I'm not such a debauchee as to deceive you about mother's death. This is not a lie. Sister, let's go home and have the funeral.

Tokki's Sister: You're telling me a story in such an interesting and humorous way. But I can't believe it. I don't think what you're saying is true.

Tokki: It is the truth! Where's my brother-in-law?

Tokki's Sister: It has been nine years since he left me. I am struggling somewhere between life and death to make a living.

Tokki: Oh, my goodness. This must be a good chance for me. Well, you've said it has been nine years since my brother-in-law left you. If so, you must have had many difficulties in those years.

Tokki's Sister: To the villagers, I had to give away. . . many times for nothing.

Tokki: Oh my. If you had something to give away, you should have given some of it to me too. Are you going to. . .?

Tokki's Sister: You fool! How can a sister and a brother have that? Had I followed you and missed all opportunities, . . . what could an old woman like me do? You might sell me to a beef-soup-with-rice restaurant or just a rice-soup restaurant. What am I supposed to do if you make me suffer like that?

Tokki: No! No! That isn't the case. My goodness. You're still young—a spring chicken.

Tokki's Sister: Because you're crazy about money, it doesn't matter to you whether you can get twenty *yang*s or two hundred *yang*s for me. But don't you think I have to sell myself?

Tokki: No! That isn't the truth. Anyway, let's go home!

Tokki's Sister: What will you do for me, if it is a lie?

Tokki: If it proves to be a lie, I promise to live with you.

Tokki's Sister: What? You damn fool. You fucker. All right! Let's go!

Tokki: Let's go, sister!

Tokki's Sister: Let's go!

Tokki: [They come to the place where Miyalhalmi is lying dead.] This is it.

Tokki's Sister: Is this the place?

Tokki: Yes.

Tokki's Sister: Where is father?

Tokki: I don't know. Well, . . . He is such a difficult man. Even though he is my father, I detest him. Sister?

Tokki's Sister: Yes.

Tokki: This is the mortuary.

Tokki's Sister: The mortuary?

Tokki: Please, look.

Tokki's Sister: You couldn't give her a single package of herb medicine. Look at her face. She has died of the autumn frost.

Tokki: What is the use of talking about that?

Tokki's Sister: My goodness. Even her nose hasn't been wiped. How could you and father possibly mistreat her like this? Because you didn't clean her nose and eyes, I don't think her soul traveled to the nether world. You didn't give her a single package of herb medicine. Let's give her some medicine. Even if we give her some medicine, I don't think she is going to revive. [She goes to Sinharabi and bows to him.] Father. . .

Sinharabi: Yes.

Tokki's Sister: Well. I've checked the pulse all over her body.

Sinharabi: Yes.

Tokki's Sister: Her whole body is dead. She is dead. But. . .

Sinharabi: She is dead.

Tokki: But the place in which father used to struggle to make sister and me is still alive.

Sinharabi: What? What is still alive? I have to feel it. Let me feel it!

Tokki: It is still alive. Why are you in such a rush to feel it? I have to feel it first.

Sinharabi: Well. Are you going to feel it?

Tokki: I felt it. It is still alive.

Sinharabi: You! Damn you!

Tokki: If you still want to struggle with it, you go ahead. It's all right even in front of us.

Sinharabi: You. Don't come near your sister. [To Tokki's Sister.] You come here. Come in front of me. Don't go near him.

Tokki: We have to think about the funeral.

Sinharabi: Let's have it. Let's try to have the funeral. Tokki!

Tokki: Yes.

Sinharabi: I don't know what else we can do. If it had happened at home, we could have called the ten kings [137] and the three holy sages [138] to repose her soul. But since she has died on the road, we can't do this. So, instead, let's have a shamanistic utterance for the dead soul.

Tokki: Yes. That's a good idea. If we could afford it, we would have given a lot of offerings to the shamans to perform a rite for her. But we can't do that. So let's do it by ourselves. Sister, you play the role of shaman. Father will become the hourglass-shaped drum player. Now, come the three strings and the six musical instrument players! Play the tune of *kutkŏri*![139] I am going to dance.

Tokki's Sister: [She utters the shamanistic ravings.]

> *The dead soul.*
> *It's the dead soul.*
>
> *The first soul.*
> *On the green willow*
> *In the steep mountain.*
>
> *If it's the dead soul,*
> *Let's put it on the soul board.*
>
> *If it's a dead body,*
> *Let's put it in a coffin.*
>
> *When I look up,*
> *I see many deep valleys*
> *And mountain peaks.*
>
> *When I look down,*
> *I see a wide white sandy beach.*

[She now offers the ceremonial wine.]

On this street and that street, I am offering the holy wine. The deceased younger brother, please play in a dried gourdful of water from the well.

Hello! All of you, the audience and monks! Please help us conclude this play peacefully and safely. And all of you, including the deceased younger brother, please have a good time and return home safely.

Now let's perform an exorcism!

Ttŏngki!

Ttŏngki!

Ttŭngttŏkkung. Ttŏng ttŏngttŏkkung.

[Sinharabi, Tokki, and Tokki's Sister exit as they dance, facing each other.]

Notes

1. The Sajik-tang: The Hall of Guardian Deities.

2. Wanpo: The leader of the eight monks. In Buddhism, the monk who communicates with spirits. The basic color of this mask is maroon with wrinkles on the forehead and cheeks. This character wears a Buddhist monk's coat with the picture of a dragon on its back, a belt, and a gray four-cornered horse-hair cap with an opening on the top.

3. Omchung: The monk with scabies. The basic color of this mask is black and red with many pimples. This character wears a monk's coat with the picture of a dragon on its back. He has two small sticks. A pair of cymbals hang from his belt.

4. Mŏkchung: The over-all color of this mask is bright orange with large wrinkles on the forehead. There are a few pieces of gilded gold on the forehead and cheeks. This character wears a Buddhist monk's coat with the picture of a dragon on its back, a red belt, and gray leggings. There are more than one Mŏkchung in the play.

5. Malttugi: The servant of Saennim. The color of this mask is maroon with many wrinkles. This character wears blue armour without sleeves and a felt hat. He has a horse whip. The prefix "mal" means horse, while the affix "ttugi" refers to a stake. Thus, Malttugi literally means a stake where a horse is tied. In the old society those people who engaged in lowly professions, such as servants, often did not possess names. They were simply called Malttugi, Shoettugi [a stake where a cow is tied] or Kaettongi [dog dung].

6. The six musical instruments [*samhyŏn-yukkak*]: They include two *p'iri* [fife], one *chŏtdae* [transverse flute], one *haegŭm* [two-stringed Korean fiddle], one *changgo* [hour-glass shaped drum], and one *puk* [barrel drum].

7. Nojang: A high Buddhist monk. The color of this mask is black with white speckles. This character wears a long gray monk's coat, a red belt, and monk's hat adorned with pine branches. He has a folding fan, a bamboo stick, and a rosary.

8. Somu: A sorceress or a sing-song girl. This mask's color is white with three red dots: one on her forehead; one on either cheek. This character wears a jacket, *chŏkori*, with sleeves of many-colored stripes. There are two Somu in the play.

9. Ch'wipali: An old bachelor. This mask is painted red with a carved wooden nose and light brown hair in a pig tail. There are wrinkles on its forehead and cheeks. The slanted eyes are white with red eyeballs. This character wears a costume with a picture of a crane and a red belt. He has a branch of the flowering cherry. He also plays the role of Shoettugi.

10. The beginning of the first sentence of an ode.

11. The day, month, and year when this play is performed.

12. Sangjwa: In Buddhism, the monk who succeeds his master among many disciples. The color of this mask is white with red dots at the beginning of the eyes. There are a few pieces of gilded gold on the forehead and cheeks.

13. *Yŏmbul*: A tune of Buddhist invocation such as the repetition of the sacred name of Amitabha with a six-beat pattern.

14. *Kŭtŭrŭm*-dance: The pattern of this dance is as follows. The dancer tilts his head to the left as he raises and waves his right hand. Now he raises his left hand as he tilts his head to the right. Then he bows to the deity of heaven, stooping gradually, while holding his hands together.

15. *Sapangch'igi*-dance: In this dance the dancer faces all directions in turn.

16. *T'aryŏng*. A ballad tune.

17. *Kkaeki*-dance: A basic form of mask dance. This dance uses every part of the dancer's body. This dance is generally danced to the tune of *t'aryŏng*.

18. *P'alttukchapi*-dance: A form of mask dance. First, the dancer holds his right arm with left hand as he stoops and makes a clockwise turn. Then he puts his right foot a step forward while holding his right arm with his left hand as he makes a circle with his right hand. Then he moves one step forward. He now dances back to his original place as he turns his arm.

19. Hereafter Omchung is simply called Om.

20. This imaginary creature, represented by a bear with the nose of an elephant, the eyes of a rhinoceros, the tail of a bull, and the legs of a tiger, is said to eat metal to expel nightmares, and to purge noxious vapors.

21. The end of the Koryŏ dynasty [919 A.D.-1392 A.D.] whose capital was Songto [now Kaesŏng].

22. He is referring to a Korean chess game, *changgi*, implying that Sangjwa has an advantage over him with extra pieces.

23. A nonsense-syllable phrase which is often employed to cue the musicians as to what type of music or rhythmic beat is to be played for the ensuing dance.

24. An interjection which is often used as a cue for the next character.

25. Here the delicate meaning of the dialogue is lost because of the impossibility of an exact translation of puns. The word "wear" [*tsuda*] has the same sound as the word "use" in Korean. Hence he means that he did not borrow anything from Mŏkchung to use.

26. In the nineteenth century, the lowly people, such as foot soldiers and servants, were not allowed to wear horse-tail hats. Instead, they wore felt hats.

27. Again the exact meaning of the dialogue is lost due to the difficulty of an exact translation of puns. The word for hair brooch "*o'knu*" has a similar sound to the word for white heron [*paekno*] in Korean. The hair brooch which was worn by a high official or an envoy was usually made with jade in the shape of a white heron.

28. This is also an interjection. For an explanation, refer to Note 24.

29. A folk tale which tells of a goddess who brings smallpox to every family member.

30. *Yŏdaji*-dance: This dance requires forward movement. The dancer places both hands on the upper front of his body and, extending them forward, pantomimes the opening of his chest while his feet kick forward.

31. *Kopsawi*-dance: This dance involves the dancer retreating backward from the musicians as he waves his arms over his shoulders.

32. *Mŏngsŏkmari*-dance: This is a dance of forward movement in which the dancer moves as though he is rolling a rug. This dance is done while moving toward the musicians.

33. *Hŏrijapi*-dance: In this dance the dancer lifts his legs alternately while stepping on the same spot as he keeps his hands on his waist. This dance is often danced in front of another dancer to tease him.

34. *Pullim*: See Note 23.

35. *Samjin-samt'oe*: Originally a form of military dance. Basically this dance requires three steps forward and another three steps backward.

36. *Nalgaep'yŏgi*-dance: This dance is done by stretching and folding the dancer's arms.

37. Yŏnip: A high monk. The upper part of this mask is painted blue, while the lower part is red. This character wears a blue costume and has a fan with the picture of a flower.

38. Nunkkŭmjŏki: A high monk. This deep maroon-colored mask has oblong bumps on the cheeks. The eyebrows and thick lips are painted many colors. The unique aspect of this mask is its large round eyes which are made to blink when the player's mouth manipulates a wire attached to the eyelids. This character wears a gray full-dress with a dragon pattern.

39. *Yangban*: During the Chosŏn dynasty [1392 A.D.-1910 A.D.], civil officials were called *munban* and military officials, *muban*. The affix—*ban*—means "class," while "*yang*" implies both. *Yangban*, thus, suggests "both classes of aristocrats."

40. A famous scenic place in China which is also known for the production of beautiful mottled bamboo.

41. An abbreviation of Mŏkchung.

42. A Buddhist invocation.

43. They are degrading Buddhism by inserting "*halmi*" in an invocation. The word "*halmi*" means an old woman.

44. The word "*ŏmi*" means a mother animal.

45. Note the word "*ŏmi*."

46. Note the word "*halmi*."

47. He is implying that he is one generation higher than Wanpo because he included "*halmi*" in the invocation instead of "*ŏmi*."

48. An interjection.

49. Here the exact meaning is missing because of the difficulty of an exact translation of puns. The word for the gay quarter of blossoms and willows, "*hwaryu*," has a similar sound as the word for one day, "*haru*" in Korean.

50. This implies a visit to a house of prostitution.

51. The word *"tong"* means a street.

52. In this case, the word *"tong"* means a unit of weight used by farmers a long time ago.

53. Here the word *"tong"* means a unit of length for fabrics used by the Koreans a long time ago.

54. The word *"sae"* means a bird, thus implying this is a high pass that only birds can cross over.

55. This implies that for a girl who is passing the marriageable age, a year seems to have thirteen months when she waits for her wedding the following year.

56. The Buddhist monks are prohibited from eating meat, for Buddhism regards the killing of a living creature as a sin.

57. Haetong: Another name for Korea in the old days.

58. Chosŏn: Another name for Korea.

59. Hanyang: Today's Seoul, the capital of Korea.

60. This means Yi Sŏng-kae, a Koryŏ general, who revolted to found the Chosŏn dynasty in 1392.

61. The Six Boards of the Government: These included the Civil Office Board, the Ceremonies Board, the Revenue Board, the Punishment Board, the Public Works Board, and the War Board in the Government of the Chosŏn dynasty.

62. The Five Military Divisions: This means five army divisions during the Koryŏ period.

63. A city in North P'yŏngan-do Province.

64. The river which flows between the northwestern end of Korea and the southwestern end of Manchuria.

65. *Ch'ŏnja: The Thousand Character Text,* a primer of Chinese characters.

66. *Yuhak:* The study material for the scholars without office.

67 *Tongmongsŏnsup*: The book which contains the teachings of moral rules to govern Five Human Relations [of prince and ministers, father and son, husband and wife, brothers, and friends.] and the abbreviated history of the relationship between Korea and China.

68. *The Book of Ode [Sijŏn]:* A book which contains the Chinese poems between the first century B.C. and the eighth century A.D.

69. *The Canon of History [Sojŏn]:* A book by a Chinese scholar of the Sung dynasty.

70. *The Works of Mencius:* The writings of a Chinese philosopher, Mencius [372-289 B.C.].

71. *The Analects of Confucius [Nonŏ]:* The book which contains the characters and behaviours of Confucius and his disciples.

72. In the old society, an unmarried young gentleman wore braided hair like a pig tail.

73. This refers to a narrow wooden board used in sewing or in cutting paper in the old days.

74. It is not clear whether a boy wore a skirt in the old days.

75. A brush made with the weasel's tail hair.

76. The player of this role wears the Malttugi mask.

77. *Yang:* A monetary unit in the old days.

78. The word "new" in Korean has a similar sound to the family name, Sin.

79. It is not clear what kind of dance this is.

80. Waejangnyŏ: An old sing-song woman. The mother of Aesatang. This mask is painted white with three red dots: one on her forehead and one on either cheek. This character wears a gray jacket and skirt. She has a small wrapped bundle.

81. Aesatang: The daughter of Waejangnyŏ. This mask is painted white with three red dots: One on her forehead and one on each cheek. This character wears a pig tail in the style of unmarried girls and a peaked monk's cowl. She has a stick for a small drum.

82. It is good.

83. The sound "*k'ong*," the striking sound of a drum, has a similar sound for the word beans, "*k'ong*" in Korean.

84. The word "*noktu*" means green pea. Thus the use of the sounds "*k'ong*" and "*noktu*" provides the puns. But the sound "*k'wang*" simply means a different sound from the striking of a drum.

85. For a formal occasion, a man usually wears a pair of long loose pants which come down below the ankles. Thus it is necessary for the man to have ankle belts to keep the pant legs tight. In this case, he implies that Wanpo is stupid enough to wear his ankle belts with a pair of short pants which do not require them, since they stop above the knees.

86. An island off western Kyŏnggi-do Province.

87. See Note 8.

88. *Chara*-dance: This is a unique dance danced by Somu or Waejangnyŏ. The basic form of this dance: The dancer brings her right hand to the front of her face. Then she turns her hand upside down. Now she lifts her hand quickly and lowers it. This dance is often danced by a female to seduce a man.

89. *Kalchija*-dance: One of the basic dance forms of *kkaeki*-dance. This is generally danced by Nojang or Om. The dancer waves his sleeves this way and that, dancing with tottering steps, while moving his hips, and swaying his shoulders.

90. Shoe Peddler: There is no special mask for this character. The player of this character wears the Malttugi mask.

91. A mountain in Seoul.

92. Monkey: The basic color of this mask is deep scarlet with round eyes circled with white lines. Long hair lines the edge of its face. This character wears red armour and red leggings.

93. A simple song which is taught to a baby with finger gestures.

94. The word "*pongchi*" means a paper bag in Korean.

95. *Kopsa*-dance or *hŏt'un*-dance: A kind of improvisational dance to be followed when the dancer is in a state of ecstasy.

96. See Note 9.

97. *Kwanchachaeposal*: A Buddhist invocation.

98. Masan: A city in South Kyŏngsang-do Province. The word "*masan*" literally means the mountain of horses. Hence it implies a mountain as huge and as strong as many horses.

99. P'yŏngt'aek: A city in Kyŏnggi-do Province. The word "*p'yŏngt'aek*" means a flat marsh, thus suggesting that it is impossible for such a place to split into two pieces.

100. The hissing sound which is often made to chase a snake away.

101. *Kkach'igŏlŭm*-dance: A form of dance which is modeled on the walking pattern of the magpie. The dancer lifts his legs while stepping with long strides.

102. Korean custom requires that the mourner whose parents are dead keep his hair loose until the funeral is over.

103. Here the exact meaning of the puns is lost because of the difficulty of a precise translation of them. The Korean word for topknot, "*sangt'u*", has a sound and intonation resembling the word for boxing, "*kwŏnt'u*," although they are not exactly the same.

104. Midwife: The player of this role wears the Waejangnyŏ mask with the addition of the childbirth instruments and a baby doll. See Note 80.

105. Note that both the roles of Ch'wipali and Baby are played by Ch'wipali himself. In the original printed version, only a single character, Ch'wipali, is listed. For the reader's convenience, however, the translator substitutes Baby for Ch'wipali when he speaks in the role of Baby.

106. A distorted beginning of *The Thousand Character Text*.

107. The Korean alphabet.

108. Consonant sounds of the Korean alphabet.

109. The symbol of *kiŏk* looks like a familiar shape for the traditional Korean house.

110. The sound of "*tikŭt*" is similar to the word which means "worrisome" in Korean, "*chikŭtchikŭt*," thus implying that life is tiresome and tedious.

111. See Note 5.

112. Saennim: A gentleman scholar. The over-all color of this mask is soft pink. It has a wooden nose and a bump on the left cheek. One of the most distinctive features of this mask is its upper lip, which is a cleft palate exposing the teeth. This character wears a white full-dress and a Confucian ceremonial hood. He has a fan.

113. Sŏpangnim: A young master. The player of this character wears the Sangjwa mask. See Note 12. This character wears a white full-dress and a four-cornered horse-hair hat with an open top. He has a fan.

114. Toryŏngnim: A young bachelor. This character wears one of the Sangjwa masks. He wears armour and the cap which is worn with a Taoist garment. He has a fan.

115. Shoettugi: The player of this role wears the Ch'wipali mask. See Note 9. This character wears a blue dress with wide white sleeves and open seams in the back.

116. In the old society of Korea, smoking by a member of the younger generation in front of an elder was not allowed.

117. *Hwarang*: The flower of youth in the Silla period [57 B.C.-935 A.D.]. They excelled in beauty, bravery, and military arts. The word *hwarang* often also refers to shamans.

118. One of the three major gates of Seoul during the Chosŏn period, which still stands today.

119. The prefix "*il*" means one, while "*yi*" signifies two in Korean. The prefix "*sam*" should be translated as three, "*sa*" as four, and "*o*" as five. The words "*chang*," "*kol*," and "*t'ŏ*" all invariably mean place or street in Korean. Thus this is a kind of pun.

120. The prefix "*ch'il*" means seven, while "*p'al*" is eight in Korean. The prefix "*ku*" should be translated as nine and "*sip*" as ten. The affix "*an*" should mean an inner place, "*chae*" a ridge, "*kae*" a pass, and "*kak*" a pavilion. Again this is a game of puns.

121. A town in North P'yŏngan-do Province.

122. Here he implies that he should insert Shoettugi's head into his anus.

123. The beginning of *The Thousand Character Text*.

124. He is implying that only the affixes should be read when they are read together.

125. P'odobujang: The police chief. The color of this bearded mask is white. This character wears a Korean overcoat, *turumagi*, a horse-hair headband, and a horse-hair hat.

126. *Saemachi*: A tune for *P'ansori*.

127. A mountain north of Seoul.

128. *Kŏmmu*-dance: A sword dance. Today this dance is no longer included in the performance. This dance has been forgotten.

129. Sinharabi: An old man. This whitish mask bears the expressin of an old man with many wrinkles and a gray beard. This character wears a white full-dress and a red belt.

130. Miyalhalmi: An old woman. The color of this mask is light brown with the expression of an old woman. One of the distinctive features of this mask is its asymmetrical mouth in the shape of a half moon.

131. Tokki: The son of Sinharabi and Miyalhalmi. The player of this role wears the Malttugi mask. See Note 5. The word "*tokki*" means an ax in Korean. This character wears blue armour without sleeves and a felt hat. He has a whip.

132. Tokki's Sister: The player of this role wears the Waejangnyŏ mask. This character wears a mourner's dress and has a bell and a fan. See Note 80.

133. He is referring to the four hermits who went to a mountain during the Han dynasty in China to avoid war.

134. Here the delicate meaning is somewhat lost because of the impossibility of a precise translation of puns. The word "*kkakwi*" literally means an instrument which is used for the carving of wood, while "*tokki*" is used for cutting.

135. She is referring to his name, Tokki, which literally means an ax.

136. The area where a public cemetery was located in Seoul in the old days.

137. He is referring to the ten great kings who are supposed to rule the world of the dead.

138. The three holy sages in ancient Korea who supposedly created the land of Korea in a legend.

139. *Kutkŏri*: A tune derived from farmers' music of Kyŏnggi-do Province.

Illustrations

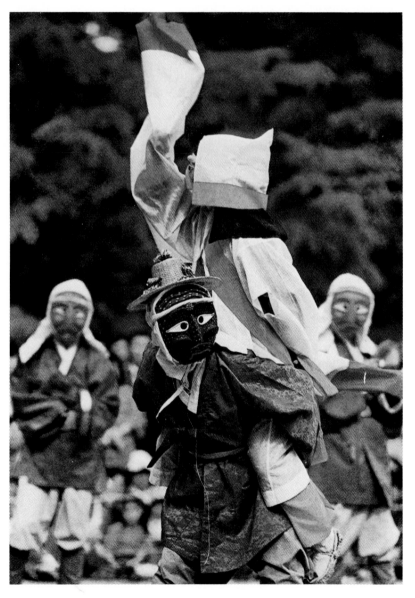

Figure 1
Yangju *Pyŏlsandae*: A dance by Aesatang, a young woman, on the back of Mŏkchung I, who wears the Malttugi mask, in Scene 3, Act V.

Figure 2
Hahoe *Pyŏlsin-kut*: Yangban, an aristocrat, flirts with Punae, a concubine, in Scene 5.

Figure 3
Tongyŏng *Okwangdae*: A funeral scene for Halmi, an old woman, in Act IV.

Figure 4
Suyŏng *Yayu*: Yŏnggam, an old man, and Halmi, an old woman, in Act III.

Figure 5
Pongsan *T'alch'um*: A dance by Nojang, an old monk, and somu, a sing-song girl, in Scene 1, Act IV.

Figure 6
Kkoktu Kaksi: A funeral scene in Scene 7.

Hahoe *Pyŏlsin-kut*

Introduction

Origins and Purposes

For a long time, until the first quarter of the twentieth century, the performance of Hahoe *pyŏlsin-kut* had been a traditional custom in Hahoe Village, North Kyŏngsang-do Province, [1] as a part of the village festival. The word *pyŏlsin* broadly means an exorcism or an incantation practiced by shamans or by fishermen, [2] while *kut* denotes a spectacle or a show. A compound of these two words, thus, implies an incantatious spectacle.

The origin of Hahoe *pyŏlsin-kut* is not clear. An earlier form of this drama, according to some scholars, had probably already been performed in various fashions long before it was adopted by the village of Hahoe. One theory suggests that the origin of this drama can be traced back to the ritual ceremony practiced by the fishermen of the southern coast, [3] while another theory implies that this drama may have its genesis in many forms of ritualistic heaven worship practiced by the people in the Hahoe region throughout history. [4] A third theory claims that it was a spontaneous creation of the oppressed people in the old society. [5]

At Hahoe Village there were two types of festivals: The *tongje,* the village festival, which was performed every year and the *pyŏlsin-kut,* the special festival, which, on a larger scale, was held only every tenth year. The *tongje* was simple and performed by only a handful of participants, but the *pyŏlsin-kut,* with which we are particularly concerned because it included the production of a play, required far greater and more elaborate preparation. All of the villagers were asked to participate in the special festival.

The *pyŏlsin-kut* was not exclusively for the people in Hahoe, but for the people of the neighboring regions as well. For the festival, the spectators flocked to the village from all over the central part of the country; this created great congestion and a festive mood in this otherwise sleepy hamlet.

To perform this festival, the master of ceremonies, the players, and other helpers all took a holy bath to cleanse themselves and boarded together in the same house. This building was confined with divine straw rope, thereby strictly prohibiting outsiders from entering. Another important regulation was that every inhabitant of the village was strictly forbidden to eat meat during the festival. This was done to avoid suffering that would result from breaking the taboo of uncleaness.

Regardless of its origins, Hahoe *pyŏlsin-kut* appears to have had a number of important purposes: first, the ensuring of prosperity for the village as exhibited in the first scene; second, the expulsion of evil spirits, demonstrated in the second scene, and the prevention of demons from entering into the village; and third, the entertainment of the audience.

Masks

Today only nine of the original twelve wooden masks of Hahoe *pyŏlsin-kut* remain. No one knows exactly what may have happened to the other three. One theory suggests that two of the three were stolen by the people of Pyŏngsan, a neighboring village. Giving credence to this speculation is the existence of two such masks in Pyŏngsan. Another theory is that the three missing masks were stolen by a Japanese scholar and taken to Japan. Further investigations need to be carried out to determine whether or not the two Pyŏngsan masks indeed belong to Hahoe, and to pursue any other information as to their whereabouts.

The nine existing masks are Kaksi [young woman], Chung [monk], Yangban [aristocrat], Ch'oraengi [clown servant of Yangban], Sŏnpi [scholar], Imae [servant of Sŏnpi], Punae [concubine], Paekjŭng [butcher], and Halmi [old woman]. Besides these nine human masks, there are two animated Chuji masks which represent the imaginary winged lions. The three missing masks are Ch'ongkak [young bachelor], Pyŏlch'ae [civil servant?], and Ttŏktari [old man]. These masks were missing when the village held its last tenth year festival in 1928.[6]

When the masks were not in use, they were generally enshrined in the Sŏnang-tang, the Shrine of the Village Guardian Deity.[7] The masks were regarded as sacrosanct by the villagers. It is said that if any of the participants of the festival had a relationship with a woman during the festival, a monstrous and strange thing would happen in the village. Thus the villagers believed that the masks served as protective gods, possessing the power to expel evil spirits and demons from the village.

For these reasons, as well as for their inviolable sacredness, the villagers worshipped the masks as though they were omnipotent gods who commanded supernatural power. If the villagers had not regarded them as sacred, they might have destroyed the masks at the end of each performance as demanded in some other forms of mask-dance drama in Korea. At the end of each festival, however, they returned the masks to the shrine.

The task of mask making in Hahoe was supposedly closely related to the divinities. The literary documents to verify this assumption are yet to be found, but it is said that the masks were made only by a man instructed by divine message in a dream. Concerning mask making, there is a well-known legend about the Imae mask in Hahoe. One night in his dream, a young bachelor, Hŏ Ch'ongkak, was ordered by a deity to make the Imae mask. So he took a holy bath, purified himself, and commenced the task of making the mask in a building to which admission was strictly forbidden by virtue of the divine rope being stretched around it. In the village there was a young girl who loved Hŏ Ch'ongkak dearly. One day, unable to control her love for him, she went to the building and made a hole in the door through which she peeped. Hŏ Ch'ongkak suddenly fell dead with blood streaming from his throat; the mask was left unfinished. Even today this mask does not have a chin. This legend is a definite indication of the serious nature of mask making at Hahoe.

No document has been found which varifies the production dates of the Hahoe masks. The difficulties of determining their production dates are further compounded by the fact that no mask bears the name of its maker. Some scholars suggest that a few of these masks are products of the Koryŏ period [918 A.D.-1391 A.D.] when Buddhism flourished.

The facial expression of some Buddhist sculpture can be characterized as mobile, fluid, and excitable—like the images of Buddha—while Confucian art of the Chosŏn dynasty [1392 A.D.-1910 A.D.] expresses serenity and calm. In addition, the Confucian art emphasizes the well-proportioned arrangement of the human figures, but strikingly lacking in the Hahoe masks are such emotionless, impassive, and orderly feelings.

Contrary to the Confucian art, the expressiveness of the Hahoe masks is great. They appear to change their expression when one looks at them from different angles. For example, they have fixed expression when viewed in a direct line of vision. When they are tilted downward, their expressions convey gloomy and somber feelings, while they appear to express some degree of exuberance when tilted upward. Thus the characteristics of the Hahoe masks are extremely rich and fluid, even metamorphic. This nonstatic quality might well be the influence of the Buddha images of Koryŏ.

The Play

No original play script of Hahoe *pyŏlsin-kut* is now extant. It is also unknown who was responsible for the beginning of this drama or when it began. Despite the fact that this drama has a long history and some excellent theatrical qualities, its importance was never recognized by scholars until recently. As a result, this festival drama remained nothing more than a village play until the first quarter of the twentieth century.

Hahoe *pyŏlsin-kut* does not have a single straight plot line; each scene has its own independent plot. Although the play has no over-all plot, it is tenuously held together by means of its themes: ridicule of the transgressing Buddhist monks, the corruption of the upper class, and mockery of insensitive local officials.

Notes

1. It has been reported that presently some well-intended young people in Antong, North Kyŏngsang-do Province, are trying to revive this drama.

2. Han'gŭl Hakhoe, *K'ŭn sajŏn* [Seoul: Ulyu Munhwasa, 1957], Vol. III, p. 1370.

3. Song Sŏk-ha, *Han'guk minsokko* [Seoul: Ilsinsa, 1963], pp. 27-28.

4. Yi Tu-hyŏn, *Han'guk kamyŏngŭk* [Seoul: Munhwa Kongpobu, 1973], pp. 159-160.

5. Yae Yong-hae, *In'gan munhwaje* [Seoul: Omungak, 1963], p. 109.

6. Since 1928 no special festival has been held at Hahoe.

7. Presently they are housed at the National Museum.

The Play

Scene 1

[At the beginning of the new year according to the lunar calendar, the master of ceremonies and the players go to the Shrine of the Village Guardian Deity.

There they erect a pole of the Village Guardian Deity, approximatley forty to fifty feet tall, with five pieces of cloth of five different colors and a divine bell on the top.

In addition, a pole approximately twenty to thirty feet tall of the Deity of the Homesite is erected. Five pieces of cloth of five different colors decorate the top of the pole.

Then they begin to pray for the descent of the deities so that they can perform the festival. When the deities are supposedly descended, the divine bell begins to ring.

Now the master of ceremonies and the players march to the playground where this drama takes place. They play music as they march past the Shrine of the National Deity and the Shrine of the Three Deities.[1]

They let the poles of the Village Guardian Deity and the Homesite Diety stand. When the bell of the former pole begins to ring, the play begins.

At this time, the villagers, believing that they will be blessed by hanging their clothes on the pole according to a shamanistic belief, begin crowding forward to toss their garments on it.]

Scene 2

[Two players in red costumes enter with the heads of Chuji[2] in their hands. These are the imaginary winged lions that were said to eat tigers.

Then they dance in four directions as they wave the heads of Chuji to the tune of the music. The purpose of this scene is to ensure a safe performance of this play by expelling the devils and demonic animals. As they dance, they noisily clack the mouths of the Chuji open and shut.]

Scene 3

[This scene is not performed by the players. It is played by a shaman who wears a rabbit-like mask with long ears.

Since there is no shaman presently living who performed the role, there is no way of knowing the details of the dance. This mask is no longer extant.]

Scene 4: The Transgression of the Monk

Kaksi[3]: [She enters and dances.]

Monk[4]: [He enters and looks at Kaksi, who continues to dance, with a suspicious expression.]

Kaksi: [She pantomimes as if urinating. Then she continues to dance.]

Monk: [He picks up a handful of dirt from the spot where Kaksi urinated and, smelling it, smiles in a grotesquely lascivious manner.]

Kaksi: [Realizing Monk's presence, she expresses astonishment. Then she and Monk begin to dance together in a circle.]

Monk: [He at last runs off with Kaksi on his back.]

Ch'oraengi[5]: [He looks back and signals with his hand as if urging someone to come quickly.]
Yangban[6]: [He walks in arrogantly.]

Ch'oraengi: [He goes to Yangban and whispers something in his ear.]

Yangban: [He clicks his tongue in great disapproval.]

Sŏnpi[7]: [Accompanied by Imae,[8] he enters and makes a disdainful gesture in the direction in which Monk carried Kaksi.]

Yangban: Oh, what a disorderly world!

Sŏnpi: Damn it. What ugly behavior?

Yangban: [Ch'oraengi and Imae embrace each other. Realizing that they like each other, Yangban beats them with his fan.]

Scene 5: Yangban and Sŏnpi

[Yangban, Sŏnpi, Ch'oraengi, and Imae are already on the playground.]

Punae[9]: [She enters dancing capriciously, looking at Yangban and Sŏnpi alternately, in order to entice them.]

[Yangban and Sŏnpi both express the psychological conflict caused by their passionate desire for the woman and the moral prohibition of their social standing. Unable to control their emotions, however, they begin to express their jealousy of one another in physical gestures and dance.]

Yangban: [He is suddenly angry at Sŏnpi.] How dare you act in such a way in front of me?

Sŏnpi: How on earth can you behave that way toward me?

Yangban: Well. Do you mean your lineage is as noble as mine?

[Imae and Ch'oraengi imitate their masters' exaggerated display of power in pantomime.]

Yangban: Of course, my lineage, body, and limbs are superior to yours.

Sŏnpi: Why is that so? Explain it!

Yangban: I am a son of a *sa-daebu.*[10]

Sŏnpi: What? A *sa-daebu?* I am a son of a *p'al-daebu.* [11]

Yangban: What on earth is that?

Sŏnpi: A *p'al-daebu* is twice the importance of a *sa-daebu.*

Yangban: My grandfather is a *munha-sijung.* [12]

Sŏnpi: Bah! A *munha-sijung?* Is that all? Who on earth would do that kind of thing? My father is a *munsang-sidae.* [13]

Yangban: A *munsang-sidae?* What is that?

Sŏnpi: Above the gate is higher than beneath the gate. A *sidae* is higher than a *sijung.*

Yangban: I've never heard of such a strange thing.

Sŏnpi: Is it the best thing in the world to have a tall body with long limbs?

Yangban: What else can be more important than those?

Sŏnpi: First a man must have high scholarly achievement. I've read all of *Sasŏsamkyŏng.* [14]

Yangban: What? *Sasŏsamkyŏng?* Who would bother with that kind of thing? I've read *P'alsŏyukkyŏng.* [15]

Sŏnpi: What on earth is that? What is *Yukkyŏng?*

Ch'oraengi: Even I know about *Yukkyŏng.* Don't you know it? They're the eighty thousand volumes of the Buddhist doctrines, the chanting of the monks, the spectacles of the blind, the Chinese balloon flowers in the drugstore, the menstruation of virgins, and the annual salary of the farm servant.

Imae: That's right. You're correct.

Yangban: You don't know the things that even these two know about. A scholar like you doesn't know *Yukkyŏng.*

Sŏnpi: [Clicking his tongue.] We are much the same. Let's stop arguing. Call out Punae.

Yangban: Punae!

Punae: *Uh—-k!*[16]

> [Yangban and Sŏnpi dance merrily with Punae. Soon each is trying to monopolize her.]

Paekjŭng[17]: [He enters with an ax and a pair of ox testicles.] Buy the balls, gentlemen!

Yangban: Damn you! Why do you shout for the balls? We're dancing in high spirits.

Paekjŭng: Don't you know about the balls?

Ch'oraengi: Chicken eggs. Eye balls, Birds eggs. And His Excellency's testicles.

Paekjŭng: That's right! Correct. The testicles!

Sŏnpi: Damn you! What do you mean by the testicles?

Paekjŭng: Don't you know about the ox balls?

Yangban: You uncivilized fool! Why do you have to talk about ox balls? I don't want to buy them. Get out quickly!

Paekjŭng: Ox balls are good for virility. A superior tonic.

Sŏnpi: What? Good for virility? If so, I must buy them.

Yangban: No! He asked me to buy them first. They're my testicles.

Sŏnpi: No! They're mine. Absolutely!

> [Yangban and Sŏnpi pull the ox testicles in different directions.]

Paekjŭng: My goodness. Don't break my balls!

Halmi[18]: [She disperses Yangban and Sŏnpi in two directions. As she takes the ox testicles.] There is only one pair of testicles. Yangban claims these ox testicles are his, but Sŏnpi screams that they belong to him, while Paekjŭng shouts that they are his. Whose testicles are they? In all my sixty years, I've never seen fighting over ox testicles before. I've never seen it before.

Scene 6: The Housekeeping

[Halmi sings a song as she sits at a loom, weaving. The content of her song is said to be about her life-long suffering and housekeeping.]

Ttŏktari [19]: You've been weaving all your life. But you're not able to have a new cloth nor can you hang a cloth on the top of the Pole of the Homesite Deity. [20]

Halmi: This has been my fate. What else can I do?

Ttŏktari: Try to hang your cloth on the pole of the Homesite Deity. Then fortune will begin to walk into your house.

Halmi: As you know, I was born under an unlucky star. Ttŏktari, you're a chatterbox.

Ttŏktari: You've eaten all the herrings which I bought at the market yesterday, haven't you?

Halmi: Yes. For our last supper I ate nine while you had one. For breakfast, I ate nine while you had one. So we ate both strings of herrings.

Ttŏktari: Ha, ha, ha! Well. You eat too much. It's no wonder you don't have any more teeth left. [He begins to sing. [21]]

Scene 7: Killing an Animal

[Paekjŭng dances as he pantomimes the killing of an ox and the peeling off of its skin.

Then he gestures to the audience to buy the ox heart and testicles as well as other things. [22]]

Scene 8: Repayment of the Grains

[While all members of the players play as they sing and dance, Pyŏlch'ae[23] enters and shouts at them to repay the government grains.

The players appear flustered. But the arrogant Pyŏlch'ae behaves in a highhanded manner toward them.[24]]

Scene 9: The Wedding

[The wedding ceremony for Ch'ongkak[25] and Kaksi takes place.

Believing that they will be blessed with fortune and prosperity, the villagers compete with each other in presenting their mats to the newly wed couple.]

Scene 10: The Bridal Room

[The wedding night of Ch'ongkak and Kaksi. As soon as Ch'ongkak falls asleep, Kaksi opens the wooden chest. Monk, her paramour, jumps out of the chest and murders Ch'ongkak.]

Scene 11: The Street Scene

[The performance of this scene takes place in the street which runs in front of the village on the last day of the festival.

The villagers prepare the ceremonial offerings. Then the players dance to the tune of the music.

The purpose of this scene is to prevent demons from entering Hahoe Village.]

Scene 12: The Shrine Festival

[At midnight on the final day of the festival, all members of the festival enter the Shrine of the Village Guardian Deity and pray for the village's safety from calamities in the coming year.

Then they go to the Shrine of the National Deity and the Shrine of the Three Deities where they also perform their last prayers. Thus the festival comes to an end.

They then return to their homes, from which they have been absent for approximately fifteen days.]

Notes

1. The Shrine of the Three Deities [The Samsin-tang]: The deities who supposedly created the land of Korea in legend. They are Whan-in, Whan-ung, and Whan-kŏm.

2. Chuji: They are simplified animal masks representing lions.

3. Kaksi: Young woman. This mask has a tightly closed mouth and narrow, asymmetrical eyes.

4. Monk: This mask has a separate chin attached to the cheeks with cords. On the forehead, there is a small growth. The eyes are narrow, while the mouth is three-quarters open, conveying a broad smile.

5. Ch'oraengi: Servant of Yangban. This mask has protruding eyes located in deep eye sockets beneath thick eyebrows. An asymmetrical mouth displays saw-blade-like teeth. There are several prominent skin pores between the nose and lower lip.

6. Yangban: Aristocrat. The hair and eyebrows of this mask are painted a dark color. Wrinkles surround the eyes. There are several prominent skin pores beneath the nose and lower lip. A separate chin is attached with cords. The mask has a smiling, braggartly air.

7. Sŏnpi: A scholar. This mask has wrinkles near the eyes, on the forehead, and on the cheeks. A separate chin is attached with cords.

8. Imae: Servant of Sŏnpi. A mask with asymmetrical slanting wrinkles near the eyes, forehead, and cheeks. This mask does not have a chin.

9. Punae: Concubine. This mask has a symmetrical shape with rouge on both cheeks and forehead, and red lips.

10. *Sa-daebu:* A person of high rank. *Sa* means four.

11. *P'al-daebu: P'al* means eight, implying that Sŏnpi would be superior to Yangban, if there were such a thing as *p'al-daebu.* All of Sŏnpi's terms in his game of one-upmanship are inventions.

12. *Munha-sijung:* A prime minister. *Munha* literally means under the gate: *jung,* middle or medium.

13. *Munsang-sidae; Munsang:* above the gate: *dae:* large.

14. *Sasŏsamkyŏng: The Analects, Mencius, the Doctrines of the Means,* and *the Great Learning; The Books of Odes, the Canon of History,* and *the Book of Changes.*

15. *Yuk* means six. These works do not exist. He implies that he has read twice as much as Sŏnpi has read.

16. There is no explanation for this answer.

17. Paekjŭng: Butcher. This mask has dark eyebrows and hair, deep wrinkles, and a tumor-like growth between the eyebrows. A sinister smile is conveyed by the narrow eyes and slightly opened mouth. A separate chin is attached with cords.

18. Halmi: Old woman. This mask has round eyes, a wide open mouth, and many green speckles. Wrinkles surround the eyes and cheeks.

19. Ttŏktari: Husband of Halmi. This mask has been lost. As a result, there is no way of knowing what it looks like today.

20. It is said that the weaving scene has been excluded from the production of the play for the last seventy or more years.

21. The song is about the landscape of the village.

22. Long ago, the Paekjŭng mask was called Hwaekwang. In the play, he pantomimed the execution of a human criminal instead of an ox while expressing his fear of lightning [from Yae Yong-hae's *In'gan munhwajae*, p. 115.]

23. Pyŏlch'ae: It is unknown who plays the role as well as what this mask looks like.

24. The system of payment of government grains, originally a system to loan out the government grains to the farmers during the spring and collect them in the fall with interest, became a procedure that corrupt officials used to their great advantage. This scene was supposed to depict the highhandedness of the corrupt official in a satiric way.

25. Ch'ongkak: This mask has been lost.

T'ongyŏng *Ogwangdae*

Introduction

Origins

T'ongyŏng *ogwangdae*, along with *yayu*,[1] in a broad sense, belongs to the same general category of mask-dance theatre which was once popular in the region of South Kyŏngsang-do Province. Until the first decade of the twentieth century, this type of mask-dance theatre was apparently a prevalent form of entertainment in many towns in the region. Except for *ogwangdae* of T'ongyŏng and Kosŏng, however, many local theatres in the area have ceased to exist since the first decade of 1900.

T'ongyŏng *ogwangdae* may have had its genesis in the mask-dance drama once performed by the Taegwangdae-p'ae Group of Pammŏri. It is believed that this group performed until the end of the nineteenth century. Pammŏri, situated on a bank of the Naktong-kang River, was once a town with a wharf. Since this river had deep water, the town naturally became the regional center of transportation and trade for grains, salt, fish, and hemp cloth. Especially during the summer many traders and merchants of the region held an open market and this type of busy activity attracted a large number of people to the town. Thus some wealthy merchants got together and commissioned the Taegwangdae-p'ae Group [it is also believed that there were other performing groups at that time] to perform various kinds of theatrical entertainment for themselves as well as for the customers and the townspeople. A mask-dance drama was included in the repertory of the group, along with a dance performed by a boy on the shoulders of an adult, acrobatic dances, magic, and tumbling.

No one knows the precise details of the origins of the Taegwangdae-p'ae Group; to this day no document has been found which verifies its history. The forefathers of this group might have been one of the *sandaegŭk* troups. Some of these groups began to travel southward when the Chosŏn court [1392 A.D.-1910 A.D.] rescinded official recognition of *sandaegŭk* after the Office of Sandae-togam[3] was abolished in the early seventeenth century. This company might have settled in the area since Pammŏri could support a regular performing troup. As to the inception of mask-dance drama in Pammŏri, this story has come down to us. A long time ago, during the monsoon season, the Naktong-kang River was swollen with high water due to continuous rain. One day a large casket, floating down the river, reached the slope of the bank near Pammŏri. Curious about the unexpected arrival of the casket, the villagers opened it, and found the masks, properties, and the instruction needed for the performance of mask-dance drama. At first the townspeople were afraid to touch the masks. Believing that there was a relationship between the masks and the village, however, they eventually decided to perform a mask-dance drama.

It is impossible to confirm if this was indeed the beginning of the mask-dance theatre at Pammŏri. But if there is some relation between the story and the beginning of theatre in this town, it indicates that the masks and properties which were employed for the performance of the drama were probably not the product of this town. It is interesting to note that the birth place of Hahoe *pyŏlsin-kut*[4] is located on the Naktong-kang River further up stream from Pammŏri, vaguely suggesting that the mask-dance drama which was initially performed at this town might have come down the river from Hahoe Village.

Like the origins of the mask-dance drama in Pammŏri, the beginning of T'ongyŏng *ogwangdae* is also shrouded in uncertainty. One theory suggests that the aforementioned Taegwangdae-p'ae Group toured widely in the region, including T'ongyŏng and Kosŏng and that it was from this itinerant company that the people in T'ongyŏng learned the drama which they soon developed into their own form of theatre, T'ongyŏng *ogwangdae*. The people from Kosŏng learned this drama from the productions at T'ongyŏng.

A second theory says that the people from T'ongyŏng traveled out of their area to see the performance of the Taegwangdae-p'ae Group rather than this company having come to them. Impressed by the theatrical aspects, the people from T'ongyŏng went home and began to perform their own imitation of what they had seen in Pammŏri.

Despite the differences in these two theories, both clearly indicate that it was the mask-dance drama performed by the Taegwangdae-p'ae Group from which today's T'ongyŏng *ogwangdae* developed. Whatever its origins, the performance of *ogwangdae* in T'ongyŏng, as a part of the village festival, took place during the second half of the nineteenth century.

The village festival in honor of the Deity of the Earth was held according to the lunar calendar on New Year's Eve. It was designed to rid the town of the evil spirits and demons of the past year and to ensure prosperity, a good harvest, and an abundant catch of fish in the coming year. The Navy of the Chosŏn court was stationed in the town and for the festival they provided approximately thirty musicians for this annual activity. The performance of *ogwangdae* was preceded by a parade. In the procession, in addition to the Navy musicians, were many people wearing masks representing various characters. The wearers of the Pibi mask and the Kkamakwi mask performed solo dances. The procession was led by the wearer of the Monk mask. He recited the Buddhist invocation and scriptures as he entered the peoples' homes to chase the demons and evil spirits out. [5]

Meanwhile the society of performers of *ogwangdae*—the earliest known is called the Uihŭng-gye (the society of justice and prosperity)—would call a meeting approximately two weeks prior to New Year's Day. At this time they would ask for contributions to purchase the necessary musical instruments and peaked cowls for the performance. Then they would visit individual households in town where they would play music until the fourth day of the month to raise money. These activities were finally followed by the performance of *ogwangdae* at the local Buddhist temple court on the evening of the fifteenth day.

The performance of *ogwangdae* in T'ongyŏng was allegedly carried out by the Uihŭng-gye between approximately 1880 and 1910. We are not certain as to which group was responsible for performances prior to this one. This group was then replaced by the Ransa-gye [the society of epidendrum] whose existence lasted approximately ten years. In the

1930s the second group gave way to the last group, the Ch'unhŭng-gye [the society of spring and prosperity].[6] T'ongyŏng *ogwangdae* was kept alive mainly by this group until the beginning of World War II.

Presently this drama is not being produced on a regular basis. There are only a few known survivors capable of playing characters in this thirty-one-role drama. A full-scale production of this drama demands not only the regular players, but the participation of approximately ten additional people. Today the Senior Citizens Association of Ch'ungmu [T'ongyŏng] and the Ch'ungmu Association of the Important Intangible Cultural Property are responsible for the preservation of this drama.

Masks

The origins of the masks for the mask-dance drama of Pammŏri, which have been regarded as the prototype of the T'ongyŏng masks, are by no means clear. As we have already mentioned, according to one legend, the masks, packed in a casket, reached Pammŏri during a flood. Ever since then the townspeople have used these masks for the performance of the drama as well as for the village festival.

It is said that the original masks were made of paulownia wood. When they were burned in the great fire in 1909, the town soon replaced them with a new set of wooden masks. These wooden masks were assumed to be the prototypes of the T'ongyŏng masks. Curiously enough, not a single wooden mask is found among the T'ongyŏng masks today. All of the present masks are made of dried gourd with the added materials being paper, wood, and split bamboo. A further intriguing point is that no masks from Pammŏri have survived. As a result, there is no way of comparing the present masks with the original masks from Pammŏri.

Dance and Music

D ance—along with its witty dialogue and songs—is an integral
part of the production of *ogwangdae*, as it is in many other
forms of mask-dance drama in Korea. The dance which is
employed for the performance of this drama is generally called
tŏtpaegi-dance. It was once characterized by brisk, vivacious qualities,
but over time this dance has lost its vigorous, sprightly nature,
becoming increasingly slow and languid. This dance is usually danced
to the accompaniment of *kutkŏri*, a tune derived from farmers' music,
played mainly by small gongs. Unlike the many structured dance forms
of Yangju *pyŏlsandae*[7] and Pongsan *t'alch'um*,[8] the basic patterns of
this dance are improvised.

For the production of this drama, as in the case of Yangju
pyŏlsandae, six musical instruments are predominantly used.[9] The
accompanying music is mainly the slow tune of *yŏmbul*, rhythmic
t'aryŏng, and *kutkŏri*.

The Play

W e are not certain as to the exact meaning of *ogwangdae*.
The literal meaning of *o* is five, while *gwangdae* broadly
implies actor, mask, shaman, or puppet player. The
combination of these two words, thus, generally means a drama of five
actors or five masks. Another relevant point is that *ogwangdae* from
T'ongyŏng has a five-act structure, remotely suggesting that this word
might have resulted from the dramatic structure of the play.

Until recently, the script of *ogwangdae* in T'ongyŏng had been
orally preserved from player to player. The script which we have today
is the result of some scholars having written it down in the present
text. This five act drama has a loosely constructed form without an
over-all unifying plot.

The language of this drama is generally made up of the colloquial
discourse of the common people, although it is not totally devoid of

poetic expression. The play also abounds with puns, witty talk, and down-to-earth language.

Notes

1. *Yayu:* A traditional form of mask-dance drama which was once popular in the area of Tongrae and Suyŏng, South Kyŏngsang-do Province.

2 *Sandaegŭk:* A form of traditional mask-dance drama which was popular throughout the later period of the Koryŏ dynasty [918 A.D.-1392 A.D.] and the Chosŏn dynasty.

3. Sandae-togam: An office of the Chosŏn Court, The Master of Revels, which administered and controlled the performance and the players of all performing arts. It was abolished in the early seventeenth century.

4. Hahoe *pyŏlsin-kut:* A form of festival mask-dance drama which was performed in every tenth year at Hahoe Village, North Kyŏngsang-do Province.

5. Yi Tu-hyŏn, *Han'guk kamyŏngŭk* [Seoul: Munhwa Kongpobu, 1972], p. 328.

6. Yi Tu-hyŏn, pp. 328-329.

7. Yangju *pyŏlsandae:* A form of traditional mask-dance drama which was developed in the Yangju area, Kyŏnggi-do Province.

8. Pongsan *t'alch'um:* A form of traditional mask-dance drama which was developed in Pongsan, Hwanghae-do Province.

9. They include one *chŏtdae* [transverse flute], two *p'iri* [fife], one *haegŭm* [two-stringed fiddle], one *changgo* [hourglass-shaped drum], and one *puk* [barrel drum].

The Play

Act I
The Leper Mask

[Muntungi[1] staggers onto the playground and toward the musicians as he dances to the tune of *kutkŏri*,[2] covering his face with both sleeves.

He wears a white jacket and trousers. The light side of his trousers is rolled up above his knee.

He has a small hand drum in his right hand, while he grasps a small drumstick with his left hand.

As he dances, he covers his face. He blows his nose and sits down suddenly. He sings a song.]

> *Oh, my sad fate!*
> *The three generations*
> *Of my paternal and maternal ancestors,*
> *Including my unreliable father,*
> *How many sins did all of you commit?*
>
> *You must have committed all sorts of sins*
> *To make me suffer from this infernal disease.*
> *I'm in this miserable shape*
> *With this wretched appearacne.*
>
> *Woe is me!*

[He blows his nose.]

> *Father!*
> *I'm tormented.*
>
> *With this miserable shape*
> *And wretched appearance,*
> *What can I do*
> *Even though I'm an aristocrat?*

There's no use in having money.
I must free myself
From all social restraints
To enjoy myself before I die.

There's no hope in my life.

[To the tune of *kutkŏri,* he dances. He exits.]

Act II
The Satirical Masks

[Wŏn Yangban,[3] Tulchae Yangban,[4] Hong-paek,[5] Mŏkt'al,[6] Son-nim,[7] Pitturumi,[8] Chori-jung,[9] and Malttugi[10] enter one by one as they dance. Then they form a line in front of the musicians.]

Wŏn Yangban: Gentlemen!

All Yangban: Yes!

Wŏn Yangban: Today, we're bored to death. Let's call Malttugi and poke fun at him.

All Yangban: Yes, let's do that!

Wŏn Yangban: Damn you, Malttugi!

Malttugi: Yes---s, sir!

Wŏn Yangban: The young master turned around in both directions, right and left. He then killed a cow to make an hourglass-shaped drum, murdered a horse to make a barrel drum, slaughtered a dog to make a hand drum, and beat a small gong from Ansŏng and a large gong from Wunpong. When Hangwu[11] was dancing a sword dance at a feast, I was confused in my mind. So I lay down upon a high pillow in a thatched hut. But, I, an aristocrat, could not sleep with the cantankerous noise made by all sorts of dissolute fellows. They should be exiled to Wunpong and Tamyang after they slept with their mothers. Since we're already here, let's dance a while before we go.

[In a *pullim.* [12]]

Ch'ŏchŏl.
Ch'ŏchŏl.
Ch'ŏchŏl.

[They all dance to the tune of *kutkŏri.*]

Maltuggi: *Shee—e!* The village court is large. One thousand peaks and hilltops are picturesque. There are ten million thread-like willow branches swinging proudly in the spring wind, while the honey bees and butterflies seek the flowers. But I don't see a single human being on earth. From where are you calling me? Here's my greetings to you.

All Yangban: *Om. . .aehaem.*

Malttugi: Nine different greetings and nine different assorted salutations. Nine times two, that is, eighteen different bows. If you don't receive them, all you aristocrats, your tongues will be pulled out.

Wŏn Yangban: You! Dissolute plebeian. You've insulted the aristocrats. Do you still wish to live? What is this season? It's March: the best month of the spring. When the western sun travels over the hill and the horse by the river neighs sadly, the aristocrat sitting in the hall of thatched roof, calls his eldest son for admonition. Then he walks down to the tavern to have his first drink. . . Then, a second drink. . . Then, a third drink follows.

Malttugi: How many heroes and heroines were there?

Wŏn Yangban: There were Princesses Yŏngynag and Nanyang, Chin Ch'ae-pong, Paek Nŭng-p'a, Kae Sŏm-wŏl, Sim Mo-ran, and Kim Ok-sŏn, including all sorts of first-rate beauties. They appeared in front of the aristocrats. Now my legs begin to swagger. Let's dance for a while.

[In a *pullim.*]

Ch'ŏlchŏl!

Ch'ŏlchŏl!
Ch'ŏlchŏl!

Malttugi: *Shee—e!* [Both the music and dancing stop.] Since the weather has been hot and humid, all sorts of aristocrats have gathered here like frogs near the lotus pond. . . or like the piglets in the country road. They are sitting there in a row as though they are lanterns of all sizes on the gates of the ten thousand houses in the capital city during the Lantern Festival. As if they call their stepfather at the civil service examination, they're now just calling Malttugi. . . You! All you dissolute fellows!

Wŏn Yangban: You wretched fellow. You plebeian! You've insulted the aristocrats. Do you still wish to live?

Malttugi: Ha! Ha, ha, ha! . . . Are you all aristocrats? If so, let me hear about your family history.

Wŏn Yangban: You plebeian! What's the use of knowing our family history?

Malttugi: I see. You have a disgraceful family history. So you don't want to tell me about it. It has been many years since I came to your village to live. Since then, I've checked out your family history. [To Wŏn Yangban.] Your family has had eight *kisaeng*. [13] The *kisaeng* who served so many men raised you. Then how can you be proud of yourself being the son of an aristocrat? [To Tulchae Yangban.] You're a son of a servant girl who served many masters. In that case, how can you proclaim that you're an aristocrat? [To Hongpaek.] You have two fathers while you have only one mother. One half of you is the creation of Mr. Red, but the other half is made by Mr. White. That's why you have two colors on your face. If so, how can you proudly say that you're an aristocrat?

All Yangban: You! Damn you!

Malttugi: [To Mŏkt'al.] Your mother conceived you out of wedlock. You were also born under the wooden floor of an inn during the time of impurity. So your body is completely black. Then how can you proudly say that you're an aristocrat?

All Yangban: You! Damn you!

Malttugi: [To Sonnim.] You're the son of an old servant. Because your mother was unvirtuous, the Goddess of Smallpox left marks on your face. Are you still proud of yourself as the son of an aristocrat?

All Yangban: You! Damn you!

Malttugi: [To Pitturumi.] You can't be proud of yourself as being a son of an aristocrat. Your family suffered from epilepsy and paralysis. So you've a twisted, deformed body. Are you still proud of being a son of an aristocrat?

All Yangban: You! Damn you!

Wŏn Yangban: You plebeian! You've slandered and defamed the family of the aristocrat. Now let me hear about your family history.

Malttugi: I will let you hear about my family history. All my ancestors—needless to say more than eight generations before us—including our grandfather, passed their civil service examinations when they were young and became the Regional Commander of the army and the Commander of the Capital Division. What do you say about that? You fool! My father passed his examination at the age of twenty and became the Governor of P'yŏngan and Chinwŏn . At the age of only two, he carried the bows inlaid with yellow and black buffalo horns and became the Army Commander of the Capital. What do you think about that? You dissolute fellows! Anyone who raises a disturbance is a stupid fellow. Anyone who is simple-minded is an idiot. No matter whatever you say, you're worse than the servant who cleans my guest house. In spite of everything, you're still calling me "You! Damn you!" It's not only totally disgusting but also repulsive.

All Yangban: [In a singsong tone.]

> We're begging you.
> We're begging you.

We're begging you, Mr. Pak.
Please, listen to us, Mr. Pak.

Please, save us!
We're all awe-stricken.

Please, save us, Mr. Pak.

Malttugi: Listen. Your behavior merits nothing less than death. But, as a human being, I can't kill you. So you must correct your behavior. Return to your homes and never change your minds.

All Yangban: Ye--s!

Malttugi: Return to your homes together.

All Yangban: Ye--s. [They all sing.]

Olssigu chŏlssigu.
O-ŏlssiguna chŏlssiguna.

Olssigu chŏlssigu chihwaja chonnae.
Olssigu chŏlssigu chihwaja chonnae.

[They dance *tŏtpaegi*-dance[14] to the tune of *kutkŏri*. Then they exit.]

Act III
Yŏngno Mask

[Yŏngno[15] enters to the tune of *kutkŏri*, making the sound of *ppi—-! Ppi—-!* Now Pibi Yangban[16] enters.]

Pibi Yangban: Hey! Damn fool!

Yŏngno: "Hey! Damn fool!"

Pibi Yangban: Look. You beggar. You're again imitating exactly what I say. Hey, you! What are you?

Yŏngno: I am Yŏngno from the sky.

Pibi Yangban: Did you say you're Yŏngno from the sky?

Yŏngno: Yes.

Pibi Yangban: If you're Yŏngno, you ought to stay in the sky. Why did you come down to earth?

Yŏngno: I came to eat up all the aristocrats because they behave badly. So far, I've eaten ninety-nine of them. As soon as I eat one more, I can fly high back to the sky.

Pibi Yangban: I'm not an aristocrat.

Yŏngno: You're wearing a full-dress. You must be an aristocrat.

Pibi Yangban: I wear a full-dress?

Yŏngno: That's right.

Pibi Yangban: I'll take off my full-dress.

Yŏngno: You'll still be an aristocrat

Pibi Yangban: Will I still be an aristocrat even if I'll take it off?

Yŏngno: That's right.

Pibi Yangban: You, damn fool. Your tongue should be pulled out.

Yŏngno: *Ppippi---!* [He makes a sound.]

Pibi Yangban: You fool! Stop that noise. You son of a thief. You fool!

Yŏngno: Yes?

Pibi Yangban: If I give you some delicious food, will you spare my life?

Yŏngno: First, I must eat it. Then I'll decide.

Pibi Yangban: You must eat it first?

Yŏngno: That's right.

Pibi Yangban: Can you eat a serpent?

Yŏngno: Yes, I can eat a serpent.

Pibi Yangban: Can you eat a snake?

Yŏngno: Yes, I can eat a snake.

Pibi Yangban: You son of a thief. You can eat a serpent and a snake?

Yŏngno: *Ppippi---!* [He starts to attack Pibi Yangban as he makes the sound.]

Pibi Yangban: Please! Can you eat a frog?

Yŏngno: I can eat a frog, too.

Pibi Yangban: Can you eat a tadpole, too?

Yŏngno: I can eat a tadpole.

Pibi Yangban: You thief. You can eat a frog and a tadpole? Including. . .

Yŏngno: *Ppippi---!*

Pibi Yangban: Please, stop that sound! Do you really have to eat me?

Yŏngno: Yes, I must.

Pibi Yangban: Do you really have to?

Yŏngno: Yes.

Pibi Yangban: In that case, we must decide whether you can eat me or I can kill you with my stick. Let's have a duel. Strike! [They start to fight as they dance to the tune of *kutkŏri* and the sound of *ppippi*. Pibi Yangban runs away to the tune of *t'aryŏng*[17] chased by Yŏngno.]

Act IV
The Prostitute Mask

[Halmi Yangban[18] enters with Chaeja Kaksi[19]]

Halmi Yangban: Oh! I had such a sweet dream last night. It must have meant I was going to meet a beauty like you today. You're such a beautiful woman.

Chaeja Kaksi: Is that right? You're such a gallant gentleman.

Halmi Yangban: Ha, ha, ha! There's a saying: "We have an enemy within a yard, but there's a friend a thousand miles away." That must mean ourselves. [He sings.]

> *Love, love, my love!*
> *Tung, tung, tung, my love!*
> *You're my love.*
>
> *Even when I look at you*
> *From the right side,*
> *You're still my love.*
>
> *Tung, tung, tung, my love!*

Halmi Yangban: Oh, I have a pain in my foot.

Chaeja Kaksi: Should I massage your foot?

Halmi Yangban: Well, let's go into the house.

Chaeja Kaksi: Oh, I have a pain in my stomach.

Halmi Yangban: You have a pain? Where?

Chaeja Kaksi: My lord. For some time now, I've been having a craving for fruits and food. Now I'm having pains in my lower stomach. I also have a fever.

Halmi Yangban: That's right. It has been almost a year since we met each other. You're in labor, aren't you?

Chaeja Kaksi: Please go to the market and buy some delicious food for me.

Halmi Yangban: I must call Mongdori. Hey, Mongdori!

Mongdori[20]: Ye--s!

Halmi Yangban: Come out with my knit backpack.

Mongdori: Ye--s, master. Here's your knit backpack.

Halmi Yangban: Listen. I'm going to the market to buy some food. Meanwhile, take care of the house. Be careful!

Mongdori: Yes, sir. I'll take care of the house. Please buy a lot of delicious food.

Halmi Yangban: [To Chaeja Kaksi.] While I'm gone, don't run around with other men to have fun. Take care of yourself.

Chaeja Kaksi: Don't worry. Have a good trip.

Halmi Yangban: I trust you. [He exits.]

Chaeja Kaksi: Hey! Mongdori!

Mongdori: Yes.

Chaeja Kaksi: The master is gone. Let's have fun!

Mongdori: Yes, let's have fun!

Chaeja Kaksi: Go and bring Mr. Kim who lives in front of us, Mr. Pak who lives behind of us, and Mr. Chŏng who lives next door to us.

Mongdori: Yes! . . . Mr. Pak, Mr. Kim, and Mr. Chŏng, please come here! Our master is gone to the market. Let's have fun! What do you say?

Village Libertines[21]: [As they enter they sing the tune of "Myriang Arirang."]

> *Ariari-rang surisuri-rang.*
> *Arariga nannae.*
> *Arirang um-um-um arariga-nannae.*
>
> *Where is the third hill in Munkyŏng*
> *And the rippling blue water in the winding river?*
>
> *Ariari-rang surisuri-rang.*
> *Arariga nannae.*

My husband is in a full-dress.
Until the moonset, let's have fun!

Ariari-rang surisuri-rang
Arariga nannae.

Ariarirang um arariga nannae.

[All of them dance merrily.]

Halmi Yangban: [Enters.] You! You wretched fellows!

Village Libertines: Oh, my goodness! The master has returned. What shall we do?

Halmi Yangban: Damn it! What an uproar!

Mongdori: The master has returned. What shall I do? [To the Village Libertines.] Please, get out! Please, go away!

Halmi Yangban: *Ayaya—ayaya---!* [He cries out of exasperation.]

Chaeja Kaksi: My lord. My lord. Please, stop it. For my sake, please, stop crying.

Halmi Yangban: For your sake, I must stop? Ha, ha, ha!

Chaeja Kaksi: Now you're acting like a real man. My lord, we should be ashamed of ourselves. Let's get into the house.

Halmi Yangban: I don't think you're ashamed of yourself.

Chaeja Kaksi: Please! Let's get into the house. [They exit.]

Halmi[22]: [She enters as she dances to the tune of *kutkŏri.*] Where am I now?

Musician: [This role is played by one of the accompanying musicians.] This is a place where those libertines engage in their debauchery.

Halmi: Is that right?

Musician: Hello, old woman. Where are you from?

Halmi: I am from Hansan Yaep'yŏngdong, South Ch'ungch'ŏng-do Province. My husband left me many years ago. So I came to look for him.

Musician: Are you looking for your husband?

Halmi: Yes.

Musician: What does he look like?

Halmi: He has a round face and wears a blue full-dress. He has a few light pockmarks on his face. Have you seen a man like that?

Musician: Yes, I've seen him. I think I saw him a long time ago.

Halmi: Is that right? Maybe, I can find him. In which direction, did he go?

Musician: To find him, you must work hard.

Halmi: I must work hard? How hard should I work?

Musician: First, you must change your dress for a new one. Second, you must put make-up on your face. Then you must worship the Deity of the Dragon Mountain.

Halmi: Is that right? [She washes her face and puts on make-up. Then she begins to pray.] I am praying. I am praying for the Deity of the Dragon Mountain. My husband left me three years ago. Since then I have searched for him by every seaside and in every village. But I haven't found him yet. I am praying for the Deity of the Dragon Mountain. Please, let us meet each other again soon. [She finishes her prayer. To the Musician.] Is that good enough?

Musician: Yes. . . That's good enough.

Halmi: In which direction should I go?

Musician: You must search for him as if you were winding between every tooth of a comb. Then go to Pear Blossom Village and Apricot Hamlet.

Halmi: Oh, my goodness. What shall I do? I'm in trouble. What am I supposed to do in my old age? Thank you for your trouble. Rest in peace. [She sings.]

> *I'm going.*
> *I'm going.*
> *I'm going to look for my husband.*
>
> *Husband!*
> *Husband!*

Halmi Yangban: [He enters from the opposite direction from which Halmi left.] I'm told that my wife has left her home to look for me. I now feel I can hear her voice. Wife—!

Halmi: Hello! I can hear my husband's voice. Hello! Husband!

Halmi Yangban: Wife—! [He dances a hulla as he lifts his cane high in the air.]

Halmi: My husband—! [With her eyes wide open, she looks around nervously. Then she dances.]

Halmi Yangban: My wife—!

[They call each other several times as if they were singing. They approach each other and embrace.]

Halmi: Husband! Husband! You've been heartless. I didn't know you were here. You never wrote and told me your whereabouts. How could you be so heartless? [She cries.]

Halmi Yangban: [He sings.]

> *Please, don't you cry!*
> *Please, don't you cry!*
>
> *Everything is my fault.*
> *Please, stop crying.*
>
> *Now let's go to our home!*

Halmi: Husband.

Mongdori: [As he enters.] Master! The mistress is in labor.

Halmi Yangban: Is that right? Wife—!

Halmi: Ye--s!

Halmi Yangban: Clean the kitchen and bring the blind shaman for a
     ritual. Prepare for a secret formula of medicine. [Halmi makes a
     fire in the chimney opening and pantomimes fanning with her
     skirt for an easy childbirth.]

Blindman[23]: [He enters and plays his drum as he recites a sutra.]

> *First, for the eastern creek.*
> *Second, for the southern hall.*
> *Third, for the western soil.*
> *Fourth, for the northern river.*
>
> *I'm praying for an easy childbirth.*

Mongdori: Master!

Halmi Yangban: What's the matter?

Mongdori: The mistress has given birth to a baby.

Halmi Yangban: Is it a boy or a girl?

Mongdori: She gave birth to a precious boy with a chilly-pepper-like
     penis and two peanut-like balls.

Halmi Yangban: Is that right? Bring him here. [He sings as he rocks
     the baby.]

> *Tung, tung, my baby.*
> *Oho tung, tung, tung, my baby.*
>
> *When I look at you from this side*
> *You're my baby.*
>
> *When I look at you from that side*
> *You're also my baby.*
>
> *Tung, tung, my baby.*

Halmi: Husband, let me rock the baby. Hello! Baby! Yes. Yes. You're cute. Like your papa, you have a round face. [She sings.]

> *Tung, tung, tung, my baby.*
> *Are you from the sky?*
> *Are you from the ground?*
>
> *He is from the ground.*

Chaeja Kaksi: [Bluntly.] Give me the baby!

Halmi: He has arrived on a cloud. [She keeps rocking the baby.]

Chaeja Kaksi: Give me the baby.

Halmi: [She keeps singing.]

> *Tung, tung!*
> *Oh, tung, tung!*

[The baby cries. Chaeja Kaksi rushes at Halmi, takes the baby away from her, and pushes Halmi down on the ground.]

Mongdori: Master!

Halmi Yangban: What's the matter?

Mongdori: The madam fell down and died instantly.

Halmi Yangban: Is that true?

Mongdori: She has finished her last day on earth.

Halmi Yangban: My goodness. What shall I do? [He sings on behalf of the deceased soul.]

> *I'm sad and mortified.*

Halmi Yangban: Mongdori! What's the use of being sad and mortified? Inform my children of this and prepare for her funeral.

Mongdori: Oh, what shall I do? [He calls for the pallbearers. The pallbearers carry the coffin away.]

[The two mourners enter and begin to argue with each other as to who should become the chief mourner.]

Pallbearers: [They recite a funeral dirge.]

> *Ohŏ ŏhŏ—-!*

> *Lonely cloud in the sky,*
> *Don't feel sad.*

> *Ohanŏm ŏhanŏm.*
> *Oh, the wild roses in Myŏngsa-simri,*
> *Don't feel desolate in autumn.*
> *You'll return next March.*

> *Ohanŏm ŏhanŏm.*

Act V
The Hunter Mask

[Hunter[24] enters as he dances to the tune of *kutkŏri.* Lion and Baboon follow him. Hunter turns around in a corner of the playground.

Lion and Baboon perform a fighting dance. Lion eats Baboon who disappears into the former's stomach.

Hunter shoots Lion who falls to the ground. Then he dances merrily. Now he measures the length of Lion. Then he dances around Lion.

Lion stands up, shakes his body, and exits as he dances.]

Notes

1. Muntungi: Leper aristocrat. This mask, which is made from a dried gourd, is a dark maroon color and has many white leper boils. The protruding eyes are round, while its mouth is asymmetrical, slanting downward.

2. See Yangju *pyŏlsandae* [play], Note 139.

3. Wŏn Yangban: Aristocrat I. This mask has a whitish face with fur eyebrows, a black mustache, and black beard. Its mouth is open, revealing the protruding teeth. A horse-hair headband is worn. The player of this character wears a jade green cotton full-dress, a horse-hair hat, leggings, and carries a fan and cane. For an explanation of *yangban,* see Yangju *pyŏlsandae* [play], Note 39.

4. Tulchae Yangban: Aristocrat II. This mask is identical with the Wŏn Yangban mask except for the shape: This mask is oval in shape, but the Wŏn Yangban mask is roundish. The player of this character wears a green satin full-dress. He has a fan and a cane.

5. Hong-paek: Red-white aristocrat. The left side of this mask is painted white while the right side is red. This mask has fur eyebrows. The player of this character wears a satin full-dress, half white and half red.

6. Mŏkt'al: The black mask. This mask has a blackish face with red lips and asymmetrical eyes—the right eye is round, but the left one is horizontally thin. The player of this character wears a dark satin full-dress.

7. Sonnim: The pockmarked mask. This is a whitish mask with dark pockmarks and red lips. Its ears are drawn in ink. The player of this character wears a satin full-dress and a red straw hat. He has a flag with the inscription: "The Mission of the Western Spirit from the South."

8. Pitturumi: Askewed mask. The face of this mask is covered with fur. It has askewed eyes and mouth. The player of this character wears a plain jacket and trousers with a red vest.

9. Chori-jung: Monk mask. This mask has a whitish face with dark eyebrows. The player of this mask wears a gray full-dress with a white belt and a nun's cowl. He has a wooden bell with a clapper.

10. Malttugi: The servant of the aristocrats. This mask is made of split bamboo with a round rope around it. It has a darkish face with thick dark-red lips, yellow eyebrows, and a black mustache. Its large mouth is open, revealing teeth. The player of this character wears armour and a hat. He has a horse whip. For an explanation of the literal meaning of the word, "*malttugi,*" see Yangju *pyŏlsandae* [play], Note 5.

11. Hangwu: A Chinese general [231 B.C.-202 B.C.].

12. See Yangju *pyŏlsandae* [play], Note 23.

13. *Kisaeng:* Professional singing or dancing girls.

14. *Tŏtpaegi*-dance: A common dance in the region of Kyŏngsang-do Province. It is danced mainly for merriment to the tune of *kutkŏri.*

15. Yŏngno: An imaginary bird mask. This mask looks like a blue dragon head with a bird-like quality. Its body which is like a dragon is blue, patterned with red, white, and blue. This mask with a long body is manipulated by two people: the first person guides the head, while the tail section covers the second person.

16. Pibi Yangban: An aristocrat mask. This mask has a whitish face with fur eyebrows and a dark mustache. The player of this character wears a blue full-dress, leggings, and horse-hair hat. He has a fan and a cane.

17. See Yangju *pyŏlsandae* [play], Note 16.

18. Halmi Yangban: Old man. This mask has a whitish face with dark eyebrows, rouge, and red lips. The player of this character wears a blue full-dress, leggings, and a horse-hair hat. He has a fan and a cane.

19. Chaeja Kaksi: A concubine. This mask is whitish with rouge and red lips. The player of this character wears a yellow jacket and a red skirt. She has a white handkerchief.

20. Mongdori: A servant. This mask is whitish with dark eyebrows. The player of this character wears an ordinary man's attire and a towel around his forehead.

21. They do not wear masks.

22. Halmi: Old woman. This mask has a whitish face with two rouge dots on either cheek and ink drawn wrinkles and eyebrows. The player of this character wears a jacket and a short skirt.

23. Blindman: This mask has a whitish face with fur eyebrows, mustache, and beard. The player of this character wears a white Korean overcoat, *turumagi*. He has a cane.

24. Hunter: This mask has a whitish face with ink drawn eyebrows and beard. The player of this character wears a fur hat. He has a rifle and a knit backpack.

Suyŏng *Yayu*

Introduction

Origins and Masks

Suyŏng *yayu* or *tŭlnorŭm,* which literally means a play performed in the outdoors in Suyŏng, is a theatre found in South Kyŏngsang-do Province. If *ogwangdae*[1] was the predominant form of theatre in the area west of the Naktong-kang River, *yayu* was equally popular in the region east of the river.

The origin of *yayu* is by no means clear, although a few theories do exist. One theory suggests that during the second half of the eighteenth century the Navy Commander of Jwasuyŏng [presently Suyŏng] captured the mask-dance players from Pammŏri and brought them to perform a play.[2] Afterwards the townspeople decided to have their own theatre, adapting the methods learned from the captured players. A second theory indicates that during the middle of the nineteenth century the merchants of Suyŏng went to Pammŏri on business and saw the performance of mask-dance plays there. When they returned to Suyŏng, the merchants decided to present this drama.[3] A third theory suggests that Suyŏng *yayu* began with a form of indigenous theatre performed by local amateurs. This native theatre was substantially influenced by the mask-dance drama from Pammŏri.[4] The result of combining the two forms of theatre is known today as Suyŏng *yayu.*

Traditionally, the responsibility for performing Suyŏng *yayu* was carried out by the Yayu-gye [the *yayu* guild] in the town. The existence of this guild as a viable producing group ceased in the 1930s. Presently, the Transmission Committee of Suyŏng Yayu, an organization under the auspices of the national government, is responsible for the performance and preservation of this theatre.

The performance of this theatre requires eleven masks. Of these, eight represent human characters, while two depict animals. The remaining one represents a character which is neither human nor animal. Unfortunately, none of the old masks exist today. Traditionally, at the end of each performance, all of the masks were burned in order to ensure the peace and safety of the town. Since no old masks survived, there is no way of comparing the present masks with the old ones. The basic materials used to make the masks are dried gourds, bamboo, and paper. Of the eleven masks, eight masks are made from dried gourds, while two are made with bamboo frames. One is made of paper.

Preparation, Procession, and Play

Traditionally, the performance of Suyŏng *yayu* was divided into two parts: *kilnori*, the procession, and *t'alnori*, the mask play. Unlike T'ongyŏng *ogwangdae*, the procession was more important and spectacular than the mask play itself. For some inexplicable reason the procession has been excluded from the performance since the 1960s. Since then the mask play alone has been performed and it has become the only part of *yayu* to be preserved.[5] Preparation for the procession was an important event which required the participation of a large number of townspeople. These preliminaries were started during the early part of the first month of the year according to the lunar calendar.

As a part of the *yayu* performance, members of the *Yayu* Guild would begin to perform *chisin-pabki*, the Festival for Earthly Deities, at every household in the town. This began on the third or fourth day of the month and lasted approximately ten days. This festival served two important purposes: first, they could request contributions from each household; and secondly, it symbolized the chasing away of evil spirits from the house and the welcoming in of prosperity.

The Festival for Earthly Deities was headed by Su Yangban, the main character in the play. During the festival, he performed exorcism for the Deity of the Household at each home, while the rest of the participants danced boisterously and sang the following song.

> *If a baby boy was born*
> *Three years after the house was built,*
> *He would become a loyal subject.*
>
> *If a colt was born,*
> *It would become a winged-horse.*
>
> *If a baby girl was born,*
> *She would become an exemplary woman.*
> . . .[6]

Then Su Yangban continued the exorcism in the kitchen, where the jars of soy sauce were kept, at the well, in the stable, in the storeroom, in the outer toilet, and finally, he would perform the last ritual at the house gate. There he recited an incantation such as "When we clean the earth there emerges the golden nugget just as ten thousand prosperities enter when we open the gate." When Su Yangban completed his incantation, the family would entertain the players by bringing out wine and fruits, along with incense. They would also pledge a contribution for the upcoming *yayu* performance. This festival lasted until the thirteenth day of the month.

Meanwhile, some members of the Yayu Guild would spend several days making the masks, costumes, cowls, properties, and other necessary items. As soon as they completed the preparations, they performed *t'alje*, a sacrificial ceremony for the masks, to pray for a safe performance.

Then *sibak*, tryouts for the various roles, was also held. During these tryouts any aspiring player who wished to secure a role would perform a scene in front of a group of veteran players who were the adjudicators. The most coveted roles were those of Su Yangban and Maktugi. To be cast in one of these roles, a player had to be an accomplished dancer who could also speak wittily.

On the fifteenth day, all of the players and musicians dressed in full costume and mask and performed a number of sacrificial offerings to various deities. On the sacrificial table, there were fruits, wine, and dried meat. The first offering was held at the village shrine for the Earthly Deity and the Guardian Deity of Suyŏng. This was followed by the offering to the Dragon Deity at the village well.

While the sacrificial offerings were held, preparation of the playing area took place. Traditionally, there was neither a formal stage nor an auditorium for the performance of Suyŏng *yayu*. The market square of the town was simply converted into a temporary playing area with the installation of lanterns for illumination. Tall poles with flags were erected in the middle of the market square. Then numerous ropes were drawn between the poles in the manner of a spider's web. To these ropes approximately two to three hundred lanterns of different sizes and shapes were suspended. The lanterns were lighted with wax or candles. The area which was confined with the suspended lanterns became the "playground," while the perimeter outside of the illuminated region became the auditorium or "house."

At sunset, most of the townspeople began marching to the playground from the area of the town well, approximately three quarters of a mile away. The participants in this parade were divided into a number of small groups: The Lantern Company, the Orchestra, the Procession Company, the Eight Fairies, the Nanpong Company [the company of libertines], and the Yangsando Company [the folk song company].

The Lantern Company, which led the parade, was made up of several dozen children with lanterns. The Orchestra consisted of three small gongs, one large gong, and five hourglass-shaped drums. Several dozen grownups made up the Procession Company which marched and sang songs to the tune played by a single hourglass-shaped drum. The Eight Fairies were represented by the local professional singing or dancing girls. Su Yangban, the main character of the parade and mask play, rode on the back of the lion which consisted of a four-man team. Both the Nanpong Company and the Yangsando Company were made up of ten adults, and they also sang songs in chorus throughout the parade.

When the parade companies arrived at the playground, they began to dance boisterously. Regardless of their age or sex, the audience joined in this wild dancing for approximately three to four hours. Finally, with the welcoming entrance of Su Yangban, who has been resting in the costume hall, the mask play started.[7]

As has been the case until recently, this play, as well as all other forms of the the traditional Korean drama, was transmitted orally from the older players to their disciples. As far as the dramatic structure is concerned, there is no marked difference between this drama and other traditional plays from Korea. This four-act drama is made up of a number of different subjects. For example, Act I is about the five aristocrats who are outwitted and ridiculed by their servant. Act II is concerned with an aristocrat who is killed by an imaginary bird from the sky. One of the major characteristics of this play is its abundance of poetry.

Notes

1. *Ogwangdae:* Another form of mask-dance theatre in South Kyŏngsang-do Province.

2. Kang Yong-kwŏn, "Suyŏng yayu-gŭk," *Kukŏ kukmunhak* [1964], p. 244.

3. Song Sŏk-ha, *Han'guk minsokko* [Seoul: Ilsinsa, 1960], p. 210.

4. Sim Wu-sŏng, *Han'guk ŭi minsokgŭk* [Seoul: Ch'angjak kwa Pip'yŏngsa, 1975], p. 22.

5. Sim Wu-sŏng, p. 24.

6. Kang Yong-kwŏn, pp. 244-45.

7. This section of the book is based largely on Kang Yong-kwŏn's publication, "Suyŏng yayu-gŭk," *Kukŏ kukmunhak*, pp. 243-247.

The Play

The Parade Songs

[Players, musicians and audience assemble at the village well, then singing parade songs to musical accompaniment, march to the performance site.]

[1] *The mountain.*
The mountain.
Suyŏng-san Mountain.

Ah, Paektu-san Mountain
Washed by the rain and snow.

[Refrain]

Aehaen ae—haehaenghen.
Ae-haehaeng—aehaeng.

[2] *The River.*
The River.
The Suyŏng-kang River.

The A'pnok-kang River
Filled with the rain and snow.

[Refrain]

Aehaen ae—haehaenghen.
Ae-haehaeng-aehaeng.

[3] *Over the western mountain*
The sun is setting,
While the rising moon
Casts her reflection
On the eastern lake.

[Refrain]

Aehaen ae-haenghen.
Ae-haehaeng—aehaeng.

[In addition to the above song, they may sing many more folk songs to the tunes played by the musicians. When they arrive at the playground, they begin to dance boisterously.]

Act I
The Yangban Scene

[Toward the end of the boisterous dance, which has been danced by the players and the audience, Su Yangban[1] enters. Thus the act begins.

Su Yangban is followed by Ch'a Yangban,[2] Setchae Yangban,[3] Netchae Yangban,[4] and Chongga Toryŏng[5] who enter one by one. They are also collectively called *ogwangdae.*[6]

Now those who have been dancing gradually leave the playing area, leaving only the five aristocrats. They stand in a single line, while the musicians sit in front of them.

Su Yangban is in an official outfit with a belt and a hat. He has a fan made of delicate silk. He is an aristocrat of fifty with a dignified air.

Ch'a Yangban is in his seventieth year with a pink face and gray hair. He wears a white outer coat and a fur hat. He has a long bamboo pipe.

Setchae Yangban is a man of no intelligence in his thirties. He has many white spots on his face. He wears a short blue coat and a tall four-cornered horse-hair hat. He has a red fan.

Netchae Yangban is a man of frivolity in his twentieth year. He wears a short red coat. He has a fan.

Chongga Toryŏng is in his mid teens. He displays an air of frivolity and intelligence like a young boy who is studying for a civil service examination. He wears a young boy's outfit.

This act calls for a number of different dances such as *kopsawi-*dance,[7] *mŏngsŏkmari-*dance,[8] *hwajang-*dance,[9] *yŏdaji-*dance,[10] and *kkaeki-*dance.[11] In this play, they are commonly called *tŏtpaegi-*dance.

Depending upon the character, however, each dance varies slightly. The dignified dance by Su Yangban can be called an aristocratic dance, while the slow dance by Ch'a Yangban is classified as an old man's dance. The fast dance by Setchae Yangban and Netchae Yangban can be called a youth's dance, but the frivolous dance by Chongga Toryŏng is called a boy's dance. The jumpy dance by Maktugi,[12] with a horse whip, is probably the most sprightly in this act.]

Su Yangban: [As he waves his fan.] *Shee—-e!* [The music and dancing stop. In a half sing-song and half chattering tone.]

> *The dog which barks loud*
> *Is neither lofty nor benevolent.*
> *It barks since it has lost its master.*
> *The young lords are standing*
> *In four directions.*

> *When they kill a horse*
> *To make a barrel drum with its skin,*
> *When they slaughter a cow*
> *To make an hourglass-shaped drum with its hide,*
> *When they play small gongs,*
> *When they play large gongs from Wunpong,*
> *When they set up a tent,*
> *When they make wine,*
> *When they make rice cakes,*
> *And when Hang Chang-yŏng dances a sword dance*
> *At a feast in the hall with a large door,*[13]
> *I feel as lazy as if I've returned*
> *From an accomplished and meritorious service.*

> *So I build a grass thatched hall by a mountain*
> *And fill the library*
> *With ten thousand volumes of Books of Odes*
> *And Canon of History.*

> *Then I fill the golden keg with wine*
> *While I keep a beautiful woman.*

Now I hang a kŏmun'go [14] on the wall
As I reply to her
With a poem of the southerly wind.

You imbeciles!
You're waiting for the verdict
For your mistakes.

As if you're an aristocrat
You're playing boisterously
In front of my guest house
Late in the night.

Unpak kkaeng̈ kkaeng.

[He waves his fan to the musicians. Then the rest of the aristocrats dance for a while.]

Su Yangban: *Shee-e!* [The music and dancing stop.] We're the sons of aristocrats. Since it is almost time for the civil service examination, we must prepare for the journey.

Ch'a Yangban: Let's prepare!

Setchae Yangban: That's right. We must.

Netchae Yangban: Let's do it!

[They all agree.]

Su Yangban: [To Ch'a Yangban.] You're the oldest. You must start a game of rhyming words.

Ch'a Yangban: Well, how about the word "tight?"

Setchae Yangban: I'm for the word "thin."

Su Yangban: "Tight." "Thin." "Tight-thin." [He repeats these words as he waves his fan. They all dance one by one for a few minutes to the music.] *Shee-e!* [The music and dancing stop.] For a long time, we've been told that we should take a servant with us when we take the examination. We must call Maktugi. What do you say?

All: [They all agree and stand in a line.] You, Maktugi!

Chongga Toryŏng: Maktugi! Maktugi! [When he calls Maktugi in a
frivolous manner, Su Yangban scolds him as he hits him in the
face.]

Su Yangban: You must call him in a dignified way. Maktugi! Like this.
[Chongga Toryŏng stands, nodding.] Well, let's compose a poem,
each one of us.

All: Let's do it!

Su Yangban: [He sings.]

> *When Yi Sang-sa*
> *Meets Ka Lin-sŏn*
> *For the first time*
> *On the river.*

Ch'a Yangban: [He sings.]

> *When I come to the country,*
> *Wearing a pair of leather shoes*
> *Leaning on a bamboo cane,*
> *I find a grand waterfall.*

> *This is the green mountain*
> *With a three thousand foot waterfall*
> *Which I've heard of in ancient times.*

> *The Milky Way,*
> *Fell from the nine heavens,*
> *Which I've gazed upon with doubt*
> *Is not a false one as I expected.*

> *After plunging my head into the water*
> *To wash off my worldly thinking,*
> *I walk down the stony lane*
> *And find Chŏnyo who is ploughing*
> *And Saho*[15] *who are playing checkers.*

[Setchae Yangban and Netchae Yangban sing songs one by one.[16] Chongga Toryŏng sings *Ch'ŏnja*[17] to the tune of *t'aryŏng*.[18]]

Su Yangban: Each one of us composed a poem and recited it. Now we have to sing a song together.

All: [They begin to sing "The Song of the White Sea Gull."]

> *You, the white sea gull,*
> *Don't fly away,*
> *Flapping your wings.*
> *I'm not here to catch you.*
>
> *When I open the south gate*
> *And play a gong,*
> *I see the mountain and stream*
> *In the dawn.*

[Now they dance to the music. Then they begin to sing again.]

> *Oh, time and tide*
> *And spring.*
> *Don't pass away!*
> *The youth suddenly gets old.*
>
> *Oh, the lovely thing.*
> *Oh, the lovely thing.*
> *I see the mountain and stream*
> *In the dawn.*

[They enjoy themselves as they dance to the music.]

Su Yangban: *Shee—e!* [The music and dancing stop.]

Ch'a Yangban: We've called Maktugi. But he hasn't come yet. Shall we call him again?

Setchae Yangban: That plebeian is as mean as dog dung. He should have come immediately. Why should we call him again?

[They argue with each other whether or not they should call

him again. They finally decide to call him.]

All: Damn you! Maktugi! [They call him loudly to the tune of *odoktogi t'aryŏng*, [19] which is interlaced with dialogue between Su Yangban and Ch'a Yangban.]

"Odoktogi T'aryŏng"

Odoktok odoktogi.
Every month in spring and autumn
Has the bright sunlight.
The bright and cheerful also is the moon.

P'ungsu tatangsil.
P'ungsu tatangsil.

Su Yangban: Did you say the moon was bright?

Ch'a Yangban: Was it the full moon?

Su Yangban: You didn't know it, did you? The magpie was flying southward in the moonlight between the stars.

Yongt'a yongt'a yongt'a.
Chiralro hŏlsin yonjabarigoma.
Ah ŏhŏhŏ hŏhŏ hŏlt'aeroguna.

[They dance.]

Look at that aristocrat
How he behaves!

Look at that aristocrat
How he behaves!

He is carrying his horse-hair hat on his back
As he is staggering this way and that.

Su Yangban: Staggering this way and that?

Ch'a Yangban: He must be drunk.

Su Yangban: You don't know it. You don't know it. When he was lying down intoxicated from drinking in the mountain, he was again asking about Plum Village. [20]

> *Yongt'a yongt'a yongt'a.*
> *Chiralro hŏlsin yŏnjabarigoma.*
> *Ah ŏhŏhŏ hŏhŏ hŏltaeroguna.*

[They all dance to the music.]

> *To the steep Suyŏng-san Mountain*
> *I stroll quietly,*
> *Stripping off the willow leaves.*
> *Then I throw them here and there*
> *In the splashing deep, deep water.*

Su Yangban: In the splashing deep, deep water.

Ch'a Yangban: He must be throwing rocks in the pond.

Su Yangban: You don't know it. You don't know it. It was a man who was crossing the river.

> *Yongt'a yongt'a yongt'a.*
> *Chiralro hŏlsin yŏnjabarigoma.*

[They all dance for a while.]

Su Yangban: *Shee—e!* [The music and dancing stop.]

Setchae Yangban: Maktugi is from an arrogant family, including his stepfather. So we must call him again. What do you think?

Netchae Yangban: Should we call him again? What shall we do? We are insulted by him. We're all aristocrats.

[They argue whether or not they should call Maktugi again.]

Ch'a Yangban: We're going to be insulted plenty enough.

Su Yangban: I can't be the only person to be insulted. So I must divide it among all of you. If the insult will amount to ten bushels, Ch'a Yangban must take five bushels while Setchae Yangban and Netchae Yangban must share two bushels each other. Then the rest of it will be given to Chongga Toryŏng. That'll do it. What do you say?

Ch'a Yangban: Hey! Su Yangban. Do you mean that you're not going to take even a dishful of insult?

[When the rest of them insult him, Su Yangban finally decides to take up the responsibility.]

Su Yangban: I'm going to take all the insult. So let's call him again.

All: Damn you! Maktugi!

[Maktugi, wearing a craggy mask and an outer jacket, *magoja*, enters. He has a horse whip on his shoulder. A silk towel is tied around one of his legs.]

Maktugi: [He speaks in a half singsong tone to himself.]

When I look out
I see the wide village court.

I also see a thousand mountain peaks
And ten thousand valleys
When ten million willow branches
Sway proudly in the spring wind.

Over the lake water
I see the snow flakes
Flying in the autumn wind
While the thin ice lasts only a moment.

When the burial rite is ready
There'll be no human beings in the world.
But there's Maktugi's greetings!

Su Yangban: You! Damn you! I, an aristocrat and an official, can beat a plebeian like you to death. For the killing of you, my punishment wouldn't be any more than exile.

Maktugi: Where would you be sent in exile?

Su Yangban: I don't think it would be worse than Kilju, Myŏngch'ŏn, Sansu-kapsan, Puryŏng, Ch'ŏngjin, or a fern field in Hamkyŏng-do Province.

[When Su Yangban repeats Kilju as he waves his fan, the rest of the aristocrats do the same. Then they and Maktugi dance to the music.]

Su Yangban: *Shee—e!* [The music and dancing stop.] You! Damn you! Maktugi! Did you greet Toryŏng?

Maktugi: No, sir!

Su Yangban: Toryŏng is standing there. He is as fancy as a swallow. He just took a bath. When he sits he looks like a peony. When he stands up he appears like a flower. His face looks as bright as the moon between the clouds. His mouth looks like a water lily when he opens it half way. He is as tough as a bean and he is as baneful as poison. Go quickly and greet him.

Maktugi: I'm not sure whether he is Toryŏng in a blue cloth, or a blockheaded Toryŏng, or Toryŏng who is the key-keeper for the hall with three rooms, or Toryŏng who was born under the sacrificial table on New Year's Eve. Toryŏng, here's my greetings for you!

Su Yangban: You, Maktugi. It is almost time for the civil service examination. Why did you have to go your own way?

Maktugi: I've been everywhere looking for you.

Su Yangban: Where?

Maktugi: Because you were very chivalrous and frequented the wenching house when you were young, I went to the house of the eight beauties. [21]

Su Yangban: So?

Maktugi: I went to the house of Nanyang Princess, Yŏngyang Princess, Chin Ch'ae-pong, Paek Nung-p'a, Kye Sŏm-wŏl, Chŏk

Kyŏng-hong, and Mae Ch'un-un. But I found neither you nor any son of a bitch.

Ch'a Yangban: Damn you. Did you say "any son of a bitch?"

All: [They are extremely disturbed by Maktugi's way of talking.]

Su Yangban: [To Ch'a Yangban.] You must go and ask him quietly.

Ch'a Yangban: [He asks Maktugi something quietly.]

Maktugi: I meant I looked for him in every different house. [22]

    [Ch'a Yangban returns and explains what Maktugi told him to Su Yangban.]

Su Yangban: Good! Did he really look for me like that?

Maktugi: I even went to Chong-ro in Seoul to look for you.

Su Yangban: And?

Maktugi: I went to Il-gwanan, Yi-kolmok, Sam-ch'ŏngdong, Sa-chikkol, O'-gungt'ŏ, Yuk-joap, Ch'il-kwanhŏn, P'al-gakje, Ku-rigae, and Sip-jakkol. [23] I went everywhere. But I found neither you nor any son of a bird.

Setchae Yangban: Damn you. Did you say "any son of a bird?"

    [All of them try to talk to Maktugi in a harsh way. Then Ch'a Yangban asks Maktugi something quietly.]

Maktugi: I meant I went there to look for him carefully. [24]

Su Yangban: Carefully?

Maktugi: I looked for you in every room in every town in the eight provinces.

Su Yangban: Then?

Maktugi: I went to Il-Wŏnsan, Yi-Kanggyŏng, Sam-Muju, Sa-Masan, O-Samrang, Yuk-Mulgŭm, Ch'il-Namch'ang, and P'al-Pusan. [25] I went everywhere. But I didn't find a single son of mine.

Netchae Yangban: A son of yours? Damn you!

[They are again angry with Maktugi and try to ask him all kinds of questions. Then Ch'a Yangban asks him quietly.]

Maktugi: I meant I looked for him all the way. [26]

[Ch'a Yangban goes to Su Yangban and explains what Maktugi has said.]

Su Yangban: I see. He looked for me everywhere.

Maktugi: I went to your house to look for you.

Su Yangban: Then?

Maktugi: When I entered your house, I found that everyone had gone out: all the male servants had gone to the market; the girl servants were at the laundry; the young lord went to school with his books; and the farm servants had gone to the field to plough. The house was quiet. Then your mother asked me to climb. [27]

Ch'a Yangban: Damn you! She asked you to climb?

Setchae Yangban: Damn you. Did she ask you to climb the wall?

Netchae Yangban: Damn you! Did you say she held your hand?

[When all of them ask him different questions, Maktugi goes to Ch'a Yangban.]

Maktugi: I meant she asked me to climb the bank of the river.

Su Yangban: Then?

Maktugi: [He sings.]

> *When I opened the door to the room*
> *I found a yellow silk painting*
> *On the blue silk wall.*
>
> *There was a blue silk painting*
> *On the yellow wall.*

I saw a falcon
Flying into the gallery
Where there was a painting of pheasants.

Then I saw the pheasants
Flying into the room
Which had the painting of falcons.

When I looked at a wall
I found the picture of Yu Hwang-suk
From the Han dynasty.
He was going to see Teacher Chegal
Who was studying in the Waryong Hillcock
Which was surrounded by the clouds in the wind.

Yu asked a boy about Iktŏk
Who was sleeping,
Holding his hands together,
While trying hard to open his eyes
Which were as large as those of a whale.

Now attempting to see the village court,
He was holding back the long stream of cloud
Which was beginning to cover the area.

When I looked at another wall
I found the picture
Of the four hermits from Sang-san Mountain.

They were playing checkers.
One of them had black checkers
While the other had white ones.
The third hermit
Was trying to help one of them
While the fourth one
Was boiling the water for tea.

The boy was taking a nap in the pine forest
With a white feather fan in his hand.

When I looked at another wall
I saw the picture of the sacrificed King T'ang
With cropped hair and a pair of scissors.
Wearing a full dragon dress,
He was going to the Dragon Palace.

When I looked at another wall
I found the picture of Kang T'ae-gong
From the East Sea.
He was fishing on the beach,
Wearing a beggar's hat
Pulled way down over his face.

When I opened the eastern window
I found a picture
Of ten thousand flowers and willows
Blooming and swaying on Rabbit Mountain.

In the picture,
The pleasant King Sun was trying
To comprehend the troubles of the people
In the poem of the southerly wind
While he was playing a five-stringed harp.

I saw pictures of a royal and opulent peony,
The royal subject's sunflower
Which was blooming in Suyang-san Mountain
Under the moonlight between the clouds,
And the chrysanthemum
Which was enjoyed by To Yŏn-myŏng, a hermit,
Who resigned from his post
Of an annual salary of five bushels of grains
To enjoy music, poetry, and a pastoral life.

I also saw a picture of gourd flowers
Which looked like the four hermits,
Who were wearing hemp clothes,
Sleeping on the stone pagoda,

Casting their canes away.

There was also a picture
Of a fresh youthful looking China Pink Flower
Which was admired
By a youthful looking general
Who met the grayish True Man of Taoism
To make the country prosper.

Through the beautiful silk window
I also saw a picture of fragrant wild roses
Which inspire passionate glances
When a white pony was trotting
In the field at twilight.

I also saw the picture of Sa An-sŏk
Who, holding the hand of a beautiful woman,
Was entering into the temple
In the mountain by the river far away,
When the water birds were flying over.

In the lotus hall
I saw a picture
Of the beautiful five-colored peacock
In the midst of the clouds and fog,
The picture of a singing oriole
In the spring willow,
The picture of a magpie
Which was building a bridge over the Milky Way,
The picture of a pair of love-birds,
Which were flying up and down
As they circled around,
The picture of geese
Which were bringing the news
After a long flight over the water,
The picture of white herons
Which were looking at each other
In the middle of the stream,

The picture of a talkative parrot,
The picture of a dancing crane,
And the picture of a sea gull
Which was swimming in the mirror-like water.

While these birds were flying around,
I could not finish all the sight-seeing.

Then your mother opened the cupboard
To bring out all sorts of wine bottles.
There was a long-necked bottle,
A short-necked bottle,
A coral bottle,
A watermelon-shaped bottle,
And a porcelain bottle of the Koryŏ dynasty. [28]

There was one thousand day old wine
Of eternal youth from an exotic land,
The nine day old peony wine from Dragon Mountain,
The pine needle wine for the hermits in the mountain,
And the wine of the passing summer.
They were neither too hot nor too cold.

The little abalonies from Tongrae
And the large abalonies from Wulsan,
Sliced with a silver knife,
On the brass dishes
Were brought on to the table from T'ongyŏng.

Both your mother and I began to drink
And soon we became tipsy.
Since we were still young,
We decided to light a candle for us
In the same room. [29]

[When Maktugi's half singsong and half chattering becomes too long, it is said that the rest of the characters may entertain the audience either by playing a game or doing some nonsensical things.]

Ch'a Yangban: *Shee—e!* [Embarrassed. He convinces the rest of the aristocrats to be orderly. Then he goes to Maktugi to confirm whether or not it is true what he has said. Then he discusses the matter with all of the other aristocrats except Su Yangban.]

All: [In chorus.]

> *We're all ruined.*
> *We're all ruined.*
> *The household of the aristocrat is ruined.*

> [Refrain]

> *The wall is destroyed.*
> *The temple is destroyed.*
> *And everyone is destroyed.*

> *The dark clouds are lifting*
> *Over yonder mountain.*
> *When the sun rises*
> *The sky becomes blue.*

> [Refrain]

> *The wall is destroyed.*
> *The temple is destroyed.*
> *And everyone is destroyed.*

> *The sesame seed is playing.*
> *The perilla seed is also playing.*
> *If so, why can't the castor bean play, too?*

> [Refrain]

> *The wall is destroyed.*
> *The temple is destroyed.*
> *And everyone is destroyed.*

Ch'a Yangban: *Shee—e!* [The music and dancing stop.] Now let each one of us return to our farm, fishing ground, factory, or school.

All: [In chorus.]

> *Ka—ri kalgana puuta.*
> *Ka—rikalgana puuta.*
> *I want to go with you.*
>
> *Ka—ri kalgana puuta.*
> *Ka—ri kalgana puuta.*
> *I want to go with you.*
>
> *After I bid farewell to my servant*
> *I want to go with you.*
>
> *After I sell all the fertile land*
> *I want to go with you.*

[The four aristocrats and Maktugi exit as they sing the above song. The disappointed and lonely Su Yangban alone remains on the playground.]

Act II
Yŏngno

[This scene is a kind of follow-up scene of the previous act. In this scene Yŏngno,[30] an imaginary bird, gains complete supremacy over Su Yangban. One of the unique characteristics of this scene is the mask and the costume of Yŏngno.

While Su Yangban remians alone on the playground, the animal-bird-like figure, Yŏngno, wrapped in a dark cloth, appears. It is difficult to distinguish whether this savage-looking figure is a man or an apparition.

The dark figure begins to pull Su Yangban's cloth as it makes the sound "*pipi pipi.*" The shocked Su Yangban tries to snatch back his cloth. They repeat this action a few times. Finally the dark cloth is removed from Yŏngno, revealing his hideous-looking mask. When the astonished and pale Su Yangban, who is scared out of his wits, tries to escape by walking backwards, Yŏngno follows him closely.]

Su Yangban: What are you?

Yŏngno: I am Yŏngno.

Su Yangban: Where have you come from?

Yŏngno: I've committed a crime in the sky. So I came down to the mundane world.

Su Yangban: What have you done?

Yŏngno: I've eaten creatures in the water and on the land. So far, I've eaten ninety-nine aristocrats. If I eat one more, I can return to the sky.

Su Yangban: [Shocked. Trembles.] I am not an aristocrat.

Yŏngno: Even if you were not an aristocrat, I would eat you.

Su Yangban: I am a piece of iron.

Yŏngno: I'd like to eat a piece of iron because it's chewy.

Su Yangban: I am a shadow.

Yŏngno: If you were a shadow, it would be easy for me to drink you.

Su Yangban: [He is unable to either advance or retreat. He thinks for a moment.] What is the thing that you're most afraid of?

Yŏngno: I'm not afraid of a pretentious aristocrat. But if a real aristocrat shouts at me, I may run away from him.

Su Yangban: I see. My great-great-grandfather was the prime minister. My great-grandfather was the chief of the Civil Office Board. My grandfather was the son-in-law of the king. I am an official of the Royal Academy. As you see, I am truly a real aristocrat. You! Yŏngno! Go away! Quickly! Right now!

Yŏngno: Good. I must eat that kind of aristocrat so I can return to the sky. [He covers Su Yangban with his dark cloth and drags him off-stage.]

Act III
Yŏnggam and Halmi

[More than any other scene in this play, this act contains numerous burlesque and comic elements. But there are also some tragic elements as well.

This scene illustrates the system of polygamy in the old society with the triangular love relationship between Yŏnggam,[31] Halmi,[32] and Chedae Kaksi.[33]

A pale and tired Halmi, in her rumpled dress, leaning on her bamboo cane, enters and sits down. She places a piece of broken mirror in front of her and applies make-up on her face while pushing her hair back. Then she stands up.]

Halmi: [She sings.]

My husband.

[Yŏnggam enters. The player of this role may wear any of the five aristocrats' masks in the play.]

Yŏnggam: [He sings.]

My wife.

[As they call each other, they dance for a while, circling around the playground. Then Halmi carefully looks at Yŏnggam.]

Halmi: [She sings.]

The larva-like horse-hair headband,
The rat-tail-like hat strap,
The turtle-like jade beads
On the two strings of your horse-hair hat,
The amber hat decoration,
And the horse-hair hat from T'ongyŏng.

What has happened to all of them?
Why are you wearing a crushed bamboo hat?

Yŏnggam: [He sings.]

> *This is my fate.*
> *What shall I do about my fate?*

Halmi: [She sings.]

> *What has happened*
> *To your silk padded leather shoes?*
> *Why are you wearing*
> *Such a worn out pair of shoes?*

Yŏnggam: [He sings.]

> *That is my fate.*
> *What shall I do about my fate?*

[He exits.]

Halmi: [She goes in front of the musicians and dances for a while. Then she urinates. Stands up. Now she asks a musician.] Hello. Have you seen my husband?

Musician: [This role is played by one of the accompanying musicians.] What does your husband look like?

Halmi: He is a splendid looking man. He is clean looking with a broad forehead and wears a four-cornered horse-hair hat. He is also well mannered. Like an aristocrat, his manner of speaking is sweet and gentle.

Musician: A few minutes ago, I saw an aristocrat like that. He went in that direction.

Halmi: [She sings.]

> *My husband.*

[She exits.]

[Yŏnggam and Chedae Kaksi, his concubine, enter and dance, facing each other, for a while. At this moment, Halmi enters at a corner of the playground. She looks at them carefully. When her eyes and those of Yŏnggam meet, the latter blocks her access to Chedae Kaksi with his body. Then Chedae Kaksi exits quickly. The jealous and angry Halmi begins to beat her chest with her fists and starts to argue with him.]

Halmi: Who was that bitch? [Due to her anger, she is short of breath.]

Yŏnggam: What's the matter with you? It doesn't matter who she was. [He also expresses his anger because he misses Chedae Kaksi. They argue back and forth for a while.] Didn't I leave three temples,[34] two *yang*s [35] and eight pennies, and three sons with you? I left enough money for you to live comfortably. I walked away by myself from the house. Why are you trying to make such an ugly argument with me?

Halmi: [Stunned. She beats her chest with her fists.] Well. With two *yang*s and eight pennies which you left I bought ten mackerel to bid you farewell. Out of the ten, you ate one while I had nine.

Yŏnggam: What? You ate nine while I had only one? Well. What has happened to our three sons?

Halmi: [Heaving a sigh, she beats her chest with her fists. Then she wipes away her tears.] The oldest son, while wood cutting, fell asleep under a tree. He was hit by a pine cone and killed. [The shocked Yŏnggam stares at her.] The second son was drowned while trying to catch a mud fish in a ditch. [The angry Yŏnggam holds his bamboo pipe in his mouth.] The third son died of a nervous disorder he caught in Kyŏnggi-do Province while he was playing happily.

[The angry Yŏnggam throws down his bamboo pipe and kicks Halmi. She wails. Then she falls down in a swoon. The confused Yŏnggam pleads with the musician to bring a doctor.]

Doctor: [He enters. This character does not wear a mask. He is in an outer coat and wears a horse-hair hat. When he comes to Halmi, he checks her pulse.] She is suffering from a sudden fever. It's incurable. [He applies acupuncture to Halmi. Then he exits.]

[Yŏnggam pleads with the musician to call the blind man.]

Musician: Blind man! Blind man!

Blind Man: [He enters with a hand drum. He wears an ordinary outfit without a mask.] Where are you calling me from?

Yŏnggam: Here! Here! Please recite a Buddhist sutra to make her recover from her death.

Blind Man: [He begins to recite a sutra as he beats his hand drum.] Mrs. Sim, who is from the village of Suyŏng, Pusan, South Kyŏngsang-do Province, swooned unfortunately. Her body is at the moment of death. Gods of heaven and earth, please show your mercy and save her life. I am reciting a true incantation of the Buddhist scripture, *Kwanchachaeposal.*[36] Please be harmonious and merciful. I am spraying water to the east to cleanse the temple court. Now I am spraying water twice to the south to make the place clean. Now I am spraying water thrice to the west to clean the earth. Now I am spraying water four times to the north to make the temple court clean. The three heavenly dragons, please come and recite the true words and send mercy to protect us. . .

[While he is reciting the sutra, Halmi dies. As a result, Blind Man, who is embarrassed, exits quickly. Yŏnggam goes to the musicians and asks them to bring some pallbearers. Seven or eight pallbearers with towels around their forehead enter. They carry the body of Halmi away as they recite a Buddhist invocation.]

"The Yŏmbul Song."

The mountain beyond there
Is it Pukmang-san Mountain?[37]
Let's go quickly and busily!

[Refrain]

Ninansil nanyo.
Ninansil nanyo.
Namuamiyŏmbul-ira.

If it is the way of no return,
What's the use of going fast?

[Refrain]

Ninansil nanyo.
Ninansil nanyo.
Namuamiyŏmbul-ira.

The dreary Pukmang-san Mountain in autumn
Where heroes are buried
For the last ten thousand years.

[Refrain]

Ninansil nanyo.
Ninansil nanyo.
Namuamiyŏmbul-ira.

This lonely and homeless soul.
Let's take it to the world of paradise!

[Refrain]

Ninansil nanyo.
Ninansil nanyo.
Namuamiyŏmbul-ira.

Act IV
The Dance by Lion

[The inclusion of the lion dance by the people of this area is a puzzling factor, considering that this animal is not indigenous and is only found a good distance away on the continent.

The lion may symbolize the magnificent sea, the natural background of Suyŏng. The combative and aggressive nature of the lion may also symbolize the characteristics of the ancient people of this area.

The huge lion[39] enters, led by Maktugi, as it dances. Maktugi exits. The lion mask is the largest among the masks employed for the performance of Suyŏng *yayu*. The lion head covers the first player, while its body, which is made with a blanket or a bed sheet, is manipulated by one to three players.

Coordination among the players is a must in order to enable them to dance harmoniously. When the lion dances to the music, a tiger enters and dances, too. They dance together boisteriously, in a fighting fashion, as they snarl at each other.

After they have danced for a while, the lion finally kills and eats the tiger. This scene is acted out in a grand and heroic dance by the two animals.]

Notes

1. Su Yangban: Aristocrat I. This mask which is made with a dried gourd has a dark beard, eyebrows, and hair. One of the unique characteristics of this mask is its moveable chin. For a meaning of *yangban,* see Yangju *pyŏlsandae* [play], Note 39.

2. Ch'a Yangban: Aristocrat II. The over-all color of this mask is bright pink with gray hair, indicating the age of the character.

3. Setchae Yangban: Aristocrat III. This mask has a gray beard with dark hair.

4. Netchae Yangban: Aristocrat IV. This mask has a dark beard and mustache.

5. Chongga Toryŏng: A young lord. This is a boyish-looking mask.

6. *Ogwangdae:* This word commonly refers to the above five aristocrats in this play. Also a form of mask-dance drama in South Kyŏngsang-do Province.

7. See Yangju *pyŏlsandae* [play], Note 31.

8. See Yangju *pyŏlsandae* [play], Note 32.

9. *Hwajang*-dance: One of the basic forms of dance employed for the performance of Korean mask-dance drama.

10. See Yangju *pyŏlsandae* [play], Note 30.

11. See Yangju *pyŏlsandae* [play], Note 17.

12. Maktugi: Servant. This mask which is made with a dried gourd is painted red. There are thirteen large jagged pimples on its face. For a literal meaning of Maktugi [Malttugi], see Yangju *pyŏlsandae* [play], Note 5.

13. This is a kind of paradoxical way of talking in Korean.

14. *Kŏmun'go:* A Korean string instrument with six strings.

15. He is referring to the four hermits who went to the mountain to avoid the war during the Han dynasty of China.

16. It is not clear what kind of song they sing.

17. See Yangju *pyŏlsandae* [play], Note 65.

18. See Yangju *pyŏlsandae* [play], Note 16.

19. *Odoktogi:* A ballad tune which is popular in Chaeju-do Island.

20. This may imply that he is thinking of visiting a house of prostitution.

21. He is referring to the eight beautiful lovers of Yang So-yu, the main character, in *Kuunmong,* an old novel.

22. Here the delicate meaning of the dialogue is lost becaue of the impossibility of an exact translation of puns. The word "son of a bitch" [*kaesaekki*] has a similar sound to the word "every" [*kaegae*] in Korea.

23. The prefix *"il"* means one, while *"yi"* signifies two in Korean. Likewise, *"sam"* is three; *"sa"* is four; *"o"* is five; *"yuk"* is six; *"ch'il"* is seven; *"p'al"* is eight; *"ku"* is nine; and *"sip"* is ten. Here Maktugi is playing a game of puns.

24. Here again the exact meaning is missing because of the difficulty of an exact translation of puns. The word "bird" [*sae*], if it is repeated twice, has the same sound as the word "carefully" [*saesae*] in Korean.

25. For an explanation, see Note 23.

26. The word "my" [*nae*], if it is repeated twice, has a similar sound to the word "all the way" [*naenae*] in Korean.

27. This implies that they made love.

28. The Koryŏ dynasty [918 A.D.-1392 A.D.].

29. This implies that they went to bed together.

30. Yŏngno: This is a goblin-like mask with horns and large jagged pimples.

31. Yŏnggam: An old man. The player of this character wears a white jacket, trousers, outer coat, and a horse-hair hat.

32. Halmi: An old woman. This whitish mask has rouge dots on either cheek. She is the wife of Yŏnggam. The player of this character wears a white jacket and a dark yellow skirt. A dried gourd utensil is slung from her belt. She has a bamboo cane.

33. Chedae Kaksi: Concubine. The player of this character wears a yellow jacket and a red skirt.

34. The three temples may include a temple for Buddha, a temple for Sakyamuni, and a temple for the Medicine Deity.

35. See Yangju *pyŏlsandae* [play], Note 77.

36. A Buddhist invocation.

37. Pukmang-san Mountain: A mountain near Nakyang, China, which is supposed to have many graves. Pukmang-san Mountain commonly implies a graveyard in Korean.

38. *Namuamiyŏmbul-ira:* A distorted Buddhist invocation.

39. A large bamboo lion mask which is covered with a mane made of yellow, green, purple, and black wool and cotton yarn. The diameter of the mask is approximately eighteen inches.

Pongsan *T'alch'um*

Introduction

Origins

A splendid form of mask-dance theatre commonly called *t'alch'um* [1] is found in Hwanghae-do Province, a portion of west-central Korea now a part of North Korea.

For the past few hundred years, this folk mask-dance drama has been a popular form of theatrical entertainment in every major town in the province. It can generally be categorized into three regional groups: first, the one which is performed in the western plains, centering around Pongsan and Hwangju; second, in the southeastern plains including Kirin, Sinwŏn, and Sŏhŭng; and the third which is treasured in such coastal towns as Haeju, Kangnyŏng, and Ongjin. Of these three groups, the theatres in Pongsan, Kangnyŏng, and Haeju appear to be the most popular and have kept the art alive until the present-day. The rest of the local versions are no longer performed and some of them have even vanished from memory.

Not a single historical document remains by which to verify the inception of these various groups. In the instance of the Pongsang *t'alch'um,* there exists a story which sheds some light on its origin. A long time ago, there was an old high Buddhist monk who had devoted his life to prayer for Buddha. As a result, he was not only greatly admired, but also practically worshiped as a living Buddha. Meanwhile, there was a young clergyman, an acquaintance of the high monk, who whiled away his time by indulging in intemperate drinking and debauchery. Disregarding his own faults, he was extremely jealous of the high esteem enjoyed by the old monk. He made several attempts to tarnish the old monk's reputation, but failed each time. One day, in a fit of jealousy, the young monk bribed a local professional sing-song girl, well-known for her peerless beauty and talent for singing and dancing, to ensnare the high monk. Overwhelmed by her beauty, winsomeness, and dexterity, the old monk succumbed to his desire for her, disregarding his vows to Buddha. When the story of his transgression was revealed, hatred and antipathy for the old monk spread far and wide. A scholar in the area wrote this mask-dance drama to discourage other monks from making similar mistakes, as well as to ward off the demoralization of the people.[2]

Since this story has come down to us only in the form of a legend, it is difficult to know for certain if it accurately represents the beginning of this theatre. Possibly the story does explain the reason for including scenes in the play where the fallen Buddhist monks are derided.

A second theory suggests that the mask-dance theatre of Hwanghae Province is an off-shoot of *sandaegŭk*, another kind of mask-dance theatre from which the present Yangju *pyŏlsandae* allegedly originated. There are some similarities between Pongsan *t'alch'um* and Yangju *pyŏlsandae*. For example, at least five scenes in Pongsan *t'alch'um* deal with the same subjects and characters which appear in Yangju *pyŏlsandae*. In addition, certain dialogues in Pongsan *t'alch'um* are almost identical with those of Yangju *pyŏlsandae*.

During the early seventeenth century the Chosŏn court withdrew official sanction for *sandaegŭk*, which essentially meant that the players of this theatre were no longer supported by the government. As a result, some of them apparently toured Hwanghae-do Province. Of course, a number of them eventually returned to the Seoul area, with the remainder settling down in such large towns as Pongsan, Haeju, and Kangnyŏng. It is possible that these itinerant performers, who once served in the Chosŏn court, were the progenitors of the mask-dance theatre in the province. In the past few hundred years, then, each town has developed its own versions of this theatre.

If these itinerant players of *sandaegŭk* were indeed the progenitors of mask-dance theatre in the region, then the theatre in Hwanghae-do Province has a history stretching back approximately three hundred and fifty years. Despite its apparently long history, we know very little about its birth, development, and early performance.

According to one story from the region, an important rehabilitation of this theatre took place during the eighteenth century. A man known as An Ch'o-mok, a lowly official of the local government, made some changes in the performance of this theatre. When An returned from exile on an island off the coast of South Chŏlla-do Province, he replaced the wooden masks with paper ones and introduced some new forms of dance. Ever since then, it is believed that paper masks have been employed for the performance of this theatre.[3] In addition, the lower officials in the local government assumed the major responsibility for its production.[4]

Given this perspective, though it is difficult to prove, it can be postulated that this mask-dance theatre has definitely undergone significant changes throughout its history.

Despite the fact that the first three hundred years of its history is incomplete, information on the activities of this theatre during the past fifty years has become much more available, if not plentiful. With the exception of a few major companies by the beginning of the twentieth century a majority of the local performing groups had vanished. Of the remaining theatres, Pongsan *t'alch'um* is regarded today as the most well-known, and is widely accepted among the scholars and critics as the most representative mask-dance drama of this province.

Until 1938 the performance of mask-dance drama was an integral part of the annual Tano Festival. This major holiday was held on the fifth day of the fifth month according to the lunar calendar. Between 1939 and 1945 this theatre was shut down in every town by the occupying Japanese forces. The Japanese military, who started the Sino-Japanese War on July 7, 1938, declared that no mass entertainments could be allowed, ostensibly because this would disrupt the war efforts. In fact, this was their means of suppressing the nationalistic culture of Korea.

According to people from the area who fled to Seoul during the Korean War, the performance of this mask-dance drama was revived after World War II and again became a popular part of the annual Tano Festival. But presently this theatre does not thrive in its native area; the North Korean Government, virtually forbidding its theatre to resemble past forms, discourages the performance of folk plays. They regard the mask-dance drama as backward and not sufficiently revolutionary. And Pongsan *t'alch'um* is one of them.

During the Korean War, a few players of this theatre managed to migrate to Seoul. With other interested people they made an important attempt at reviving this theatre in South Korea. In 1958 the performance of Pongsan *t'alch'um* was held in Seoul as a part of the National Folk Arts Festival. A few players from the north and some volunteers hastily formed the Pongsan T'alch'um Company and represented the folk theatre of Hwanghae-do Province during this event. Another giant step for the preservation of this drama was taken in 1967. The government of the Republic of Korea, recognizing this heritage, designated this theatre an Important Intangible Cultural Property. Since then this theatre has been supported by the government. The Pongsan T'alch'um Company made two international tours: to the United States in 1977 and to Western Europe in 1978.

Players, Stage, and Performance

Until the close of the nineteenth century, the players of mask-dance drama in Hwanghae-do Province were the lowly municipal officials. These were men who inherited the menial professions of stewards and petty officers. And just as they followed their fathers' professions in the local government, they assumed the roles which their fathers had performed whenever this drama was produced. Thus they acquired performing skills in this theatre while young men. It is said that some roles were played by members of the same family generation after generation.

Traditionally, only men played in this theatre. But during the Japanese occupation this long tradition was broken when some local professional sing-song girls, *kisaeng,* began to participate in the performance, playing the roles of Sangjwa and Somu. The use of sing-song girls brought about another change. These girls appeared in the production without masks in order to show off their beautiful faces. [5]

Although the social position of these local civil servants was never high, the players of this theatre were not looked down upon. The present players of both Pongsan and Kangnyŏng *t'alch'um* in Seoul are no longer lowly government officials as their predecessors were during the Chosŏn dynasty, but they are selected from a wide variety of social background.

As in the case of all other forms of traditional mask-dance theatre in Korea, the Hwanghae variety had neither a permanent theatre structure nor a formal stage. Traditionally, the performance took place outdoors. The production of this drama needed no theatrical scenery. Thus any open-air space could be easily converted into a temporary playground. Spectators would surround the playing area and leave a narrow path for the players to make their entrances and exits to the nearby temporary costume room. The dimensions of the playground varied, ranging from a few hundred to several hundred feet in diameter.

Until the beginning of the twentieth century Pongsan *t'alch'um* took place on a sandy terrace at the bottom of a hill located near the river. It is reported that this stage was raised approximately a foot above the ground. This unconventional construction was apparently to improve the audience's view.

The mask-dance theatre in Pongsan moved to Sariwŏn in the 1920s and began to use the temporary two-story structure which was built for the Tano Festival. This makeshift structure was partitioned into twenty-eight compartments which encircled slightly more than half of the circular playground. Three of these compartments were reserved for the players' dressing rooms. The remaining cubicles were rented out to local merchants as temporary restaurants for the duration of the festival. The proprietors of these restaurants would issue special invitations to their regular patrons who would then come to eat and drink while watching the performance from the upper level of the temporary auditorium. Members of the audience who could not afford to pay for food and drink at the restaurants would watch the play while standing on the ground. There was no admission fee.

Since the performances took place outdoors at night, several blazing bonfires were set around the playground for illumination. This type of lighting was particularly effective for displaying the colorful masks; it accentuated their mysterious expressions during the performance.

Today both companies of Pongsan and Kangnyŏng *t'alch'um* in Seoul share the same indoor stage. The performing area is raised approximately two feet above the auditorium floor. The rectangular stage of this converted theatre has a kind of proscenium opening.

According to some documents, the Chosŏn court frequently sponsored the production of *sandaegŭk* to entertain foreign envoys, especially those from China. For this purpose, the court often dispatched companies of players to northern cities situated along the route the dignitaries would travel from the Chinese border to Seoul. Considering the inconveniences of travel during that time, it was difficult for the players to reach such remote cities as P'yŏngyang and Hwangju. It was not only time consuming, but expensive. As the players often arrived too late, the court sometimes mobilized local troupes of performers to take their places. The old companies of Pongsan and Hwangju were believed to have been called upon frequently for this purpose. Mask-dance drama troupes were also often summoned by the local magistrates to perform upon the occasion of their birthdays, their children's weddings, and other important public ceremonies. However, for the past one hundred years the performance of this drama has been limited exclusively to the Tano Festival.

Approximately a month prior to the Tano Festival the players and the persons who were involved in the performance would take their holy bath. Then they would begin to lodge together in the local Buddhist temple where rehearsal of the play, mask-making, and the construction of properties, took place. Approximately forty people took part in the preparation and performance. [6]

The production of this drama was an expensive venture; it meant money for the lodging of forty people, the making of masks and properties, and frequently the purchasing of new costumes. No single official or citizen was responsible for these expenses. Until the end of the Chosŏn court, costs for the production was customarily borne by the local citizens each year in the form of a tax. Although the citizens were willing to pay the expenses for the production in good times, it was not an easy task to collect enough money when famine hit the farmers. From 1910 to 1930 the method of raising funds for the production was changed. During that period expenses were mainly the responsibility of the local merchants, who rented the temporary compartments to open makeshift restaurants, and the wealthy citizens.

Masks, Properties, and Music

All masks employed for the production of Pongsan *t'alch'um* are typified by their fantastic and outlandish appearances. For example, the masks for the eight Mŏkchung are far more rugged than the masks for the same characters in the plays from Kangnyŏng and Haeju. Each grotesque-looking mask has seven protuberances covered with beaten gold: two on the forehead, two between the eyebrows, two on the lower cheeks, and one on the chin. Another interesting characteristic of the masks from Pongsan is that they are usually quite asymmetrical. The size of the mask is comparatively smaller than the masks from the other regions. All masks are made of paper except those of the lions. Because of these grotesque qualities, the Pongsan masks are often referred to as "demonic masks."[7]

It is not known exactly when the production of this drama began to use paper masks. According to some scholars, wooden masks were employed in the original performances. Approximately two centuries ago, the wooden masks were allegedly replaced with paper masks.[8] It is not exactly clear why the wooden masks gave way to the paper ones. But it is presumed that the production of wooden masks was not only too expensive but also too time consuming.

Traditionally, the performance of this drama took place at night on the fifth day of the fifth month and lasted until dawn. At the end of the performance the players customarily tossed their masks, properties, and frequently their costumes, into the blazing bonfire; this was done while bowing solemnly and keeping their palms together. They were burned because the people believed that once the masks and properties were used for the production of this drama they were bedeviled with demonic spirits. To get rid of the devils and cleanse the players and audience, it was necessary for them to burn the bewitched masks. Thus the masks and properties, which were constructed for the performance with great labor and much expense of time, became ashes and smoke after a single use. Each year the process began again and posterity was deprived of these rich examples of those earlier creations. The present company in Seoul burn neither the masks nor the properties after each performance and they are used again and again.

The mask making was usually entrusted to one or more players skilled in this type of handicraft. Since there were no old masks which survived as models, the mask maker had to depend entirely upon memory. Without a model it was impossible for the mask maker to recapture the exact essence of the old mask. Throughout history, therefore, it is conceivable that the appearances of these masks have changed somewhat.

To make a mask a clay model was created for each visage. When this clay archetype dried, several thin layers of glue-soaked parchment paper were laid on it a layer at a time. When it was completely dry, the paper mask was removed from the clay. After that, the mask was painted according to the characteristics of each persona; items such as fur eyebrows, beard, and mustache were added where necessary. The lion masks, which were the largest, were never made of paper. They were made of dried willow branches, then covered with parchment paper, after which, they were ready for painting. When it was completed, a piece of dark cloth was sewed along the edge of the mask. This cloth was used to cover the back of the wearer's head.

Although it has been reported that sometime ago the expenses for costumes of Pongsan *t'alch'um* were often levied on the local shamans, no verifying document has been found. Whether or not they belonged to the shamans, the costumes used for the production of this drama were as sumptuous as those which were worn by the sorceresses.

As in all other traditional mask-dance theatre of Korea, both music and dance were an integral part of the production. The relatively small group of musicians for the production was usually made up of two *p'iri* [fife], one *chŏtdae* [transverse flute], one *haegŭm* [two-stringed Korean fiddle], one *changgo* [hourglass-shaped drum], and one *puk* [barrel drum]. During the performance, the musicians played a variety of tunes, including *yŏmbul*,[9] *t'aryŏng*,[10] and *kutkŏri*.[11] Then the players would dance numerous dances.[12]

The Play

The script of Pongsan *t'alch'um* is the work of anonymous artists. Until as late as the 1930s, the script had only been orally transmitted.

The dramatic structure of this play lacks any organic aspects. There is no single unifying plot, only a few scenes are connected in terms of subject matter. The appearance of characters in the play is consistent with this lack of organic structure. Most of the characters appear only once during the play. The irregular appearance of characters contributes to the creation of totally independent scenes. The lack of organic structure, the independent plot in each scene, and the one-time appearance of characters are all attributed to the oral preservation of this theatre.

Comic satire in the play is aimed mainly at two groups of people from the elite class in the society: the immoral Buddhist monks and the degenerate aristocrats. For example, Nojang, a high monk, who is lured to the mundane world by his disciples, not only enjoys the popular songs but also succumbs to the coquettish wiles of a young sorceress. For this, he is derided by many different types of common people. The arrogant aristocrats also become targets of ridicule. For example, the three aristocratic brothers who are ready to travel to the capital city to take their civil service examination become the target of derision. The two brothers have cleft palates, to suggest that they are the children of a gay blade who contracted a venereal disease as a result of frequenting a brothel. In this scene their servant calls them *yangban*, aristocrat, not because they are retired ministers, but because to him the word, *yangban*, refers to "a little table with dog-foot-shaped legs." When they demand that their servant find temporary lodgings for them, they are further ridiculed when he quickly constructs a makeshift pigpen for that purpose.

Curiously enough, unlike some other traditional plays in Korea, Pongsan *t'alch'um* is devoid of satire against the government officials. It is not clear why the corrupt officials are spared ridicule here. Although there is no concrete evidence to this effect, it is possible that the traditional players of this theatre, being lowly civil servants, were reluctant to satirize their occupational superiors.

Pongsan *t'alch'um* is filled with poetry, songs, witty dialogue, puns, and some Buddhist prayers. Some poetry in the play is incomplete or lacking in logical sense, while other lines are brilliant. Besides the poetry and songs, this play also contains a great deal of bawdy language which appears to be quite intuitive and spontaneous.

Notes

1. *T'al* means mask, while *ch'um* suggests dance in Korean. The compound of these two words, thus, implies mask-dance.

2. Ch'oe Sang-su, *Haesŏ kamyŏngŭk yŏngu* [Seoul: Taesŏng Munhwasa, 1967], p. 74.

3. Ch'oe Sang-su, p. 12.

4. Yi Tu-hyŏn, *Han'guk kamyŏngŭk* [Seoul: Munhwa Kongpobu, 1973], p. 277.

5. Yi Tu-hyŏn, p. 280.

6. Kim Yang-ki, *Chosen no kamen III* [Tokyo: Sinko Bijutsu Shuppan, 1967], p. 60.

7. Ch'oe Sang-su, p. 17.

8. Yi Tu-hyŏn, p. 278.

9. See Yangju *pyŏlsandae* [play], Note 13.

10. See Yangju *pyŏlsandae* [play], Note 16.

11. See Yangju *pyŏlsandae* [play], Note 139.

12. Refer to the Notes of the play translation.

The Play

Act I
The Dance by Four Sangjwa

[Four Sangjwa,¹ in Buddhist monk's coats and peaked cowls, enter. Red sashes are slung across their shoulders. Their entrances are made in the following way. A Mŏkchung,² carrying Sangjwa I on his back, rushes onto the playground. Then he recites a *pullim*³ and circles around the playground to the tune of *t'aryŏng*.⁴ Now he puts Sangjwa I down in front of the musicians and exits. The remaining three Sangjwa enter the same way.

All Sangjwa stand in a line in front of the musicians and begin to dance to the tune of slow *yŏngsanhoesang-gok*⁵ played by the musicians. When the musicians change their tune to *todori*,⁶ they now dance in groups, facing each other.

When the musicians again change to a *t'aryŏng* tune, Mŏkchung I enters and falls down. All Sangjwa dance for a while. Then they exit.]

[This dance by Sangjwa, which includes the bows to the deities of the four directions, is a kind of opening ritual for the performance of this play. Originally, male players performed the roles of Sangjwa in this act. But during the Japanese occupation of Korea these roles were taken up by *kisaeng*.⁷ In addition, they often played without masks to show off their pretty faces.]

Act II
The Dance by Mŏkchung

Mŏkchung I: [He rushes onto the playground and falls down. He wears a *tŏgori*, jacket, with green sleeve to which wristlets are attached. The right side of the jacket is red while its left side is blue. Two large bells are fastened to his knees. A willow branch hangs on his lower back. While lying down, covering his face with his sleeves, he begins to make movements with his body, beginning

with his toes. When he finally begins to move his whole body, he
makes three turns and crouches. At the fourth turn, he barely
stands up. Then he falls down again. Finally, he stands up. Now he
looks to his right and his left while still covering his face with his
sleeves. Then he makes a vigorous shimmy shake with his whole
body as he waves his sleeves over his head. Finally, he removes his
sleeves from his face, revealing his grotesque-looking reddish-
orange mask. When the musicians play a fast *t'aryŏng*, he dances
kkaeki-dance[8] boisterously, circling around the playground, waving
his sleeves and lifting one of his legs.]

Mŏkchung II: [He rushes onto the playground. When he slaps
Mŏkchung I in the face with his sleeve, the latter exits.[9] Now he
runs around the playground. Then he looks to his right and left.]

    Shee—e!
    Ah-ah't-shee—e!
    Ah-ah't-shee—e!

[The music stops. The rest of the Mŏkchung make their
entrances in a similar manner.]

Since there was no calendar in the mountains,
Unknown to me came the change of seasons.[10]

When the flowers bloom,
It must be the spring season.

When the leaves on the trees grow,
It must be the summer season.

When the leaves of paulownia fall,
It must be the autumn season.

When the white snow flakes
Fall on the green pines and bamboo,
It is none other than the winter season.

I, originally a libertine of the country,
Have been engaging in a hermit-like existence

In the mountains.
But when I hear the sound of music,
I lose my interest in prayer to Buddha.

With this elegant music
Shall I have some fun?

[In a *pullim*.]

Although my hair is gray,
My mind is still young.

[He begins to dance to the tune of *t'aryŏng* for a while.]

Shee—e!

After learning the proper etiquette,
We must wait for the last day of our lives.
After having the religious service,
We must entertain our guests.

Since that's what they've told us, I must say here are my
greetings.

[In a *pullim*.]

The setting sun in the scenic spot,
The pear-blossom pavilion
. . .

Mŏkchung III: [He enters, running. Then he slaps Mŏkchung II in the
face with his sleeve. Mŏkchung II exits. Now he makes one round
of the playground. Then he stands somewhere in the middle as he
looks to his right and his left.]

Shee—e!
Ah-ah't-shee—e!
Ah-ah't-shee—e!

[The music stops.]

After coming here

I glance in the four directions.
Then I clearly see the four words:
"Indifference, purity, peace, and tranquility."

When I look to the east,
I clearly see King Chu Mun, an eternal sage,
Who is traveling to Wisuyang
To seek out T'aekong Mang. [11]

When I look to the south,
I obviously find Chin Mok-kong
During the war perid. [12]
He is traveling
To the Village of Prosperous Agriculture
To seek out Kon-suk.

When I look to the west,
I clearly see the picture
Which portrays O Ch'a-sŏ in war time. [13]
He is traveling to Napu-san Mountain
To seek out Son Mun-ja.

When I look to the north,
I definitely see the picture
Which portrays Hang Chŏk,
The strongest man
Of the disturbed period
Of the Ch'u and Han dynasties. [14]
He is traveling to Kiko-san Mountain
To seek out Pŏm A-pu.

When I look straight ahead,
I see many friends of mine.
They are enjoying the sound of music.

So, I, too,
For a while,
Should have fun.

[In a *pullim*.]

When the dark clouds fill the sky,
Nothing is seen...

[He dances to the tune of *t'aryŏng*.]

Shee—e!

[The music stops.]

After learning the proper etiquette,
We must wait for the last day of our lives.
After having the religious service,
We must entertain our guests.

Since that's what they've told us, I must say here are my greetings.

[In a *pullim*.]

This cuckoo, that cuckoo,
And the cuckoo in the steep mountain
. . .

Mŏkchung IV: [When he enters, Mŏkchung III exits.]

Ah-ah't-shee—e!
Ah-ah't-shee—e!
Shee—e!

The clear water in the calm and wide pond
Appears like the loyal spirit.
The tangled rains in the three rivers
Are the souls of the five children.

Paek-yi and Suk-jae,[15] and Chang Ui,
Who could placate the kings of all nations,
Could not appease the King of Hell.
So they, too, became the sad ghosts
Of the cuckoos in the spring breeze.

Much less,
Our lives are as fleeting as the dew on the grass.
If so, why not have some fun
When we hear such music?

[In a *pullim.*]

The mottled bamboo
With twelve knots from Sosang
. . .

Shee—e!

After learning the proper etiquette,
We must wait for the last day of our lives.
After having the religious service,
We must entertain our guests.

Since that's what they've told us, I must say here are my
greetings.

[In a *pullim.*]

The swing which sways over the willow
. . .

Mŏkchung V: [When he enters, Mŏkchung IV exits.]

Ah-ah't-shee—e!
Ah-ah't-shee—e!
Shee—e!

When I return to the five lakes
I find no clams.
But the sea gulls from the large frog island
Fly to red grass beach,
While the geese from the three lakes
Fly to the hall of lotus.

When I arrive at the Simyang-kang River
The tune of *pip'a*[17] ceases.

But I still find the same old wind and moon.
Which So Tong-p'a enjoyed
On the Chŏkpyŏk-kang River
In the autumn night.

Now I see Jo Maeng-dŏk,
A valiant hero of the day,
And An Chae-jae,
The kindest and most affectionate man
In history.

When I moor the boat by the Koso Castle,
I hear the peal of a bell from the Hansan-sa Temple
And the sound of "*tung tung*" from the pleasure boat.

Shee—e!

Here are my greetings.

[In a *pullim*.]

When the moon sets
The birds chirp.
Then the white frost fills the sky
...

Mŏkchung VI: [When he enters, Mŏkchung V exits.]

Ah-ah't-shee—e!
Ah-ah't-shee—e!
Ah-ah't-shee—e!
Shee—e!

If the mountain is not high,
It is beautiful and handsome.

If the water is not deep,
It is blue and calm.

If the ground is not wide,
It is even and flat.

If there aren't too many people,
They grow and prosper.
The moon and crane become pairs
While the pine and bamboo
Complement each other's green color.

The beautiful mountain
By the river in another world
Where Sopu and Hŏyu[18] were idle.

The Ch'aesŏk-kang River under the bright moon
Where Yi Chŏk-sŏn had fun.

The Chŏkpyŏk-kang River
Under the moon in the autumn sky
Where So Tong-p'a enjoyed himself.

In these pavilions of music and poetry,
I, too, like to have fun before I go.

[In a *pullim.*]

The Hansan-sa Temple
Outside of the Koso Castle
· · ·

Shee—e!

After learning the proper etiquette,
We must wait for the last day of our lives.
After having the religious service,
We must entertain our guests.

Since that's what they've told us, I must say here are my
greetings.

[In a *pullim.*]

Yi Paek is riding a whale
High in the sky
· · ·

Mŏkchung VII: [When he enters, Mŏchung VI exits.]

> *Ah-ah't-shee—e!*
> *Ah-ah't-shee—e!*
> *Shee—e!*

After the creation of the darkness,
The yellow sky, and earth,
The sun and the full moon rise.

After the formation of heaven and earth,
All things in the universe prosper.

Since it is the right spring season,
To see the scenery of the mountain and river,
I, wearing a pair of straw sandals,
Leaning on a bamboo cane,
With a gourd full of water,
Came to the countryside.

Then I, again, find the mountain
Filled with the beautiful red and yellow colors
Which I saw last year, too.

The green pine and bamboo
Appear luxuriant and verdant,
While the butterflies,
Having slept
In the splendid flowers and swaying plants,
Fly away, disappearing.

The oriole flying high above the willow
Appears like a golden nugget,
While the dancing butterflies between the flowers
Fly like snow flakes.
So this must be paradise. [19]

The slender willow branches,
Like green threads,
Swaying in the yellow mountain in spring,

Must be the five willows of Yŏn-myŏng. [20]

Since the waterfall cascades,
Making crystal marbles,
From the precipitous cliff,
Splashing like silver jade,
It must be the beautiful mountain by the river
Where Sopu and Hŏyu exchanged their discourses.

Since birds sing,
It must be the season of eternity.

When I look into the hall
I find many gallant men,
Playing *haegŭm,* [21] fife, flute, drum,
And hourglass-shaped drum,
While they dance this way and that.
This must be the pavilion of music and poetry.

So, I, too, shall have fun before I go
. . .

[In a *pullim.*]

The deep valley with a thousand peaks
Reaching the thick clouds.

Shee—e!

After having the proper etiquette,
We must wait for the last day of our lives.
After having the religious service,
We must entertain our guests.

Since that's what they've told us, I must say here are my greetings.

[In a *pullim.*]

The peach blossom in Jade Village
And the ten thousand trees in spring.
Each one of them. . .

[Sometimes this character also has the following lines.]

Ah-ah't-shee—e!
Ah-ah't-shee—e!
Shee—e!

Wherever the governor goes,
There must be a governor's office.
Wherever the military commander goes,
There must be a tavern.
Wherever there are profligates,
There must be a pavilion of music and poetry.

I, too, originally, was a libertine.

Since I came to this pavilion of music and poetry,
I shall have some fun before I go.

Mŏkchung VIII: [When he enters, Mŏkchung VII exits.]

Ah-ah't-shee—e!
Ah-ah't-shee—e!
Shee—e!

When I walk into the mountain
By the river of the thousand *ri*, [22]
Wearing a pair of straw sandals
And leaning on a bamboo cane,
I find a splendid waterfall.
This must be the beautiful Yo-san Mountain.

I've heard rumors of a three thousand foot waterfall.
But I no longer doubt the existence of
This falling silver river
That reaches to the heavens.

When I walk down
The winding narrow stony lane,
By the Silver River,
I find the four hermit scholars [23]
Playing checkers.

Sopu is handling the reins of a cow
For an unknown reason,
While Hŏyu, washes his ears,
Rolling up his sleeves,
Sitting by the stream.

When I walk down further
Hearing the beautiful melodies of music,
What I find is obviously
A pavilion of music and poetry.

So, I, too, shall amuse myself for a while.

[In a *pullim.*]

When a tiger appears
By an eastern river,
Rilroraebi hwŏl hwŏl. [24]

Shee—e! Anaya-a. [25]

[The music and dancing stop. He calls out the other monks.]

All Mŏkchung: Yea!

[The rest of the seven Mŏkchung enter simultaneously and stand in a line in front of the musicians.]

Mŏkchung VIII: We're originally all monks. But since we've found a beautiful pavilion of music and poetry, why shouldn't all of us dance together?

All Mŏkchung: Yea—a! [They all answer together.]

[In a *pullim.*]

The pear blossom pavilion,
The sunset, and the eastern sky

. . .

[They all dance *mutdong*-dance [26] to the music as they circle around the playground. All exit.]

Act II
Scene 2: The Drum Scene

[Two Mŏkchung enter and perform the following scene. The drum is already placed in the middle of the playground.]

Mŏkchung I: [He walks to the middle of the playground.]
Anaya.[27]

Mŏkchung II: [As he follows Mŏkchung I.] *Kuraeae.*

Mŏkchung I: Aren't we monks? Let's try to play the drum.

Mŏkchung II: *Anaya.*

Mŏkchung I: *Kuraeae.*

Mŏkchung II: You've said we should play it while we're naked, haven't you?

Mŏkchung I: Yes, we should play it like that.

Mŏkchung II: [As though he still cannot believe what Mŏkchung I has said.] *Anaya.*

Mŏkchung I: *Kuraeae.*

Mŏkchung II: Did you really say we should take off our clothes and play it?

Mŏkchung I: Yes, we should play it.

Mŏkchung II: [As though he still thinks what Mŏkchung I has said is strange.] *Anaya.*

Mŏkchung I: *Kuraeae.*

Mŏkchung II: Did you really say we should take off our clothes before we play it?

Mŏkchung I: You fool! I said we should play the drum.

Mŏkchung II: [As he tries to take off his clothes.] *Anaya.*

Mŏkchung I: *Kuraeae.*

Mŏkchung II: [Partially removing his clothes.] Did you really say we should take off our clothes and play it?

Mŏkchung I: Ha, ha, ha! You fool! Let's play the drum.

Mŏkchung II: [He takes off his jacket.] *Anaya.*

Mŏkchung II: [He puts his jacket on the ground. As he grasps his pants belt.] You said we should take off our clothes before we play. So I've taken mine off.

Mŏkchung I: You fool. You've really taken off your clothes. [With his fan, he suddenly strikes the drum.] I meant to play this drum.[28]

Mŏkchung II: You stupid imbecile. This drum is called *pŏpkko.*

Mŏkchung I: Ha, ha, ha! . . . Is that right? If so, let's play *pŏpkko.* Put that large round drum on your head.

Mŏkchung II: *Anaya.*

Mŏkchung I: *Kuraeae.*

Mŏkchung II: Did you say I should put the large round drum on my head?

Mŏkchung I: Yes, on your head.

Mŏkchung II: [As he holds the drum.] *Anaya.*

Mŏkchung I: *Kurae-ae.*

Mŏkchung II: You told me I must put it on my head, didn't you?

Mŏkchung I: You fool. You must put it on your head.

Mŏkchung II: [As he holds the drum in front of him.] *Anaya.*

Mŏkchung I: *Kurae-ae.*

Mŏkchung II: You told me I should put it on my head. So, I did.

Mŏkchung I: Let me see it.

Mŏkchung II: Look. [He lets Mŏkchung I look at the drum.]

Mŏkchung I: Hold it a little higher.

Mŏkchung II: Yes.

Mŏkchung I: [He suddenly strikes the drum with full gusto.]

Mŏkchung II: Oh, my penis! Damn, you fool! I told you to play the drum. But you hit the head of my penis. I'm bleeding white blood.

Mŏkchung I: You clumsy fool! I told you to put it on your head. But you pressed it against your penis. [29] [He strikes Mŏkchung II in the face.] I meant this head.

Mŏkchung II: You fool. You're as foolish as your grandfather. This is my Lord Head.

Mŏkchung I: Ha, ha, ha! Put it on your Lord Head.

Mŏkchung II: *Anaya.*

Mŏkchung I: *Kurae-ae.*

Mŏkchung II: On my Lord Head?

Mŏkchung I: Yes, the large round drum.

Mŏkchung II: [He puts the drum on his head.] *Anaya.*

Mŏkchung I: *Kurae-ae.*

Mŏkchung II: I put it on my Lord Head.

Mŏkchung I: Let me see it.

Mŏkchung II: Go ahead.

Mŏkchung I: A little more.

Mŏkchung II: Go ahead.

Mŏkchung I: [He suddenly strikes the drum with full gusto.]

Mŏkchung II: Oh, my head. I told you to strike the drum. But you hit my Lord Head. Oh, my head aches.

Mŏkchung I: *Anaya.*

Mŏkchung II: *Kuraeae.*

Mŏkchung I: I didn't mean it. Let's have some fun. Play the drum.

Mŏkchung II: You fool. You should have said that before. That's a good
idea.

[They stand on either side of the drum holding it. Another
player in the mask and costume of Sangjwa enters and plays the
drum from the front as he dances while a third Mŏkchung enters
and holds the drum. They play the drum while dancing for a
while.]

Mŏkchung I: [He shouts loudly.] Get out! Get out!

Sangjwa: [He stops playing the drum and exits.]

Mŏkchung II: [In a *pullim.*]

> *The pear blossom pavilion,*
> *The sunset, and the eastern sky*
> . . .

[All three Mŏkchung dance to the tune of *t'aryŏng.* They exit.]

Act III
The Dance by Satang

[Satang,[30] in an embellished costume, either walks onto the
playground or rides in an open palanquin. She is followed by seven
Kŏsa,[31] who play a variety of drums, including the hourglass-shaped
ones.

Holapi Kŏsa[32] enters carrying a rolled straw mat on his back,
dancing without regard to the tune played by the musicians. When he
finds Satang, he is excited. Once in a while, he feels Satang's dress and

face. Now he tries this and that with her.]

Kŏsa I: [As he sees Holapi Kŏsa.] *Sulrŏngsu,*

All Kŏsa: [They all answer together.] *Yaeaeyit.*

Kŏsa I: Arrest Holapi Kŏsa!

All Kŏsa: *Yae-ae-yit.* [All of them go to Holapi Kŏsa to arrest him.]

Holapi Kŏsa: [Surprised. He runs here and there, escaping from them.]

All Kŏsa: [They return to the playground. Now they begin to play with Satang while singing "Nolryang Sagŏri"[33] and playing the drums.]

"Nolryang I"

The growing buds on the tree.

Ae-ae-ae-ae-ae-ae.
Ku-u-u-u-kyong.
Ka-ae-ae-ae-ae-ae-ka.
To chae-ae-ae-ae-ae-ae-ka.
Chil-ŏp-ŏp-ŏp-toup-ta-ha.
Matle-ul-nae-ae-ae-ae-ae-ae-ya-ha.

Ae-yina-a-ha.
Tuya-ae-ae-yi-na-ae-wŏl.
Naegu naeroguna.
Ma-a-a-rul-yae-ae.

Ae-ae-ae-ro.
Ji-yi-yi-yi-yi-yi.
Ae-ae-yae.
Rochi-yi-yi-yi.
Nae-ae-wol-naeroguna.
Ae-ae-aero-chi.
Yi-yi-yi.
Yi-yi-yi.

"Nolryang II"

Ae-ae-ae-ae-ae-ya.
Ae-ae-wŏl naeroguna.
Aeraduya ae-ae-ae-ya.
Ae-ae-wŏl naeroguna.

Bidding farewell to my life,
Into the green mountan,
I'm entering.
Ae-ae-ya ae-ae-wol naeroguna.

When the spring water falls,
The geese are flying,
Flapping their wings,
The tall exuberant pine
Suddenly loses its branches and twigs.

Chihwaja chŏlsiguna.
Olsigodo chot'a.

Listen to me!

Bidding farewell to my life,
Into the green mountain,
I'm entering.
Ae-ae-ae-o-o-ya.
Ae-ae-wŏl naeroguna.

When the twilight spreads its sleepy wings,
Where does the cuckoo in the village shrine
Want me to go?
Where does it want me to go?

When I walk over this mountain
I find a cuckoo.
On the yonder alp,
There's another cuckoo, too.

E-ae.
The elegant figure of a young maiden,
In my vision, still lingers,
While, in my ear, her voice rings.

I'm praying.
I'm praying for supplication.
Ae-ae-ae.
It's March in Yukkuhamdo.

Olsiguna cholsiguna.
Tampul tampul ssaeindo sarang.
Love, love, my love.
Climb the old pine on the curious rock.
Hwi hwi ch'ing ching.

Love ties me round and round,
Like the love grass, the round shrub,
The gourd vines,
And the round stick for rolling cloth.
The love which knotted in my heart.

Ae-ae-ae-na ae-ael naeroguna.

"A'psan T'aryŏng"

Na-nae-ae-ae no-na-no.
AAe-ae-ae-ae-yi na-no-o.
Na-na-ae-ae-ae-ro.
Sin-hajiro-huna-a-a.

Strophe:

The Buddhist monk from Tobong
On the love seat in the Yŏmbul-sa Temple
In Kwach'ŏn-kwana'k-san Mountain.
Ae-ae-yi.
He is encircled by three curtains.

Antistrophe:

Ae-ae-ae-ae-ro.
Chi-yi-yi-yi-yi.
Jiroguna maul-nae-ya.
Ah-ah-ah.
Ae-ae-ae-a-e-ae-ro.
Saniiroguna-ah-ah.

Strophe:

The white pony is ready to go.
He kicks the ground with his hooves,
While the lord laments, dropping tears,
As he hold her jade-like hands.

Antistrophe:

Don't you cry.
Don't you cry.
Please don't you cry.
If you cry too long,
You may fall out of our love.

"Twitsan T'aryŏng"

Naji-na-a saniroguna-ae.
Ae-ae-ttu-ya na-a-ae.
Na-na-chiroman saniroguna.
Ae-ae.

Strophe:

The weeping sounds of grass and trees
In the south east wind
Make my heart tear into pieces.
Ae-ae.

Antistrophe:

The sounds of falling leaves
Scare me as if the Chinese soldiers are coming,
While the flapping sounds of a bird
Makes me wonder whether it's a trident.

Strophe:

If I take her, it must be preordained tie.
If I leave her, it's a mutual love.
Mutual love and separation.
When I reincarnate as a butterfly
I'll fly back and forth to her garden.
Ae-ae.

Antistrophe:

What medicine should I take
To cure the disease from her?
Should I take a cold medicine
Or a tonic with peppermint?
No, I must be cured with her sweet talk.

Strophe:

Should I follow my lover?
Or should I not?
I must follow my lover to the capital,
Riding a blue pony, like Ch'a Yong,
To cross the river.
Ae-ae.

Antistrophe:

Ae-ra.
I can't leave my lover.
Ae-ra.
I can't leave my lover.
The thumb is being pulled
While the little finger
Is torn into three pieces.

Oh my!
If my mother finds out
I'll be slashed.

When I think about our affection
I can no longer leave my lover.
Ae-ae.
Even if it means death to me.

"Kyŏngbalrim"

Strophe:

It's the edge of the sky and earth.
Ae-ae-yi.
When the day becomes turbulent
The three mountains fall half way
Under the clear sky,
Making them into the island of white herons.
Ae-ae.

Antistrophe:

Where are you begging me to go?
Why do you keep begging and begging me
To go to Ch'ŏngyong in Ansan?

Strophe:

It's the waterfall in Sŭrak-san Mountain.
Ae-ae.
The Tonggu Pass, the Manri Pass,
The Yakjam Pass, and the Nuemori Yongsan-map'o.
Ae-ae.

Antistrophe:

Kim Tok-sŏn from Yŏnsan
Built the North Gate In Suwŏn
And became a meritorious subject.
After drinking three bowls of the imperial gift wine,

Wearing a horse-hair hat,
Leading Mo Hong-kap in the front
While having Kwŏn Sam-tŏk behind,
Along with the ten thousand boys,
Accompanied by the loud court music,
He is marching on the open road to the capital,
While begging at every excuse.
Ae-ae.

Strophe:

As if it's going to be windy,
Ae-ae,
Half of the tree is dancing.
As if it's going to be flooded,
The magic clouds are covering
The ten thousand year old mountain.
Ae-ae.

Antistrophe:

Let's go to see the Eight Views in the West: [34]
The Hwanghak Tower in Samdŭng,
The Kansŏng Tower in Sŏngch'ŏn,
The Mujin Terrace in Kaech'ŏn,
The Yaksan Terrace in Yŏngbyŏn,
The Inp'ung Tower in Kanggye,
The T'onggun Pavilion in Uiju,
The Paeksan Tower in Anju,
And the Yongkwang Pavilion in P'yŏngyang.

But it's said the best place to have fun
Is the Pubyŏk Tower by the Taedong-kang River.
Ae-ae.

Strophe:

Kŭmkang-san Mountain in Kangwŏn-do Province.
Ae-ae.

There're clearly fifty-three Buddhas
Who came from the west countries of China
On the branches of elm trees
Behind the Yuch'ŏm-sa Temple
In Kŭmkang-san Mountain in Kangwŏn-do Province.

Antistrophe:

Let's go to see the Eight Views in the East: [35]
The Kyŏngp'o Terrace in Kangnŭng,
The Naksan-sa Temple in Yangyang,
The Mangyang Pavilion in Uljin,
The Samil Bay in Kosŏng,
The Chuksŏ Tower in Samch'ŏk,
The Wŏlsŏng Pavilion in P'yŏnghae,
And the Ch'ŏngkan Pavilion in Kansŏng.

But it's said the best place to have fun
Is the Sinhŭng-sa Temple in Sŏrak-san Mountain.

Act I
Scene 1: The Dance by Nojang

[All Mŏkchung, carrying Nojang's cane, enter as they drag Nojang[36] onto the playground from the costume hall to the tune of *t'aryŏng*. In fact, Nojang is holding one end of his cane, as he follows them.]

Nojang: [He wears a monk's robe, a cowl, and a long rosary. A red sash is slung across his shoulder. He covers his face with a silk gauze fan. Now he slowly lets his cane go and stops following the Mŏkchung. Without realizing that Nojang no longer holds one end of his cane, all Mŏkchung keep going as they pull it. Suddenly, one of them finds out that Nojang is no longer following them.]

Mŏkchung I: *Shee—e!* [The music stops.] *Anaya-a.*

All Mŏkchung: *Kurae-ae.*

Mŏkchung I: I thought we brought out Master Nojang. But we find him nowhere. We've been fooled by this cane.

Mŏkchung II: *Anaya-a.*

All Mŏkchung: *Kurae-ae.*

Mŏkchung II: We must search for him. What do you think? I must go and look for him.

[In a *pullim.*]

The dark clouds reach the high sky
And the sky is not seen

. . .

[He goes near Nojang as he dances to the tune of *t'aryŏng.* Then he returns. All other Mŏkchung also dance as they remain in their places. Now all of them go toward Nojang and return as they dance one by one.]

Mŏkchung II: *Shee—e!*

All Mŏkchung: *Kurae-ae-yi.*

Mŏkchung II: When I went to the east to look for Master Nojang, I found the sky was cloudy as if it was going to rain.

Mŏkchung III: *Anaya-ya-a.*

All Mŏkchung: *Kurae-ae.*

Mŏkchung III: I must go and examine the situation carefully.

[In a *pullim.*]

The peach blossom in Jade Village
In mid-spring.

. . .

[He goes to Nojang as he dances and returns.] *Shee—e!* [The music and dancing stop.] *Anaya.*

All Mŏkchung: *Kurae-ae-yi.*

Mŏkchung III: When I went there I didn't find a cloud in the sky. But there was the peddler's pottery. They were glazed dark brown.

Mŏkchung IV: *Anaya.*

All Mŏkchung: *Kurae-ae-yi.*

Mŏkchung IV: I must go and examine this.

> [In a *pullim.*]
>
> *The sunset in the eastern sky*
> *And the pear-blossom garden*
> . . .

Mŏkchung IV: I examined the situation carefully. It was a load of charcoal owned by a peddler.

Mŏkchung V: *Anaya.*

All Mŏkchung: *Kurae-ae.*

Mŏkchung V: I must go and examine this in detail.

> [In a *pullim.*]
>
> *The place where the mountain is green*
> *While the water is blue*
> . . .
>
> [He goes and returns.] *Shee—e!* [The music and dancing stop.] *Anaya.*

All Mŏkchung: *Kurae-ae-yi.*

Mŏkchung V: I examined them carefully and found the sky was overcast. So a huge serpent came out.

Mŏkchung VI: A huge serpent? *Anaya.*

All Mŏkchung: *Kurae-ae-yi.*

Mŏkchung VI: This time, I must go and examine it.

[In a *pullim.*]

The ceremonious willow
In the spring air
. . .

[He goes and returns.] *Shee—e! Anaya.*

All Mŏkchung: *Kurae-ae-yi.*

Mŏkchung VI: I've no doubt that it was a huge serpent.

Mŏkchung VII: *Anaya.*

All Mŏkchung: *Kurae-ae-yi.*

Mŏkchung VII: How is it possible for a huge serpent to come?
There're so many people. I must go and check it out.

[In a *pullim.*]

Although my hair is gray,
My mind is still young
. . .

[He goes and returns.] *Shee—e! Anaya.*

All Mŏkchung: *Kurae-ae-yi.*

Mŏkchung VII: You fellows said it was a huge serpent, pottery with a
dark brown glaze, or a bundle of charcoal. But it was obviously
Master Nojang whom we dragged in.

Mŏkchung VII: *Anaya.*

All Mŏkchung: *Kurae-ae-yi.*

Mŏkchung VIII: It can't be. I must go and check it out.

[In a *pullim.*]

The mottled bamboo
With twelve knots
. . .

[He goes and returns.] *Shee—e! Anaya.*

All Mŏkchung: *Kurae-ae-yi.*

Mŏkchung VIII: He was definitely our Master Nojang. We all know that his favorite thing in the world is "The Song of the Sea Gull." Let's sing it for him.

All Mŏkchung: That's a good idea.

Mŏkchung I: *Anaya.*

All Mŏkchung: *Kurae-ae-yi.*

Mŏkchung I: I must go and ask him whether he wants to hear "The Song of the Sea Gull." [He goes to Nojang.] Master Nojang, may we roll "The Song of the Sea Gull" and gently stuff it into your ear?

Nojang: [Nods.]

Mŏkchung I: [As he returns.] *Anaya.*

All Mŏkchung: *Kurae-ae-yi.*

Mŏkchung I: When I asked him whether we should roll "The Song of the Sea Gull" and gently stuff it into his ear, he nodded like a hungry dog which shakes its head to its master for food.

All Mŏkchung: [In chorus.]

> *You, white sea gull*
> *Don't fly away,*
> *Flapping your wings.*
> *I'm not here to catch you.*
> *His Majesty has deserted me.*
> *So, to keep you company,*
> *I've come.*

[They all sing as they dance to the tune of *t'aryŏng.*]

Mŏkchung II: *Anaya.*

All Mŏkchung: *Kurae-ae-yi.*

Mŏkchung II: Let's stop singing "The Song of the Sea Gull." How about "Ododogi T'aryŏng?"[37]

All Mŏkchung: Good!

Mŏkchung II: I must go and ask him. [He goes to Nojang.] Master Nojang, may we roll "Ododogi T'aryŏng" and gently stuff it into your ear...?

Nojang: [Nods.]

Mŏkchung II: [As he returns.] *Anaya.*

All Mŏkchung: *Kurae-ae-yi.*

Mŏkchung II: When I asked him whether we should roll "Ododogi T'aryŏng," he shook his head like the head of a penis being masturbated.

All Mŏkchung: [They sing in chorus to the tune of *t'aryŏng* as they dance, jerking their shoulders.]

> *Ododogi Ch'un-hyang.*
> *When the moon is bright and pleasant*
> *Kkittuduttang kkittuduttang kkittuduttang.*
> *The great monk from Sinch'ŏn*
> *Is coming to the deep valley and high peak.*

Mŏkchung III: *Anaya.*

All Mŏkchung: *Kurae-ae-yi.*

Mŏkchung III: We can't leave Master Nojang alone like a lonely pillar in the blaze. It is against our principles and religion. We must serve him. What do you say?

All Mŏkchung: You're right. [All of them go to Nojang and pull one end of his cane.]

> [In a *pullim*.]

> *When the dark clouds reach high*
> *And no sky is seen*
> *...*

[When they come to the middle of the playground, some of them try to dance in front of him to the tune of *t'aryŏng* while others follow him. Nojang drops his cane and falls down. One of the Mŏkchung quickly clasps the end of the cane and follows them. They continue for a while. One of them turns around and discovers that the person who is following is not Nojang. He is shocked.]

Mŏkchung IV: *Shee—e!* [The music and dancing stop.] What has happened to Master Nojang? Who's that fellow?

Mŏkchung V: What's happening? Master Nojang has completely disappeared. It must be due to the lack of our spiritual devotion to Buddha. All of us must search for him.

All Mŏkchung: Yes, you're right. [They look for Nojang as they dance to the tune of *t'aryŏng*. One of them finds Nojang lying down on the ground. He is surprised.]

Mŏkchung VI: *Shee—e!* [The music and dancing stops.] Something has gone wrong.

All Mŏkchung: What is it?

Mŏkchung VI: I found Master Nojang lying down in the corner of the playground. He looks dead.

Mŏkchung VII: *Anaya.*

All Mŏkchung: *Kurae-ae-yi.*

Mŏkchung VII: I must go and see whether he is really dead or not.

[In a *pullim.*]

When the dark clouds reach high
No sky is seen
. . .

[He runs to the place where Nojang is lying down and comes back.] *Shee—e! Anaya.*

All Mŏkchung: *Kurae-ae-yi.*

Mŏkchung VII: We're really in trouble.

Mŏkchung VIII: Why are we in trouble?

Mŏkchung VII: Our Master Nojang is in a state of double submission, tranquility, and peace.

Mŏkchung VIII: Ah, ha! You're talking such nonsense. "A state of double submission, tranquility, and peace?" What do you mean? Ah, I see. You mean he has trembled and wiggled. Then he has stiffened himself to death. Do you mean that?

Mŏkchung I: *Anaya.*

All Mŏkchung: *Kurae-ae-yi.*

Mŏkchung I: I don't think our Master Nojang can die so easily. I must check him carefully.

> [In a *pullim.*]

> *The pear blossom pavilion.*
> *The sunset in the eastern sky*
> . . .

[He goes to Nojang and returns.] *Shee-e! Anaya.*

All Mŏkchung: *Kurae-ae-yi.*

Mŏkchung I: I've examined him . . . Definitely dead. . . smells like a rotten dog in the height of summer.

Mŏkchung II: *Anaya.*

All Mŏkchung: *Kurae-ae-yi.*

Mŏkchung II: Monks must behave like monks while the mundane people should act like mundane people. According to this logic, we can't be indifferent. We're all his disciples. Master Nojang is dead. We must perform a ritual of great change and variety.

All Mŏkchung: Yes, you're right. [They bring out an hourglass-shaped drum, a regular drum, a small gong, a large gong, etc. As they circle around Nojang, they begin to perform the ritual while reciting *yŏmbul.*[38]]

Namuamit'abul
Kwanseŭmbosal.[39]

[Nojang shakes his fan.]

Mŏkchung III: *Shee—e!* [Everything stops suddenly.] *Anaya.*

All Mŏkchung: *Kurae-ae-yi.*

Mŏkchung III: *Yŏmbul* must be the medicine for him. He is beginning to revive. The thing which Master Nojang likes most is *yŏmbul.* Let's recite *yŏmbul* for a while.

All Mŏkchung: Yes. [When the musicians play the tune of *yŏmbul,* they all circle around Nojang. Nojang begins to revive, shaking his fan. When they see that Nojang is reviving, they all exit. Then they reenter, carrying Somu[40] on an open palanquin.]

Somu: [She wears a fancy costume, make-up, and a crown-like headpiece. She is sitting modestly on the palanquin as she covers her face with a fan.]

[Two Mŏkchung have lanterns while the other four carry the open palanquin. Two of them hold sun umbrellas. They enter to the tune of *t'aryŏng.* They put down the palanquin at a little distance from Nojang.]

Somu: [She puts down her fan. Then she gets off the palanquin.]

All Mŏkchung: [They exit in the opposite direction carrying the empty palanquin.]

Somu: [As soon as all Mŏkchung exit, she begins to dance to the tune of *todori.*]

[There should be no dialogue between Somu and Nojang. They ought to express their mutual feelings only through their action and dance.]

Nojang: [He tries to stand up to the tune of *todori*. Finally, he gets up. As he leans on the cane, he covers his face with a silk gauze fan. Then he looks around slowly, bending his back, to see whether there is anyone around him. Unexpectedly finding Somu, he is surprised. He quickly covers his face again with the fan; his body trembles. He crouches to the ground. Once again, he stands up and furtively peers at Somu between the ribs of his fan. It appears that he wonders whether she is a fairy, admiring her beauty. He finally realizes that she is a human being. He is still amazed by her captivating beauty. Now it seems that he is regretting his past life which was devoted only to Buddhism. He thinks he shoud live with a beautiful woman like her in the mundane world instead of being a monk. As if he is determined, he nods. He has completely capitulated to the beauty of Somu. He still keeps covering his face with the fan.]

Somu: [She dances as though she does not notice the presence of Nojang.]

Nojang: [He is determined to approach her. He attempts to lift his cane. But it is stuck to the ground. Holding his cane, he circles around it as he dances to the tune of *todori* while covering his face with the fan. He cannot lift the cane. Now he holds his fan. As he dances, he strikes the cane with the fan. Now he is able to lift the cane. Holding the cane in both hands, he carries it on his shoulder. As if he is ashamed of himself, he walks backward toward Somu.]

Somu: [She keeps dancing without paying attention to Nojang.]

Nojang: [While he is walking backward, he bumps against her. Surprised. He runs back to his original place. Now he turns around and looks at her as he fans himself. Nods. The tune of *kutkŏri*.[41] He begins to dance hand-dance as he holds the fan in one hand. Keeping the fan on his shoulder, he goes behind her. Then he sneaks around to see her face as he covers his face with the fan.]

Somu: [When Nojang tries to see her face from the right she turns to the left. When he goes to the left she turns to the right. They repeat this action a number of times.]

Nojang: [He comes in front of her and repeats the same action.]

Somu: [She turns quickly.]

Nojang: [As if he can no longer control his excitement, he tries his best to see her face, circling around her. The tune of *kutkŏri.*]

Somu: [She turns quickly in a charming manner when Nojang tries to see her.]

Nojang: [Confused as well as excited. He runs toward a corner of the playground. He stares at her as he holds the open fan. As if he is now resolved, he nods. He throws away his cane and goes toward Somu to see her from the opposite direction. For a couple of times, he repeats the same action.]

Somu: [She keeps turning quickly to avoid Nojang.]

Nojang: [The tune of *t'aryŏng.* Despite trying every method, he hasn't been able to win her heart. Now he begins to dance a hand-dance as he takes off his rosary. When he goes behind her, he checks around to make sure that there is no one around them. He removes his fan from his face and folds it. Then he holds the rosary in both hands and puts it on Somu as he dances a hand-dance. Elated. As he dances, he now makes a single circle around her.]

Somu: [She removes the rosary and throws it on the ground.]

Nojang: [Seeing Somu has thrown down the rosary, he is surprised and disappointed. He picks up the rosary and smells it. Nods. Thinking his face is not handsome enough to win her, he takes out a mirror from his pocket and looks at it, fixing his face and hat. Once more, he looks at the mirror. Nods. He circles around Somu dancing in such a way as if trying to fondle her. Now he puts the rosary on her.]

Somu: [She keeps dancing.]

Nojang: [He looks around and retreats a few steps from Somu. Holding the fan, he watches her to make sure she keeps the rosary. As though he is completely satisfied, he makes a couple of jumps. He comes in front of her to seduce her. For a while, he dances with her.]

Somu: [She dances in such a winsome way with Nojang.]

Nojang: [He dances excitedly, jerking his shoulders, while circling around her for a while.]

[The scene should portray the character of Nojang, reputed as being a living Buddha, having completely capitulated to the voluptuous beauty, coquetry, and allurement of the deft Somu.]

Act IV
Scene 2: The Dance by the Shoe Peddler

[While Nojang and Somu are dancing, facing each other, Shoe Peddler[42] enters.]

Shoe Peddler: [He wears a felt hat and carries a wrapped bundle of merchandise on his back. To the tune of *t'aryŏng,* he enters the playground.] *Shee—e!* [The music and dancing stop. Nojang and Somu stand still.] Oh-ho-o! Because I didn't study when I was young, I had to become a shoe peddler. I have to search out customers in every corner of the country. I pity my life. Anyway, I'm a peddler. To sell my merchandise, I must strut. [He walks to the tune of *t'aryŏng* to the middle of the playground. He stops.] *Shee—e!* [The music stops.] Oh! What a wonderful market! After hearing about this wonderful market, I've rushed here in spite of the great distance. I think what I've heard about this market is not an intemperate description. When I look on both sides, I see so many people that they could almost make themselves human screens against the wind. It must be a great market. What difference does it make whether it is a great market or not? They say "if there is fighting we must stop it. If it's merchandise for sale we must bargain for the price." Since I'm a peddler, I must sell my merchandise. Well. What should I sell? I have tasty roasted chestnuts. Let me sell them. First, I must sell the roasted chestnuts to a daughter-in-law who eats them in her bed, hiding from her mother-in-law.

[In a singsong tone.]

Please buy my roasted chestnuts!
Please buy my roasted chestnuts!
Please buy my chestnut candies with pepper!

Ha, ha, ha! . . . Well. There isn't a single person who wants to buy my chestnuts. I must sell shoes instead of chestnuts.

[In a singsong tone.]

The straw sandals with three meshes!
The hemp-cord sandals with six meshes!
Please buy my beautiful shoes for maidens!

Well. There isn't a single person who wants to buy shoes either. This market must not be for buyers. I came to the wrong market. I must change my direction and go to the market of good harvest. [Or he may say "If this is the case, I must go to another market."]

[In a singsong tone.]

I'm going.
Yes, I'm going.
I'm going.
To the market of good harvest.

I'm going.
Ae-yi.
I'm going
To the market of good harvest.
I'm going.
Ae-yi.

[When he walks over to Nojang, the latter strikes him in the face with his fan. Shocked. He recoils a few steps.] What is this? I've never been beaten by anyone before in my life. I see. Because he wears a monk's cowl down to his face, a blue monk's dress, a rosary, and a red sash, he must be a monk. Even though monk has different customs from ordinary people, he should have greeted me, a *yangban*. [43] Instead, he hit me.

Nojang: [He beckons Shoe Peddler to come.]

Shoe Peddler: [Suddenly becoming polite.] Oh. He wants me to come. [He puts down his merchandise and goes to Nojang. Gently.] Do you want to buy shoes? Well. What kind?

Nojang: [He points to his shoes.]

Shoe Peddler: Oh, yes. I have them. What size?

Nojang: [He indicates the size with his hand on the fan.]

Shoe Peddler: Oh. Size seven and half. Oh, yes. I have them. [He picks up a pair of shoes from the top of his merchandise wrapping and gives them to Nojang.]

Nojang: [Now he points to Somu's shoes.]

Shoe Peddler: Oh, for your daughter, too? I have them for her. What size?

Nojang: [He indicates the size with his hand on the fan.]

Shoe Peddler: [Surprised.] Oh, my goodness. Size ninety-nine? My goodness! She must have huge feet. They can be used as boats for the flood. Yes. I have them, too. [When he opens his merchandise case to pick up a pair of shoes from the bottom, a monkey jumps out. The shocked Shoe Peddler runs away. He runs around the playground to the tune of music. The monkey follows him. He stops as he stretches his arms. The monkey imitates him.] What is this? What kind of monster is this? What are you? Let me see what you are. Sit down here! You have four legs. Your body is covered with hair. You must be an animal. What kind of animal are you? Are you a dog?

Monkey[44]: [Shakes his head.]

Shoe Peddler: Are you a pig?

Monkey: [Shakes his head.]

Shoe Peddler: If so, are you a cat?

Monkey: [Shakes his head.]

Shoe Peddler: If you aren't a cat, are you a deer from a mountain?

Monkey: [Shakes his head.]

Shoe Peddler: Are you a deer with spots?

Monkey: [Shakes his head.]

Shoe Peddler: If you aren't a deer with spots, are you a rabbit?

Monkey: [Shakes his head.]

Shoe Peddler: If you're neither this nor that, are you your grandfather?
[He pushes the monkey. The monkey does the same to him.] Let
me think. Since you're imitating human beings very well, you must
be a monkey. I've been told that the animal which imitates human
beings is a monkey. You're a monkey, aren't you?

Monkey: [Nods.]

Shoe Peddler: Oh, oh! I'm glad you're a monkey. One of my ancestors
went to China as an envoy and brought a monkey with him. So I've
brought out the monkey instead of shoes. A monkey is a smart
animal like man. So I'm going to hire you to collect money. Can you
obey my orders?

Monkey: [Nods.]

Shoe Peddler: Well. I've sold the shoes to the monk. Go and collect the
money.

Monkey: [He goes behind Somu and makes obscene movements
towards her.]

Shoe Peddler: [He waits for the monkey. He shouts.] It's time for him to come back. He hasn't come back yet. I'm afraid he must have run away with the money. I must look for him. But I've no idea where he might be. When I was young I learned the art of prognostication. To find him, I must try it. [He takes out a bamboo tube from his wrapping.] When I say this to heaven and earth, please answer me quickly and smoothly. I, a foolish farmer, am looking for the monkey. Teacher Kwak Kwak, Yi Sun-p'ung, Teacher Chae-gal Kongmyŏng, and all sorts of spirits, please descend on earth and answer my. . . Ha, ha, ha! This prognostication is strange. It gives me the word "union." It must mean that he hasn't gone too far. But he has made a union with someone. I must find him. [He looks for the monkey as he walks to and fro to the tune provided by an hourglass-shaped drum. He finds the monkey on Somu's back, making obscene movements.] *Shee—e!* Ah-ha! You've made a "union" with her. Come here! [He pulls the monkey's nose. The monkey does the same to him.] You fool. Leave my nose alone! Leave it alone! You fool. I'll let yours go first. [He drops his hand from the monkey's nose.] You've made love to her. Now I must perform sodomy with you. [He makes the monkey lie down on his stomach and makes obscene movements.]

Monkey: [He stands up quickly and makes Shoe Peddler lie down on his stomach. Then he makes obscene movements over him.]

Shoe Peddler: [He stands and slaps the monkey on the hip.] You fool! What are you trying to do? You deformed creature! . . . Anyway, did you collect the money for the shoes? Let's count the money. Two times eight makes sixteen. Three times five makes fifteen. [He tries to calculate as he writes the figures on the ground.]

Monkey: [He erases everything as soon as Shoe Peddler writes.]

Shoe Peddler: Because you're bothering me, this must mean you haven't collected the money. Go and collect the money! Right now! [He sends the monkey to Nojang.]

Monkey: [He goes to Nojang and extends his hand.]

Nojang: [He doesn't give him money. But he scribbles something on a piece of paper and hands it to the monkey.]

Monkey: [He returns to Shoe Peddler and hands the letter to him.]

Shoe Peddler: Oh. Have you collected the money? What did you bring instead of money? You've brought a letter? What kind of letter? Let me read it. [He opens the letter and reads it.] "If you want to collect the money for the shoes, you must come to the corner of Firewood Street." Oh, my goodness! It must be he is going to burn me to death in fire. Let me run away from here. [He exits quickly, holding the monkey's hand to the tune provided by an hourglass-shaped drum. When Shoe Peddler and the monkey exit, Nojang and Somu begin to dance to the tune of *t'aryŏng*. After a while, Ch'wipali[45] enters.]

Act IV
Scene 3: The Dance by Ch'wipali

Ch'wipali: [To the tune of *t'aryŏng*, he staggers onto the playground as if he is drunk. He carries willow branches in his hand. A large bell is fastened to one of his knees. As he stands apart from Nojang, he speaks loudly.] *Shee—e!* [The music and dancing stop.] *Aek-k'ae-k'ae! Ah't-shee-e! Shee-e!* The damn cold or flu comes to me every year, every month, every day, every hour, and every minute.

[In a *pullim*.]

Making a round circle
While circling round
. . .

[To the tune of *t'aryŏng*, he dances a hand-dance for a while.]
Shee—e!

When the mountain is not high
It is beautiful and handsome.

When the water is not deep
It is blue and clear.

When the ground is not wide
It is even and flat.

When there aren't too many people
They grow and prosper.

When the pine and bamboo
Complement each other's green color,
The moon and a crane become a pairs.

Since the willow branches are green
It must be the spring season.

Sopu and Hŏyu idled
In the beautiful mountain
By the water in another world
When Yi Chŏk-sŏn had fun
On Ch'aesŏk-kang River under the bright moon
And So Tong-p'a enjoyed himself
On the Chŏkpyŏk-kang River
Under the moon in the autumn sky.

Hearing rumors
About the beauty of Kŭmkang-san Mountain,
I, originally a libertine,
Sought for friends in the green mountain.
But I found none.

Instead of devoting myself
To prayer for Buddha
I brought a beautiful girl to play with me.
And. . .

[In a *pullim*.]

Kking kkorang.
Kking kkorang.

[He dances jumping up and down and goes to Nojang. Now he circles around him. Then he stands in front of Somu.]

Nojang: [When Ch'wipali comes in front of him, he suddenly strikes him in the face with the fan.]

Ch'wipali: [Trembling, he recoils.] *Shee—e!* [The music stops.] *Aigu!*[46] Ah! What is this? I've never been beaten in my life before. Something hit me. Ah! What is this? Oh, I see.

In order not to hear
The mundane affairs
I stuffed my ears.
Then I went to the mountain.
But due to the lack of interest
In Buddhism, instead,
I sought the scenic beauty.

There I found
The great monk
Who was on the five mountain peaks
In the high Hyang-san Mountain under the sky.

Following the great monk
From the western mountain,
I, a mastermind young monk,
Who frequented the Palace of the Dragon King
To fondle the eight beauties[47]
On the stone bridge in the spring,
Was caught.

Becoming an accused man,
I returned to the hall of great monks,
Flanked by the chaste and modest women
Such as Nanyang Princess, Chin Ch'ae-pong,
Kae Sŏm-wŏl, Sim O-yŏn, and Paek Nŭng-p'a
Who were as elegant as slender clouds,
I had great fun with them.

Then on my way home,
Meeting friends from here and there,
I kept drinking one bowl of wine after another.

After the first, second, and third drink, my face was reddish. Then I finally came here. The mountain is steep while the trees stand thick and tall. Meanwhile, the black-eared kites, thinking I'm a piece of meat, are circling over me one by one from every direction. Maybe, they're trying to tease me. I must return to check things out again. . .

[In a *pullim*.]

Tranquility extends boundlessly
When clouds float in mid-sky
. . .

[He goes to Nojang as he dances to the music.]

Nojang: [When Ch'wipali comes to him, he suddenly strikes him in the face with the fan.]

Ch'wipali: [As he recoils.] *Shee—e!* [The music stops.] Ah. I'm beaten. Oh. What is this? I was never beaten even when I was a boy. It is blackish, shiny, and whitish. It must be gold. I don't think it's gold. Because the cunning and clever Chin P'yŏng distributed thirty thousand *yangs*[48] among the soldiers of Ch'u,[49] it couldn't be a large amount of money. If so, can it be jade? If it is jade, you must tell me about jade.

The broken jade
By Pŏm-chŏng
At the banquet in Hongmun-yŏn
Is the burnt jade.

Jade and stone are two different things. So it can't be jade. If so, can it be a ghost? If it's a ghost, you must tell me about the ghost. There can't be a ghost on a bright sunny day. If so, are you a serpent?

Nojang: [He lifts his fan ready to strike Ch'wipali.]

Ch'wipali: Oh. I'm in trouble. [Shocked. He tries to cover his face with
the willow branches which he carries.] Oh! Oh! I see. You're
wearing a lacquer-colored monk's dress, a rosary, a monk's cowl,
and a red sash. You're also leaning on a cane. You have a fan, too.
So you must be a monk. If you're a true monk, you should devote
yourself to prayer for Buddha. You shouldn't play with a beautiful
girl in the mundane world.

[In a *pullim*.]

Kking kkorang.
kking kkorang

. . .

[To the tune of *t'aryŏng*, he dances.] *Shee—e!* [The music and
dancing stop.] You monk! Listen to me. Your behavior is wrong.
You must not play with a pretty girl. Let's make a bet. Since you're
good for tinkering, you should play the role of blower, while I'll
become a thick gruel of grain flour. If you can't win, you must give
up that girl to me. If I lose the bet, I'll let you beat me on the hip.

[In a *pullim*.]

Should I make a fire
Under a pan or cauldron?

. . .

[To the tune of *t'aryŏng*, he begins to dance.] *Shee—e!* I don't
think I can endure this either. Now you and I must dance facing
each other. If you can't do it, you must do such and such a thing. If I
can't endure it, I'll do this and that.

[In a *pullim*.]

Although my hair is gray
My mind is still young

. . .

[To the tune of *t'aryŏng*, he dances. Then he stops.] *Shee—e!* I can't endure this either. Well. I'm in trouble. I'm told that a goblin must be taken care of with a club. So I must really beat him up.

[In a *pullim*.]

When a tiger appears
In the eastern region,
Kilro-raebi hwŏl hwŏl.

[To the tune of *t'aryŏng*, he goes toward Nojang as he dances.]

Nojang: [When Ch'wipali comes to him, he suddenly strikes him in the face with the fan.]

Ch'wipali: [Recoiling.] *Shee—e! Aigu.* What's happening? This fellow has really beaten me. Ha, ha, ha! He has beaten me on my heel. But I'm bleeding from my nose. The blood must have circulated upward. What shall I do about this? They say the best way to stop bleeding from the nose is to stuff it with something. But I don't think I can even find my nose. Because my face is as large as one half of Korea, I can't find it easily. I'm sure my nose must be somewhere on my face. To find it, I should start searching from the bottom. [He begins to search for his nose with his hand.] Ah. It's here. I didn't know it was this easy to find. [He stuffs his nose with something.] Oh, my. It is still bleeding. What shall I do? Once upon a time, a doctor told me I should rub my nose to stop it from bleeding. [He picks up a handful of dirt and rubs his nose with it.] Ah. It's so easy to stop it. But until now I've tried all kinds of silly things. Even if it's necessary for me to drink a handful of cold water or grit my teeth to make me strong enough to fight, I must do it. I have to chase him out. I must play with the girl.

[In a *pullim*.]

The mottled bamboo
With twelve knots
. . .

[To the tune of *t'aryŏng,* he goes to Nojang and beats him ruthlessly.]

Nojang: [Beaten by Ch'wipali, he exits.]

Ch'wipali: [Satisfied. He begins to sing as he dances.]

That's right!
That's right!
If it's not a bead decoration
It must be a nun's cowl. [50]

[He stops dancing.] *Shee—e!* [To Somu.] You bitch. What do you think of me? You only like the monk from the temple. But you don't like me because I look like a lion's molar teeth. Don't you know that the monk smells like burning fat? But I smell like perfume. Why don't you play with me?

[In a *pullim.*]

When the willow reaches the autumn sky
. . .

[He dances.] *Shee—e!* Oh. You're picking cherries. Oh. Oh! You must look down upon me because I'm a bachelor. Look! I'm going to make a top-knot with my hair. [51] [He makes a top-knot with his hair.]

[In a singsong tone.]

The top-knot
Which is as small as an ant
It tumbles loose
Even with twelve knots.

[He dances.] *Shee—e!* Look! Listen to me. I'm a country libertine. I know how to drink, sing, dance, and spend money. "Money can subjugate even goblins." This means that if I had money I could even buy a goblin. So I'm going to buy your heart with money. [He throws her some money.] Look! Catch it!

Somu: [She tries to pick up the money.]

Ch'wipali: [As he runs quickly.] Ah! [He picks up the money.] Look. According to your behavior, I can say that you're the kind of woman who wants to trade your doorknob for candies. Listen to what I say.

> Although I've spent my life
> With the most beautiful women
> At the tavern and brothel,
> You don't seem to me
> An ordinary woman in this world.
>
> Let's tie oursevles together
> With the string of T'ak Mun-kun's *kŏmun'go*. [52]
> Then shall we live together
> For the next one hundred years?

Somu: [She turns away quickly.]

Ch'wipali: Oh. You still don't like me. It must be a joke. I was wrong to pick up the money which was given to you. Here! Take the money. Take it! [He throws the money to her.] Take the money. Take it! [He throws the money to her.]

Somu: [She turns around and picks up the money.]

Ch'wipali: Oh, my goodness. She has gobbled it down. Eat my body too.

> [In a *pullim*.]
>
> *The pear blossom pavilion.*
> *The sunset in the eastern sky*
> . . .
>
> [He begins to dance.]

Somu: [She dances with Ch'wipali for a while.]

Ch'wipali: [He lifts Somu's skirt and sticks his head under it.] *Shee—e!*

My goodness. It's really hot here. I must count these. . . One, two, three, four, five, and six. . . Oh, my. Leave me alone. Good. [He picks a pubic hair from her.] Ah! This is such a long hair. It's one and half my arm's length. [Then he plucks a few hairs from his head. Now he inserts a doll between Somu's legs.]

Somu: [She suddenly begins to act as if she has a stomach pain. She drops the doll, suggesting that she has given birth to a baby. She exits.]

Ch'wipali: [He goes to the place where Somu was, dancing. He picks up the baby.]

[The role of the baby in the following scene is also played by Ch'wipali.]

Baby: [Crying.] *Ungae. Ungae. Ungae.*

Ch'wipali: My goodness. What's happening? Gentlemen in the village, please listen to me. At the age of seventy, I was able to make a baby boy. Please, don't dare come to my house. I must find a name for the baby. Should I call him the second child? No. To call him the second child, I must have the first child. Well. Since he was born on the playground, I have no choice but to call him playground. Hey! Playground's mother, please nurse him. . . [He rocks the baby singing a lullaby.]

Oh-ho tung-tung.
My baby.
Where have you been until now?

Have you been playing
With Sopu and Hŏyu
In the beautiful mountain
By the clear water?

Have you been playing
With Yi Chŏk-sŏn
On the Ch'aesŏk-kang River
Under the bright moon?

Have you been eating ferns
With Paek-Yi and Suk-Jae
In Suyang-san Mountain?

Why did you come so late?
Tung-tung. . . my baby.

Baby: Papa! Don't just rock me while singing a lullaby. Like other children, I want to study.

Ch'wipali: Well. That's a good idea.

Baby: Please let me study both books. [53]

Ch'wipali: What do you mean by both books? Do you mean the provinces of Hwanghae-do and P'yŏngan-do?

Baby: No, I don't mean that. I mean the Korean script and the Chinese characters.

Ch'wipali: Good. I'll teach you. *Hanul-ch'ŏn.* [54]

Baby: *Tta-ji.* [55]

Ch'wipali: Look! When I said *hanul-ch'ŏn,* you said *tta-ji.*

Baby: Papa! Don't teach me like that. You must teach me *The Thousand Character Text* [56] in the way it is made into poetry.

Ch'wipali: That's a splendid idea.

[In a singsong tone.]

At the Hour of the Rat [57]
The sky was created.
Then it became infinitely blue.
Now, hanul-ch'ŏn.

At the Hour of the Ox [58]
The earth was created.
Then everything began
To grow and prosper.
Now, tta-ji.

Profundity, black ink, black-red color,
And a demon in the North.
Now, kamul-hyŏn.

King, ministers, subjects, events, things,
East, west, south, north,
And the color of the middle of earth.
Now, nuru-hwang.

The heaven, earth, four directions,
And the great, vast, long tower.
Now, chip-u.

The successful generations,
Rise and fall,
Prosperity and decline of a nation.
Now, chip-ju.

The control of flood by U,
The Kija family of Ch'uyŏn,
And the nine principles
Of morality and politics.[59]
Now, nŏlbul-hong.

The barbarians of no return,
The wild field and garden,
And the three Classics of Ancient China.[60]
Now, kŏch'il-hwang.

To Yo and Sun,[61] *great sages,*
The Kyŏkyang Song,[62]
And the hazy moonlight.
Now, dal-wŏl.

The five wagonfuls of poetry and penmanship
And many deskfuls of scholar's books.
Now, ch'al-yŏng.

When the full moon sets

What is the time of night?
Now, kiul-ch'uk.

The twenty-eight stars along the zodiac, [63]
The pictures of Hato and Nakso, [64]
And many stars of mutuality.
Now, pyŏl-jin.

The cock fighting boys
And the quilts and pillows
In the brothel.
Now, chal-suk.

The unparalleled beauty,
Sweet melodies of music,
And the tableful of exquisite food.
Now, pŏl-yŏl.

The love talk
In the secluded chamber
At midnight.
Now, pep'ul-chang. [65]

Baby: Please stop it. Now teach me the Korean alphabet.

Ch'wipali: Yes. I'll teach you the Korean alphabet. *Ka kya kŏ kyŏ ko kyo ku kyu.* [66]

Baby: Papa. Don't teach me that way. You must teach me in the opposite way.

Ch'wipali: *Ka na ta ra ma ba sa a cha ch'a. Ah't-ch'a-ch'a!* I've forgotten it. *Kiŏk niŭn tikŭt.* Now let's build a house with the shape of *kiŏk.* [67] We've planned to live like *niŭn.* But we have to live like *tikŭt.* [68] *Ka kya kŏ kyŏ.* I have no place to go. I have become a man without a place to live. [69] *Ko kyo ku kyu.* My sufferings made me a man without good friends. [70] *Na nya nŏ nyŏ.* Oh. The flying bird, [71] why don't you and I become a pair? *No nyo nu nyu.* The willows and roses by the street and hedges [72] for any man, for whom are you standing there? *Ta tya tŏ tyŏ.* The sticky affection of mine is falling apart fleetingly. . .[73] *To tyo tu tyu.* The motivation of an old man who walks into the inner chamber is not clear.[74]

[He exits, holding the baby, as he dances.]

Act V
The Dance by Lion

All Mŏkchung: A beast has appeared. [Eight Mŏkchung chased by the lion[75] enter together to the playground. The lion appears ready to kill and eat all the Mŏkchung. They make one circle around the playground and exit in the opposite direction from which they entered except one who plays the role of the lion driver with a whip.]

Lion Driver: *Shee—e!* [The lion sits in the middle of the playground as he turns his head in this direction and that. Once in a while, he tries to scratch his body or tries to catch some fleas. Whenever the lion moves his head, the bells on the head ring.] This is a beast. But I wonder what kind of beast this is? It's neither a deer nor a deer with spots, nor a tiger. Well. I should ask him. You're a beast. I've never seen a beast like you before. Neither have my ancestors. Are you a deer?

Lion: [He shakes his head to indicate that he is not a deer. Once in a while, he licks his tongue.]

Lion Driver: If you're not a deer, are you a deer with spots?

Lion: [Shakes his head.]

Lion Driver: Well. You're not a deer with spots. Then are you a tiger? Or are you your grandfather?

Lion: [Shakes his head.]

Lion Driver: You fool. You're only a beast. You should be able to recognize man. Man is the lord of all creatures. You wicked fellow. You dare not try to jump on me. What kind of animal are you? I see. Now I know. An old saying says: "If a sage was born he would be followed by a giraffe. If a man of virtue was born he could be followed by a phoenix." Since our master was born, you must be a giraffe.

Lion: [Shakes his head.]

Lion Driver: No? If you're neither a giraffe nor a phoenix, what on earth are you? [Thinks for a second.] That's right! Now I understand. A long time ago, Ch'ŏn Tan in Che Kingdom defeated many thousands enemies by sending oxen with torches on their horns into the enemy camp. Because we've been playing noisily, an ox has appeared, thinking this is a battle ground. So you must be an ox, aren't you?

Lion: [Shakes his head.]

Lion Driver: You're not an ox? If you're neither an ox nor a dog, what on earth are you? Oh, I see. Now I understand. During the Tang period in China, there was a big drought in the Country of Ogye. As a result, there was a great uproar among the people. So the Dragon Deity, with his tricks, sent you the sweet rain. Then you could return to the palace of Ogye and enjoyed all sorts of prosperity. There you soon buried the king alive in the emerald well. Then you disguised yourself as the king for the next three years, and enjoyed all sorts of prosperity.[76] After this, you went to the Pongrim-sa Temple to get a copy of the Buddhist scripture. There you gave a Buddhist saint a ride on your back, pulling all kinds of tricks. This was you. I know now. So you must be a lion.

Lion: [Nods. He moves his head up and down as if he agrees.]

Lion Driver: After hearing the beautiful melodies of music, you came to play with us, didn't you? Or did you come to kill and eat your grandfather? Or do you have any other reason to come into human society? Our master, who has been regarded as a living Buddha, has practiced asceticism. So did you come to serve him with an order from Buddha?

Lion: [Shakes his head.]

Lion Driver: When you were in the Country of Ogye, your ears and eyes were fixed on pleasure. And you did all sorts of human merry-making. So you were chased by Son Haeng-Ja to the sky. After that, you barely managed to live with the gratitude of Bodhisattva. But hearing the beautiful clarion calls of music in the sky, you came down to play with us, didn't you?

Lion: [Shakes his head.]

Lion Driver: You lion! Listen carefully to what I say. Both you and I should forget about the fairy-land. I want to know the reason why you came down. Did you hear that we, all monks, tricked our master—who was devoting himself to prayer for Buddha—into apostasy? So did you come down to punish us? Are you going to eat all of us?

Lion: [Nods. He is ready to jump on Lion Driver to bite him.]

Lion Driver: [Scared.] *Aigu!* I'm in great trouble. [He retreats backward. Then he starts to beat the lion in the face with his whip.]

Lion: [He retreats helplessly a few steps and sits down.]

Lion Driver: *Shee—e!* [Still frightened.] Listen to me! Anyway, what kind of sins did we commit? We simply followed the instructions of Ch'wipali. We regret that we've behaved terribly. But we're now going to devote ourselves to prayer to become good disciples of Buddha. Can you forgive us?

Lion: [Pleased. Nods.]

Lion Driver: Well. Before we part, shall we dance to this beautiful music? What do you think?

Lion: [Nods.]

Lion Driver: Good. Now I want to know what kind of dance you wish to dance. Shall we dance *kin-yŏngsan?*[77] Or *dodori?* No, I don't think that's right. I know. Shall we dance to the tune of *t'aryŏng?*

[In a *pullim.*]

The pear blossom pavilion
And the eastern sky in Nakyang
. . .

[He begins to dance with the lion to the tune of *t'aryŏng.*] *Shee—e!* [The music stops. The lion sits down.] We've danced to the tune of *t'aryŏng.* Now we must dance to *kutkŏri.* Shall we?

Lion: [Pleased. Nods.]

Lion Driver: Oh, good! [In a singsong tone.]

Tŏng-tŏng.
Tŏngtŏk-kkung.

[They dance to the tune of *kutkŏri.* They exit.]

Act VI
The Dance by Yangban

Malttugi[78]: [He enters the playground to the tune of *kutkŏri.* He is guiding the three *yangban,* aristocrat, brothers. He wears a felt hat.]

Three Yangban: [They enter as they dance an awkward dance to the tune of *kutkŏri.* They are Saennim,[79] the oldest; Sŏpangnim,[80] the second oldest; Toryŏngnim,[81] the youngest. Both Saennim and Sŏpangnim wear white full dress, *top'o,* and many-cornered horsehair hats, *kwan.* Both of them have cleft palates: Saennim has two while Sŏpangnim has one. They also carry fans and bamboo canes. Toryŏngnim's nose and mouth are askewed. He carries only a fan. Throughout the scene Toryŏngnim does not have a single line of dialogue. He only follows whatever his two older brothers do while he strikes them in their faces with his fan once in a while, behaving frivolously.]

Malttugi: [He comes to the middle of the playground.] *Shee—e!* [The music and dancing stop.] The *yangban* are coming. I call them *yangban.* But you shouldn't mistake them for the retired members of the Noron and Soron Parties,[82] or the retired members of the Revenue Board, the War Board, and the Letter Board or the Chief of the Six Boards of the Government. What I mean for *yangban* is *yang* for the dog and *ban* for the small table with dog-foot-shaped legs. These are the two words which I use for them.

All Yangban: Damn you! What did you say?

Malttugi: Well. I don't know what you've heard from me. I said after serving as the members of the Noron and Soron Parties, the Revenue Board and the War Board, the three retired ministers are coming. That was exactly what I said.

All Yangban: [In a *pullim*.]

　　　He called us Yi Saengwŏn.

　　　. . .

[The tune of *kutkŏri*. They dance. Toryŏngnim joins them as he strikes his brothers in their faces with the fan.]

Malttugi: *Shee—e!* [The music and dancing stop. To the audience.] Hello! Listen to me! Don't try to smoke tobacco with a short pipe. You should go to a pipe shop and get varied-colored pipes and spotted bamboo pipes which are at least one and half your arm's length. Then decorate them with the six-sided rings and poulownia engravings. After that, you must smoke them one by one, taking them out from the rack like the fishing poles from Namuri in Chaeryong.

All Yangban: Oh, my goodness. What did you say?

Malttugi: What did you hear from me? Because you are coming, I told them to stop smoking and fighting.

All Yangban: [In a *pullim.*]

> *Stop the fighting.*
>
> . . .

> [The tune of *kutkŏri.* They dance.]

Malttugi: *Shee—e!* [The music and dancing stop.] Hello, musicians! Listen to me. Stop playing the Five Notes and Six Beats of Classical Chinese music. Instead, blow the peeled willow reeds and beat out the dried gourd house utensils.

All Yangban: You! What did you say?

Malttugi: What did you hear from me? I told them to play *haegŭm,* drum, hourglass-shaped drum, flute, and fife instead of making dragging rhythm.

All Yangban: [In a *pullim.*]

> *Strike them beautifully,*
> *Beautifully.*
>
> . . .

> [The tune of *kutkŏri.* They dance.]

Saennim: *Shee—e!* [The music and dancing stop.]

Malttugi: Ye-e-s.

Saennim: Instead of serving us, where have you been?

Malttugi: Ye-e-s. To look for you, I ate my soup with cold rice in the early morning. After that, I took out the old donkey[83] from the stable and brushed and brushed him. Then I rode him and took a trip to Europe, England, America, France, Germany, and the three Asian nations as easily as I stepped on soybean malt. I went to the east and the west. In addition, I traveled to Pukhyang-san Mountain, every neighborhood, every valley, every borough, every village, between the rocks, between the sands, and between the trees. But I didn't find a single fellow who looked like you. Because I was a man of high birth, I went to your home to look for you. Again I found neither you nor the young lords at home except your wife. So without taking off my felt hat and leggings, I kneeled and made it again and again,[84] while holding the whip in my hand.

Saennim: You! What did you say?

Malttugi: Ha, ha, ha! What did you hear? When I asked the health[85] of the madam, she brought out a tableful of food and drink. There were all sorts of wine bottles: a long-necked one like a crane's neck; a short-necked one like a turtle's neck; a bottle for the red whisky from China; a bottle for simple wine. She poured the drink for us. So we drank one bowl after another. For side dishes, she brought out the steamed short ribs in the large bowl, pork in the small bowl, *kimch'i,*[86] octopus, and abalone. In addition, she gave me penis-head which was left over from your hiking lunch last August.

Saennim: You fool! What did you say?

Malttugi: Ah. Listen to me. I said she gave me a porgy fish head.[87] She told me fish-head had the best taste.

All Yangban: [In a *pullim.*]

The porgy fish head.

. . .

[The tune of *kutkŏri.* They all dance.]

Saennim: *Shee—e!* [The music and dancing stop.] You! Malttugi!

Malttugi: Ye-e-s. [To himself.] Damn mother fucking *yangban.* If he's not a *yangban,* he must be half a penis[88] or a table with dog-foot-like legs[89] or a bowl of white rice[90] in the market place. Why does he have to call me "Malttugi," "Kkolttugi,"[91] "Ch'oettogi,"[92] "Maettugi,"[93] or "the broken Chŏlttugi?"[94] Why does he have to call me like a child who calls his grandfather when he sees a walnut-candy peddler?

Saennim: You! Damn you. If you've brought us, you ought to find lodging for us. Instead, why have you been wandering here and there?

Malttugi: [He draws a circle on the ground with the whip.] Ye-e-s. I've acquired this lot for the lodging and drove a few oak stakes around it. I threw some straws for cushion. I also made an opening to the sky. This is your new lodging.

Saennim: You! What did you say?

Malttugi: Ah. What did you hear? After selecting the lot which faces south, I've built a house with five pavilions according to your fortune. The house has ambered footing stones, pillars inlaid with corals, green jade, and golden waves. When we look up at them, they appear to be the lid of a coffin. But when we look down at them, they seem to be the floor covered with laminated paper. Spreading the floral design rug, I look at the writing on the east wall and I see the four words: "clarity, tranquility, peace, and silence." When I look at the west wall I see the words: "fortitude and peace exist in the hall." When I look at the south wall I see the four words: "virtue, justice, decorum, and wisdom." When I look at the north wall I see the words: "filial son and loyal subject." So this place can be a new lodging for *yangban*. For stationary, I see a chest decorated with the engravings of phoenix, a dresser inlaid with mother of pearls, a small chest, a shiny brass chamber pot, brass basin, a many-colored pipe, a mottled bamboo pipe, and some sliced tobacco. I've arranged them like pigs in the dung on the wharf.

Saennim: You fool. What did you say?

Malttugi: Oh. What did you hear? I said I moistened the tobacco with honey.

All Yangban: [In a *pullim*.]

> *The tobacco is moistened with honey.*
>
> . . .

[The tune of *kutkŏri*. They all dance for a while. They stop.

Now they pantomime, entering into their new lodging. They sit down.]

* * *

[After they've entered into the new lodging, the scene can end in the following way as well.]

Malttugi: *Shee—e!* [The music and dancing stop.] Saennim, how do you like your new lodging?

Saennim: It's very nice.

Malttugi: To make sure that all sorts of prosperity come in, I've flung open all the doors.

Saennim: Will prosperity enter into the new lodging, if you keep the doors open?

Malttugi: Yes, that's right. They say "prosperity enters through the open door." So we must keep the door open. When it enters, I must catch it. You should try to catch it, too.

All Yangban: [They are ready to stand up.]

Malttugi: Wait a second. When I shout about prosperity, you must stand up and catch it. Prosperity!

All Yangban: [They stand up and try to catch "prosperity" while running around in all directions.]

Malttugi: [He suddenly starts to beat all the *yangban* as he shouts "Prosperity! Prosperity!"]

All Yangban: [They exit chased by Malttugi.]

* * *

Saennim: *Shee—e!* [The music and dancing stop.] Hello, younger brothers! We're all *yangban*. So we must keep ourselves quiet without saying anything. But this bores us. Let's recite a *sijo*. [95]

Sŏpangnim: That's a good idea.

All Yangban: [They begin to recite a *sijo*.]

> We've lived
> Half of our lives.
> But we'll never get younger.
>
> . . .
>
> Ha, ha, ha! [They laugh.]

Malttugi: [In a singsong tone.]

> *The Nakyang Castle*
> *In the ten square ris of wasteland.*
> *The high and low tombs.*
>
> . . .

Saennim: Now let's compose some poetry.

Sŏpangnim: Brother, you must compose first.

Saennim: You must give me a rhyming word.

Sŏpangnim: Yes, I'll give you some. They are words for "mountain" and "pass."

Saennim: Oh, my. . . They're difficult. Listen to me. Whether it makes sense or not, I'm going to compose one.

> [As if reciting poetry.]
>
> When a rugged huge mountain is made,
> There's the Eastern Pass
> In the huge mountain
> By the yellow river.

Sŏpangnim: Ha, ha, ha! [The two brothers laugh together.] Your composition is fantastic.

Saennim: Why don't you compose one?

Sŏpangnim: Give me a rhyming word.

Saennim: The words are "mesh" and "nail."

Sŏpangnim: Oh. They're difficult. [He thinks for a while.] Listen to what I say.

> When the front mesh
> Of the straw sandal
> Becomes the mesh of a rag,
> The wooden shoe
> Needs a nail.

Malttugi: Sir! I also want to compose one. Please give me a rhyming word.

Saennim: They say "even a dog can understand the mood of the wind and moon if he lives three years in a house of *yangban.*" Well, . . . Since you've been living with us for a few yers, you've become quite smart. What a commendable thing. We composed our poem with two rhyming words. But I'll give you a single word to make it easy. The word is "head."

Malttugi: [As if reciting poetry.]

> When there's a dog head in the hole,
> There's a penis-head in the old pants.

Saennim: You! What a good composition! As soon as I gave you a rhyming word, you composed it. That's a good composition. Now let's try another riddle. What's the word for the thing which has a whitish mouth and spotted body?

Sŏpangnim: [He thinks for a while.] Well, . . . I don't think we can find the word even in The Dictionary of Chinese Rhyme. It's very difficult. Well. Isn't this the word for the castor-oil plant?

Saennim: Oh, brother. You're clever.

Sŏpangnim: Brother, now let me give you a word.

Saennim: Good.

Sŏpangnim: Who's the fellow who stands on the rice paddy bank leaning on the landmark?

Saennim: [He thinks for a while.] That's very difficult. Is he the owner of the rice paddy?

Sŏpangnim: Ha, ha, ha! You hit the right word.

[At this moment Ch'wipali enters quietly and stands in a corner of the playground.]

Saennim: You! Malttugi!

Malttugi: Ye-e-s.

Saennim: Arrest the fellow who has swindled seven pennies from the government fund. His face is like a ripe date and his back is like a mottled snake.

Malttugi: He is strong like a bull with huge horns. He can run as fast as a flying tiger. I don't think I can arrest him by myself unless I have your written order.

Saennim: Oh. I'll let you have it. Here's the written official order. [He scribbles something on a piece of paper and gives it to Malttugi.]

Malttugi: [He takes the paper from Saennim and goes to Ch'wipali.] Your're arrested.

Ch'wipali: Let me see the official order.

Malttugi: [He shows the paper to Ch'wipali.]

Ch'wipali: [He reads it. Then he follows Malttugi to Saennim.]

Malttugi: [He makes Ch'wipali turn his hips toward Saennim's nose.] I've arrested him.

Saennim: You. Malttugi! What kind of nasty smell is this?

Malttugi: Well. Since he has been a fugitive, he hasn't been able to brush his teeth. That's why he stinks so badly.

Saennim: If that's the case, pull out his head and stick it into his ass-hole.

Malttugi: If I knew how to pull his head and stick it into his ass-hole, I could stuff your mouth with my penis.

Saennim: [Angry. He shouts.] You! Damn you! What did you say?

Malttugi: My lord, listen to me. We're living in the period in which money is omnipotent. What's the use of killing him? Rather we should demand some money from him. So we can use it. It'll do good for both you and me. If you just pretend not to know what's happening, I'll take care of the situation.

[The tune of *kutkŏri*. They all dance for a while. All exit.]

Act VII
The Dance by Miyal

Miyal[96]: [The tune of *kutkŏri*. She enters dancing. She has a fan in one hand while a bell is held in the other. She goes to the musicians as she cries.] *Aigo. Aigo. Aigo!*[97]

Musician: [This role is played by one of the accompanying musicians.] Who are you?

Miyal: Are you asking me who I am? Hearing the sounds of music, I've dropped by to have fun for a while.

Musician: If so, you should have some fun before you go away.

Miyal: I am looking for my old husband. Before I can have fun, I must find him.

Musician: Granny, where are you from?

Miyal: I am from Makmak Village in Cheju-do Island.[98]

Musician: How did you happen to lose your husband?

Miyal: There was a war in our area. So we ran away to save our lives. Ever since then, I don't know his whereabouts.

Musician: Tell me, what does your husband look like?

Miyal: He has the color of a horse.

Musician: Is he a colt?

Miyal: No, he has the color of a cow.

Musician: Is he a calf?

Miyal: No. Not a cow or a horse. What's the use of knowing what he looks like? What purpose would it serve?

Musician: If you would tell me what he looks like, you might find him.

Miyal: [In a singsong tone.]

> *My husband's appearance?*
> *His forehead is cliff-like*
> *While his chin looks like a wooden spoon*
> *With hollow eyes*
> *And dog-foot-like nose.*
>
> *He looks like a servant*
> *With a stumpy beard*
> *And a penis-like topknot.*
>
> *His height?*
> *He is only three feet and four inches.*

Musician: Ah, I see. He just went to chase the animals into the trap.

Miyal: My goodness. How stupid! They say "the wicker worker holds a willow branch even on his death bed." [99] He still has to chase the animals?

Musician: Why don't you call him?

Miyal: What's the use of calling him? He's not here.

Musician: But you must call him at least once.

Miyal: Husband.

Musician: It's too short.

Miyal: Hu—s—band!

Musician: It's too long.

Miyal: How do you want me to call him?

Musician: You're from Makmak Village in Cheju-do Island. Call him to
the tune of *sinawich'ŏng*. [100]

Miyal: [To the tune of *sinawich'ŏng*.]

> *Chŏl chŏl chŏl-sigu.*
> *Chŏ-chŏl chŏl-chŏl chŏl-sigu.*
> *Olsigu chŏl-sigu.*
> *Chihwaja chŏljŏl chŏl-sigu.*
>
> *Where's my husband?*
> *Did he follow Sopu and Hŏyu*
> *To the beautiful mountain*
> *And the clear river?*
>
> *Did he follow Yi Chŏk-sŏn*
> *To the Ch'aesŏk-kang River*
> *Under the bright moon?*
> *Or did he go to the Chŏkpyŏk-kang River*
> *With So Tong-p'a?*
>
> *To search for my husband*
> *I went and stayed:*
> *First, in Wŏnsan for one night,*
> *Second, in Kanggyŏng for two nights,*
> *Third, in Puyŏ for three nights,*
> *Fourth, in Pŏpsŏng for four nights.*
>
> *Like Yu Hyŏn-dŏk*
> *In the period of the Three Kingdoms*
> *Who visited Chaegal Kongmyŏng*
> *In his grass thatched hut three times.* [101]

With the sincerity of King Chu Mun,
A great sage, who went to Wisuyang
To seek out T'ae Kong-mang.

With the sincerity of Hang Chŏk
In Han dynasty
Who went to Nako-san Mountain
To seek out Pŏm A-pu.

Like these people
With this and that sincerity
In my mind
I went everywhere in the country
To look for my husband.
But I still can't find him.

When I see him
I want to touch
His ears, nose, eyes, and lips.
And I want to give him a piggyback ride.
An embrace, too.

But where is he?
Why doesn't he know
How to look for me?

Aigo! Aigo!

[The tune of *kutkŏri.* She exits, dancing.]

Yŏnggam [102]: [He enters, dancing. He wears a gray monk's dress and a strange-looking fur hat. In one hand he has a cane, while his other hand holds a fan.] *Shee—e!* Without having any destination, I came here. It's good here. I hear such beautiful music. When I hear this music, I can't but think of my wife deep in my heart. Since my wife was a shaman, she might come here if she heard the music. Well, . . . Should I ask someone about her? Excuse me.

Musician: Yes. Who are you?

Yŏnggam: I lost my old wife. I am looking for her. Have you happened to see her going in this direction?

Musician: How did you happen to lose your wife?

Yŏnggam: There was a war in our area. To avoid the war, we went in different directions. Ever since then, I haven't heard anything from her.

Musician: Where are you from?

Yŏnggam: I am from Makmak Village in Cheju-do Island.

Musician: What does she look like?

Yŏnggam: She looks so ugly. I can't even describe her.

Musician: But you must tell me what she looks like.

Yŏnggam: What is the use of describing her appearance?

Musician: The world doesn't work any other way. If you describe her appearance to me, you might be able to find her. You never know.

Yŏnggam: If so, I must. Her forehead is cliff-like while her chin looks like a wooden spoon. She has deep eyes like a well and a dog-foot-like nose. Her hair is like a worn-out broom. Her face is similar to a broken dried gourd utensil. She usually carries a fan in one hand and a bell in the other. She is about three feet four inches tall.

Musician: I see. That old woman. She has just gone to the other side of the hill to perform an exorcism.

Yŏnggam: Ah. She is always crazy for exorcism.

Musician: Why don't you call her?

Yŏnggam: What's the use of calling her? She is not here.

Musician: That isn't right. You must call her.

Yŏnggam: I don't understand you. But I should do whatever you say. Wife.

Musician: It's too short.

Yŏnggam: Wi——fe!

Musician: It's too long.

Yŏnggam: How should I call her?

Musician: You're from Makmak Village in Cheju-do Island. You must call her to the tune of *sinawich'ŏng.*]

> *Chŏl-chŏl chŏl-sigu.*
> *Chŏ-chŏl-ri chŏl-chŏl chŏl-sigu.*
> *Olsigu chŏl-sigu.*
> *Chihwaja chŏl-sigu.*

> *Where's my wife?*
> *Did you follow Yi Chŏk-sŏn*
> *To the Ch'aesŏk-kang River*
> *Under the bright moon?*
> *Did you follow So Tong-p'a*
> *To the Chŏkpyŏk-kang River*
> *Under the autumn moon?*

> *To look for my wife*
> *I went and stayed:*
> *First, in Wŏnsan for one night,*
> *Second, in Kanggyŏng for two nights,*
> *Third, in Puyŏ for three nights,*
> *Fourth, in Pŏpsŏng for four nights.*

> *I went everywhere in the country.*
> *But I still can't find my wife.*

> *To see my wife*
> *I've been searching for her*
> *With feelings of longing for the rain*
> *During the seven year drought:*
> *With the feelings of longing for the sunshine*
> *During the nine year flood.*

If I happen to see my wife
I want to touch
Her eyes, nose, and mouth.
I also want to fondle
Her ink-stone-like breast tips,
Biting her shoe-sole-like tongue.

Where's my wife?
Why can't she find me?

[He goes to a corner of the playground, dancing. The tune of
kutkŏri.]

Miyal: [She enters, singing.]

Chŏl-chŏl chŏl-sigu.
Olsigu chŏl-sigu.
Chihwaja cho-t-nae.

Chŏl-chŏl chŏl-sigu.
Who is looking for me?
There is no one who should look for me.
Who is looking for me?

Is he Yi T'ae-paek
Who wants to have a drink with me?
Are they the four hermits in Sang-san Mountain
Who want to play checkers with me?

Is there anyone who wants to dance
Hakturumi-dance[103] *with me?*
Are they Paek-yi and Suk-jae
Who want to eat ferns with me
In Suyang-san Mountain?

Yŏnggam: [The tune of *kutkŏri.* He goes to Miyal, dancing, as he
sings.]

Chŏl-chŏl chŏl-sigu.
Olsigu chŏl-sigu.

Chihwaja chŏl-sigu.

Is there anyone else,
Besides me,
Who's looking for you?

Wife!
Wife!
It's me!
It's me!

Miyal: Who are you? Aren't you my husband? You're my husband. They say "sincerity even moves the heavens." Because of my sincerity, I've finally found my husband.

[In a singsong tone.]

I'm so happy.
I'm so happy.

[She clings to Yŏnggam as she dances.]

Yŏnggam: My wife. By the mercy of heavens, we've happened to meet each other again. Let's dance together.

[In a singsong tone.]

I'm so happy!
Let's interwine ourselves.

[They interwine themselves. Miyal clings to Yŏnggam behaving lewdly. When Yŏnggam falls down on the ground, Miyal crawls over his head.]

Miyal: [In a painful tone.] *Aigo!* Oh, my back aches! I've given birth to a baby boy at the age of seventy. What a happy event! I'm happy to see our son. [Dances.]

Yŏnggam: [Still lying down.] My goodness. What a splendid scene! But it's also such a precipitous place. Along both banks, there stand pine trees. Between a high mountain and a deep valley, there's a crystal clear lake with the winding bank. From here to my home, it is three thousand *ris* by land. But by sea it is only two thousand *ris*. By golly! There's no other way but to go home by boat. . . While sailing, I happened to encounter a storm. So I got stuck here. But how am I supposed to get up? I have to have a secret formula to make me get up. I see. I know it now. I am asking this question to the heaven and earth. Please answer me quickly and smoothly. I, a foolish peasant, got stuck here while I was sailing home. I am pleading to Yi Sun-p'ung, Teacher Kwak Kwak, Teacher Chegal Kongmyŏng, Chŏng Myŏng-do, Teacher Chang Yi-ch'ŏn, Teacher So Kangk-ch'ŏl, and all sorts of spirits. Please tell me the secret according to the fortune telling. [He pulls out a divination sign and reads it.] Ha, ha, ha! This is strange as well as wicked. The sign is for the sound of a cow's mew. That is, . . . the sign that a calf can stand up if he mews. *Ummae-ae!* [He gets up.] You bitch! You've disgraced me with the first child. You're the worst bitch under the sky. I'm going to wreck your vagina. Since the upper half of it looks so precipitous, I must carve out a horse-hair headband brooch[104] for a bold head. But I must make dominoes with the lower half. [He beats Miyal.]

Miyal: My husband! After such a long separation, how could you possibly beat me like this? How is it possible even if I made some mistakes?

Yŏnggam: You bitch. I don't want to hear you. What muttering!

Miyal: [She clings to Yŏnggam and begins to bite him.] Good. Kill me! Beat me to death!

Yŏnggam: My goodness. Look. She's biting me.

Miyal: Look! Husband. Since we're always fighting, the villagers are going to expel us from the village.

Yŏnggam: *Hung.* They say they're going to expel us? That's a good idea. If they want to expel us from the village, we'll go.

The boat with lust and greed
Can sail in the fair wind.
The sky is infinite
And there're as many roads
As the legs of an octopus.

Indeed,
There're loyal subjects
In the loyal land.

Why can't I survive wherever I go? Before they expel us, let's get out of the village quickly. When you and I leave the village, the lack of distinguished persons will arouse the subterranean god by disturbing the earth. Don't they know that the evil spirits and demons cannot enter into the village as long as you stand on the cold spot of the room while I sit on the warm place in our house? house?

Miyal: That might be so. But I wonder how you've spent your life ever since we were separated?

Yŏnggam: During the terrible war, I had to suffer all sorts of hardship. I had to move from one place to another.

Miyal: What are you wearing on your head?

Yŏnggam: Do you want to know?

Miyal: Yes, of course, I want to know.

Yŏnggam: Listen to what I say. When I arrived in the southern part of the country, I went here and there. But I couldn't find my livelihood. So I finally bought an instrument for tinkering. While I was carrying it around on my back, I happened to meet a player of mask-dance drama who belonged to Sandae-togam. [105] He said "there shouldn't be a tiger which didn't know Inwang-san Mountain. [106] Likewise, there shouldn't be a tinker who didn't know Sandae-togam." Then he told me I had to pay a tax. When I asked him the amount, he said it was one *yang* and eight pennies per day.

I told him it was too much because I could make only eight pennies a day. In that case, I had to add one *yang* to my daily earnings to pay the daily tax. So he beat me, tearing off my cloth and horsehair hat. Naturally, I finally lost my hat. After that, I looked into my tinkering can. Then I fortunately found a piece of dog skin fur. So I made it into a hat. Ever since then I have worn that. Now with this hat, I look like a man with the official rank of *tongji.*[107]

Miyal: What? Did you say you have some kind of official rank?

> [In a singsong tone as she cries.]

> *Chŏl-chŏl chŏl-sigu.*
> *Look at the shape of my husband.*
> *What has happened*
> *To his fancy horse-hair hat from T'ongyŏng*
> *And the turtle shell headband brooch?*

> *Now he's wearing a human-hair headband*
> *And a dog fur hat.*

> *What are you wearing, husband?*

Yŏnggam: Listen to what I say. When I left the mask-dance player, I went to Yŏngbyŏn and Hyangsan in P'yŏngan-do Province. There I met a monk. After greeting the head monk, I was allowed to stay in the temple overnight. Since I was lonely, I approached a pretty nun to make love. So the monks attacked me like a bunch of bees, beating me hard. When I ran away, I accidentally picked up a dark monk's dress. That's the reason why I am wearing this now.

Miyal: [In a singsong tone as she cries.]

> *Aigo. Aigo!*
> *Chŏl-chŏl chŏl-sigu.*

> *The sun has risen.*
> *So it's the sunshine satin.*

> *The moon has risen.*
> *So it's the moonlight satin.*

For the summer
The summer clothes.

For the winter
The winter clothes.

For him,
I made them all.

But what has happened to them?
He's wearing a monk's dress.
What has happened to them?

It doesn't matter to me any longer. But... husband. When you were living with me your face was so smooth as a satin bag for buckwheat flour. But why is your face so flushed at the slightest movement?

Yŏnggam: What? What's wrong with my face? Because I ate acorns and potatoes, my face became plump. I haven't seen you for a long time. I must ask you about our children. How is Munyŏl doing? Our oldest son.

Miyal: *Aigo.* Don't ask me about him. *Whew!* [Heaves a sigh.]

Yŏnggam: Why are you sighing deeply. What has happened to him? Let me hear about him.

Miyal: Oh, husband... Because we were so poor, he went to cut fire wood in the mountain. But he was killed by a tiger.

Yŏnggam: What? You let our son be killed by a tiger? I no longer have any relationship with you. Let's separate from each other for good.

Miyal: Hello. Husband. How can you say that after we haven't seen each other for so long?

Yŏnggam: I don't want to hear you. Without a child, what reason is there for us to live together?

Miyal: If you want, let's separate from each other.

Yŏnggam: As long as we're going to separate, there's no reason for me to keep your immoral behavior a secret. [To the audience.] Hello! Ladies and gentlemen! Listen to how this bitch venerated her husband. One day the daughter-in-law of the family in front of us brought a plateful of cake when she visited with us. If this bitch had brought the cake to me and asked me to eat it, I would have let her eat it first. Instead, while holding the plate, she asked me whether or not I wished to eat it. Then she said to herself: "If you don't want to eat it, that's all right." Then she started to eat it by herself. Of course, she didn't even give me time to answer her question. . . One cold night during a snow storm, she suddenly woke up as she kicked the quilt and my nose, making me bleed profusely. Then she started to piss so hard in the chamber pot. You know our chamber pot was made so strangely that it made such a great hissing sound even when a single fly got in it. But when she started to piss with her beehive-like vagina, and she was farting "t'ung t'ung," Tolp'ungi, who lived in front of us, rushed to our house with a hoe, thinking the river bank was broken and a flood was running wildly. Imagine! What a shameful humiliation!

Miyal: [As she points to Tolmori[108] who has been standing in a corner of the playground.] I see. You have been living with such a pretty girl. No wonder you hate me and have divulged my personal secrets. If you want to separate from me, you also ought to separate from her, too. If you hate me, you also ought to hate her, too. Is her vagina inlaid with gold rings? [To Tolmori.] You bitch! What kind of grudge do you bear against me? Before I die, I must kill you. That's all. [She jumps on her and starts to beat her.]

Tolmori: Aigu! Aigu! She's killing me. Save me! [Cries.]

Yŏnggam: [He beats Miyal.] You bitch! Why do you have to beat her? What sin did she commit? You ugly bitch! You stink!

Miyal: Because you're living with a bitch like her, you're mistreating me. I also no longer want to live with a man like you. Let's divide our properties equally between you and I. We bought them

together. After that, let's separate. Let's divide our properties!
Right now!

Yŏnggam: All right. Let's divide them. The rice paddy filled with
water, the rent-free field, the pretty maids, the ox, and the cow,
including the calf, I'll have all of them. But you can have the sandy
field which doesn't yield any crops, the male rat, and the female rat,
including the mice. If there will be new-born rats next year, you can
have them, too.

Miyal: *Aigo. Aigo!* How sad am I! Even a tree has a companion. The
flying birds and the crawling animals have their lovers. In that
case, how is it possible for us to separate from each other? We're
man and wife. But if that's what you want, let's separate from each
other. [She dances.]

> *Chŏl-chŏl chŏl-sigu.*
> *Chihwaja chŏl-sigu.*

You're going to have the rice paddy filled with water, the
rent-free field, the pretty maids, and the servants, including their
offspring. The ox and cow. . . and calves will also be possessed by
you. But you're giving me the sandy field which doesn't grow
anything. You're also saying I should have the male rats, the female
rats, and the mice. . . The new-born rats of next year, too. What am
I supposed to live with these rats? [She cries loudly.]

Yŏnggam: Well. In that case, I'll give you a little more.

Miyal: When I married you first we swore to each other that as a
couple we would maintain harmony and unity and live long lives.
Ever since then we even collected broken utensils, adding more and
more to their number. The chamber pot and ax which were bought
with our utmost sincerity should be given to me.

Yŏnggam: My goodness. How greedy you are! I'll have the thirty
thousand *yang*s in gold and silver in the rice chest. I'll also have the
chest decorated with the picture of dragon and phoenix, the cedar
chest inlaid with mother of pearls, the shiny chamber pot, and the

basin. You can have the bamboo cane, shoes, the worn-out straw sandals, the vast extension of cool breeze, the fan, the broken part of the wicker basket, and the old bamboo hat which covers the chimney top. I'll keep the ax while the ax handle will be given to you.

Miyal: You, husband. How greedy you are. You've said you'll have the thirty thousand *yangs* in gold in the rice chest, the chest decorated with the picture of dragon and phoenix, the cedar chest inlaid with mother of pearls, the shiny chamber pot, and the basin. You said I should keep only the bamboo cane, the shoes, the worn out straw sandals, the vast extension of cool breeze, and the bamboo hat which covers the chimney top. Besides you want to keep the ax. If so, what am I supposed to do with the ax handle without an ax? There will be nothing for me to do but to starve to death during the cold winter months. Husband! How am I supposed to live by myself with so many children? You must give me some more.

Yŏnggam: You deserve to starve to death.

Miyal: Look. Husband. How could you say such an unkind thing? Give me more.

Yŏnggam: You bitch! You're greedy. Did you say we should divide our properties equally? You bitch! I'm going to destroy all of them.

Tolmori: [Sharply.] My dear! Listen to what I say. Do you remember what you told me when we first met? You told me you were a sincere unmarried man. Besides you promised me you would give me one half of your fifteen acres of rice paddy as long as I would live with you, didn't you? Today I've found you have a wife. You're also arguing whether or not you two should live together, fighting about how to divide the properties between the two of you. Before you two decide how to divide the properties, you must give me the promised portion of your rice paddy.

Miyal: You bitch! What did you say? Are you saying that one half of our rice paddy should be given to you? No way! There isn't enough

even for myself. How can we give you something? We don't have a
single thing for you. Husband. Have you promised her that you'll
give her one half of our rice paddy? Give me my portion quickly.

Yŏnggam: You bitch. You're too greedy. I don't have anything for you.

Miyal: What did you say? You don't have anything for me? Did you say
you have something for her, but you don't have anything for me?
I'm very indignant. Before I die, you must die, too. [She jumps on
Yŏnggam.]

Tolmori: Please give me my portion.

Yŏnggam: I don't have anything for you either.

Tolmori: *Aigu.* I'm indignant and angry. I've been deceived by you until
this day. Before I die, you must die, too. [She jumps on Yŏnggam.]

Yŏnggam: [He escapes from the women quickly and goes to a corner
and stands there. Without knowing Yŏnggam has runaway, Miyal
and Tolmori begin to beat each other, thinking the person whom
they are beating is Yŏnggam. Miyal is knocked down.]

Tolmori: [When she sees Miyal is dying, she exits quickly.]

Yŏnggam: [He looks at Miyal.] Is she dead? What a short temper she
has. [He checks Miyal's pulse.] *Aigu!* She is dead. What a pity! I am
saddened. How is it possible for her to die so suddenly?

[In a singsong tone.]

After tasting hundreds of different herbs,
Sinnong-ssi[109] *created all sorts of medicine.*

For the lack of vigor, six flavors,[110]
Eight flavors,[111] *and sipchŏndaebo-t'ang.*[112]
For spleen and stomach aches, samch'ul-t'ang.[113]
For over drinking, taegŭmŭmja.[114]
For the symptom of phlegm, tossidodam-t'ang.[115]
For jaundice and tympanitis, onbaekwŏn.[116]
For dead drunkeness, sŏkkal-t'ang.[117]

For malaria, pulyŭm.[118]
For worms, kŏnri-t'ang.[119]
For the problem of urination, ugong-san.[120]
For constipation, yuksin-hwan.[121]
For gonorrhea, orim-san.[122]
For diarrhea, wiryŏng-t'ang.[123]
For headache, yijin-t'ang.[124]
For vomiting, pogyŏngbanha-t'ang.[125]
For a cold, p'aedok-san.[126]
For sudden indigestion, soch'e-hwan.[127]
For stomatitis, kamŏn-t'ang.[128]
For erysipelas, sŏgaksodokŭm.[129]
After sexual intercourse, ssanghwa-t'ang.[130]

The world is full of such medicines. But I couldn't give her a single package of medicine before she died. I am totally aghast. [He exits as he dances to the tune of *kutkŏri.*]

Namkang Noin[131]: [He is an old man with a gray beard. He wears a horse-hair hat. As he coughs, he enters slowly.] *Ae-haem! Ae-haem!* Well. Why are they fighting? Since they've met after a long separation, they must be having a love fight. The whole village is in an uproar. [He looks at Miyal. He finds she is dead.] Look. Madam Miyal is dead. Villagers! Look! She is dead. *Aigo.* It's such a pity. It's miserable. She is at last dead after long suffering. What shall I do? Since she is dead, I have no other way but to call a shaman to perform an exorcism to send her dead soul to paradise. . I have to call a shaman. [He exits. Several Mŏkchung enter and carry away Miyal's body. Namkang Noin enters with an incense burner and a chalice of wine on a small low table. He is followed by a shaman with a fan and a bell. As soon as Namkang Noin puts the table down, the shaman begins to perform an exorcism as she dances. Namkang Noin stands near the shaman, listening to what she says. Once in a while, he responds to the shaman saying "that's right."]

Shaman[132]: [In a singsong tone.]

This is the grave.
This is the grave.
This is the grave
For the woman from Kaesŏng.

This is the grave.
This is the grave.
This is the grave
For the woman of a family.

This is the grave.
This is the grave.
This is the grave
For the woman from Kaesŏng.

Ae-hae-ae-ae.
It's pity.
It's a misery.

Here I am.
Here I am.
To pray for the dead person
I am here.

Here I am
O-o-o.
Without accomplishing her hopes
She has become a guest in the nether world.

O-o-o.
She wanted to meet her husband
To cherish her wishes.
But she has met
With an unfortunate and miserable death.

[She cries.]

Yi-yi-yi.
The Spirit after the Death,

Please send this poor dead soul
To paradise.

On the soul board, her soul.
On the spirit board, her spirit.
Send them to the lotus blossom peak.

Olsa!

[She dances.]

Namkang Noin. That's right. That's right. Go to paradise. An exorcism is performed to send you to the good place. Go only to paradise.

[The shaman dances as she rings the bell. Then she exits.[133]]

[Thus Pongsan *t'alch'um* ends. Soon a table with wine and food is brought out to the playground. All players bow twice as they toss their masks into the bonfire.]

Notes

1. Sangjwa: There are four identical masks of Sangjwa. These whitish masks have ink-drawn hair and eyebrows. A thin ink-drawn line circles its eyes. The lips are rouged bright red. A white *t'alpo*, a piece of cloth which is used to cover the back of the head and with which the mask is tied around the wearer's neck, is attached to the mask. The player of this character wears a monk's white dress and the white peaked cowl. A red sash is slung across her shoulder. Red wristlets which cover the hands are attached to the sleeves of the coat.

2. Mökchung: Monk. There are eight almost identical masks of Mökchung. This orange-colored mask has numerous black spots on the lower half of its face. There are seven horn-like protuberances on its face: two on the forehead, two between the eyebrows, two on the lower cheeks, and one on the chin. All of the protuberances are covered with beaten gold. Vertical lines [instead of the usual horizontal ones] of black and white make up the eyebrows. Its protruding black eyes are circled by wide gilded lines which are again circled by thin black lines. The player of this character wears a jacket, a pair of short pants, and a monk's coat. A bell is attached to either knee of the player. A willow branch hangs from his lower back.

3. See Yangju *pyölsandae* [play], Note 23 and 34.

4. See Yangju *pyölsandae* [play], Note 16.

5. *Yöngsanhoesang-gok:* This music usually consists of approximately ten different tunes depending upon the instruments, and musical pieces.

6. *Todori:* A tune of music.

7. See T'ongyŏng *ogwangdae* [play], Note 13.

8. See Yangju *pyŏlsandae* [play], Note 17.

9. Originally he hits Mŏkchung I in the face with a peach tree branch or a willow branch to chase him off the playground.

10. In order to differentiate poetry from songs, no italics are employed for the former.

11. A meritorious subject of King Chu Mun of China.

12. He refers to approximately between the eighth century and the fifteenth century B.C. of China.

13. This refers to the last period of the Chou dynasty of China during which time a civil war ravaged the country.

14. The Han dynasty: A dynasty in China.

15. Paek-yi and Suk-jae: The righteous brothers of Chou in China. They attempted to stop King Chu Mun's plan to invade the neighboring state. When their attempt failed, they went into self-exile on a mountain where they starved to death by eating only ferns.

16. So Jin: A famous orator of ancient China.

17. *Pip'a:* A loquat-shaped four-stringed musical instrument.

18. Sopu: A character in a Chinese legend who was known for his integrity and uprightness. Hŏyu: A friend of Sopu.

19. This refers to the Happy Valley which is descrived in *Towha wŏngi* by To Yŏn-myŏng: [365 A.D.-427 A.D.], a Chinese pastoral poet.

20. See Note 19.

21. *Haegŭm:* A two-stringed fiddle which is held vertically on the knee of the player when played.

22. *Ri:* A unit of distance. Approximately four kilometers make ten *ris*.

23. The four hermit scholars of the Han dynasty of China who went to Sang-san Mountain to avoid the war.

24. *Kilroraepi hwŏl hwŏl.* These words do not contain any particular meaning. They are apparently used here to create some sort of rhythmic pattern to the music.

25. This word, which has no particular meaning, is employed as a cue to the rest of the characters in the scene.

26. *Mutdong*-dance: This dance employs some basic patterns of *chara*-dance. The basic movement patterns of this dance are as follows. Bring the dancer's right hand to the front of his face. Then he turns his hand upside down. Now he lifts his hand quickly and lowers it.

27. Neither *anaya* nor *kuraeae* has any particular meaning as a word. They are used as cues for the other characters.

28. Here the exact meaning of the dialogue is missing because of the difficulty of an exact translation of puns. The word for drum "*pŏpkko*" has a similar sound to the words for take off [cloth] "*pŏtko*" in Korean.

29. Here, too, the exact meaning is somewhat lost because of the impossibility of an exact translation of puns. The lowly word for head, "*daekaengi*," resembles the lowly word for the head of a penis, "*chotdaekaengi*," in Korean.

30. Satang: This mask is identical with the Somu mask. The player of this character wears a white jacket and a flare skirt.

31. Kŏsa: All masks for the seven Kŏsa are identical with those of all Mŏkchung.

32. Holapi Kŏsa: This character also belongs to the group of Kŏsa. The player of this character often carries a rolled strawbag or mat on his back.

33. "Nolryang Sagŏri": A song with little literary meaning although it contains musical rhythm.

34. This refers to the northwestern part of Korea, namely Hwanghae-do Province and North and South P'yŏngan-do Provinces.

35. This refers to the eastern part of Korea, namely Kangwŏn-do Province.

36. Nojang: This dark maroon mask has painted eyes with gold which are encircled with ink-drawn lines. Its eyebrows are gray. The protruding lips are painted rouge. There are five protuberances: two on the space between the eyebrows and three on the lower chin. These protuberances are covered with beaten gold.

37. "Ododogi T'aryŏng": A ballad tune which is popular on Cheju-do Island, a southernmost island of Korea.

38. See Yangju *pyŏlsandae* [play], Note 13.

39. *Namuamit'abul kwanseŭmbosal*. A Buddhist invocation.

40. Somu: Traditionally this role was played by a male player, wearing a mask. But recently this role has been played by a female player often without a mask.

41. See Yangju *pyŏlsandae* [play], Note 139.

42. Shoe Peddler: This skin-colored mask has ink-drawn eyebrows and beard. Its lips are rouged. The player of this character wears a black jacket and white pants. He has a bundle of wrapped merchandise, which includes a monkey, on his back. This character also often appears wearing one of the Mŏkchung masks.

43. See Yangju *pyŏlsandae* [play], Note 39.

44. Monkey: This is a reddish mask with numerous white spots on the lower part of the face. Its eyes are encircled by white and black lines. Animal fur covers its head. The player of this character wears a red jacket and trousers.

45. Ch'wipali: The general appearance of this mask is similar to the Mŏkchung masks, although it is slightly longer. There are twelve protuberances on the face: four on the forehead, six between the eyebrows, and two on either end of the mouth. It has gray hair and beard. A lock of gray hair hangs between the eyes to indicate he is an old bachelor. The player of this character wears a red jacket with green sleeves and a pair of red pants. He has willow branches. A large bell is fastened to one of his knees.

46. *Aigu:* Ouch. Oh my!

47. The eight beauties refer to the eight beautiful concubines of Yang So-yu, the hero, in *Kuunmong,* an old Korean novel by Kim Man-jung: [1637 A.D.-1692 A.D.].

48. See Yangju *pyŏlsandae* [play], Note 77.

49. An ancient state of China.

50. Here the delicate meaning of the song is missing because of the impossibility of an exact translation of puns. The words "bead decoration [*yŏngrak*] have a similar sound to the words

"nun's cowl" [*songnak*], although they are not the same.

51. In the old society of Korea, no bachelor was allowed to wear a top-knot regardless of his age. Instead an unmarried man was ordered to keep his hair braided in a pigtail by the authorities.

52. See Suyŏng *yayu* [play], Note 14.

53. Here the delicate meaning of the dialogue is missing because of the impossibility of an exact translation of puns. The words "both books" [*yangsŏ*] have the same sound as the words "two west," implying the two western provinces, namely Hwanghae-do Province and P'yŏngan-do Province.

54. *Hanul-ch'ŏn:* The beginning character of *The Thousand Character Text.* A primer of Chinese characters.

55. *Tta-ji:* The second character of *The Thousand Character Text.* Thus he means that the baby is one word ahead of himself.

56. See Note 65.

57. The Hour of the Rat [*jasi*] refers to the first hour of the twelve hour day: between eleven o'clock in the evening and one o'clock in the morning.

58. The Hour of the Ox [*ch'uksi*] refers to the second hour of the twelve hour day: between one and three o'clock in the morning.

59. This refers to the nine principles of morality and politics [*hongbŏmkuju*] in *The Canon of History [Sijŏn]*, a Chinese classic.

60. *The Three Classics of Ancient China [Samkyŏng]: The Book of Odes [Sikyŏng], The Canon of History [Sijŏn], and The Book of Changes [Chuyŏk].*

61. Yo and Sun. The two sages of ancient China.

62 "The Kyŏkyang Song". An ancient Chinese song for peace.

63. The twenty-eight stars along the zodiac.

64. *Hato* and *Naksŏ. Hato* refers to an ancient picture of China which depicts the scene of the flying horse rising from the Yellow River, while *Naksŏ* means the Eight Diagrams for Divination [*p'alkwae*] which are supposedly based on the patterns of a turtle's back.

65. Except for the beginning and occasional quotations from the ancient writings the wise talk by Ch'wipali, in teaching *The Thousand Character Text* in the form of poetry, does not always make sense.

66. The Korean alphabet.

67. *Kiŏk.* The first letter of the Korean alphabet and a familiar shape for the traditional Korean house.

68. The sound of *tikut* is similar to the word which means "worrisome" in Korean, *chigŭtchigŭt*, thus implying that life is tiresome and tedious.

69. Here the delicate meaning of the words is lost due to the impossibility of an exact translation of puns. The words "ko kyo," part of the Korean alphabet, have a similar sound to the words "the place to live" [*kŏji*] in Korean.

70. Here, too, he is referring to the words "the old friends" [*kogu*] in Korean which has a similar sound to *ko kyo* or *ku kyu*.

71. The words *na nya* have a similar sound to the word "fly" [*narun*] in Korean.

72. The willow and flowers on the street and by the hedges [*noryuchanghwa*] which can be picked by any man refer to prostitutes.

73. The word "fleeting" [*tŏtsiŏpsi*] has a similar sound to *ta tya tŏ tyŏ*.

74. The words "inner chamber" [*tojang*] have a similar sound to *to tyo tu tyu*.

75. Lion: This lion mask is usually made of wood and papier-mâché. Its protruding eyes are covered with beaten gold. The half-open mouth exhibits its teeth. The white mane surrounds the mask. The body of the lion is covered with white fur.

76. This dialogue is based on a story in *Journey to the West*, an ancient Chinese novel.

77. *Kin-yŏngsan:* A dance form from Chŏlla-do Province.

78. Malttugi: This light-brown mask has ink-drawn eyebrows. There are numerous white spots around the mouth, forming a kind of beard. Or the player of this character often wears one of the Mŏkchung masks. The player of this role wears a black jacket and white trousers, leggings, and a felt hat. He has a horse whip. For a literal meaning of this character, see Yangju *pyŏlsandae* [play], Note 5.

79. Saennim: This whitish mask has a fur beard and eyebrows. Under the nose there are vertical red scars which reach down to the upper lip. His horse-hair headband is ink-drawn. The player of this character wears a white full-dress, white trousers, white leggings, and many-cornered horse-hair hat. He has a fan in his left hand and a bamboo cane in his right hand.

80. Sŏpangnim: This mask is basically the same as the Saennim mask except it has a single cleft palate. The outfits of this character are the same as those of Saennim.

81. Toryŏngnim: This soft pink mask has ink-drawn hair parted in the center and eyebrows. The player of this character wears a white dress with blue armour, a dark blue head-cover made with cloth, *pokkŏn,* and leggings. He has a fan.

82. These refer to the political parties during the seventeenth century [Noron, Old Doctrine, and Soron, Young Doctrine,] which created intensive political struggle among fractions at the Chosŏn court.

83. Here the delicate meaning of the dialogue is somewhat lost due to the impossibility of an exact translation of puns. The word "donkey" [*nosae*] has a similar sound to old lord, "*no-saennim.*" Thus Malttugi is referring to Saennim as a donkey.

84. He implies that he made love to Saennim's wife.

85. Here, too, the delicate meaning of the dialogue is missing because of the impossibility of an exact translation of puns. The words "ask after health of someone" [*munan*] have a remotely similar sound to "kneel" [*murup-kkult'a*].

86. *Kimch'i:* Pickles made of radish, cabbage, or cucumber spiced with pepper, garlic, onion, ginger, etc.

87. Here the delicate meaning of the dialogue is missing due to the impossibility of an exact translation of puns. The lowly word "penis-head" [*chotdaegengi*] has a similar sound to porgy fish head [*chogitaegengi*].

88. The lowly words "half of a penis" [*chotban*] have a remotely similary sound to *yangban,* aristocrat.

89. The word "table" [*soban*] has a similar sound to *yangban*.

90. The words "white rice" [*paekban*] have a similar sound to *yangban*.

91. *Kkolttugi* means an octopus.

92. *Ch'oettugi* is slang for a bank around a field.

93. *Maettugi* means a grasshopper.

94. *Chŏlttugi* means a lame person.

95. *Sijo:* A kind of short lyric poem that developed in the late Koryŏ period.

96. Miyal: Old woman.This dark blue mask has many white and red spots. Its lips are rouged. The player of this character wears a white jacket and a skirt. She also wears a towel around her head. She has a fan and a bell.

97. *Aigo:* "Woe is me" or "boo-hoo" [an expression of sudden anguish].

98. A large island off the south coast of Korea.

99. This means that one cannot forget one's profession. Yŏnggam must be a hunter by profession.

100. "Sinawich'ŏng". A popular song on Cheju-do Island.

101. This refers to Yu Pi, a king of Han in China, who made three visits to Chae Kal-yang in his grass thatched hut to invite him to be his general.

102. Yŏnggam: Old man. This whitish mask has ink-drawn eyebrows and a gray beard. The player of this character wears a white full dress and trousers, leggings, and a dog-fur hat.

103. *Hakturumi*-dance. It is not clear what kind of dance this is.

104. Horse-hair headband brooch [*p'ungjam*]. A horse-hair headband brooch which is also used to hold the horse-hair hat down on the head in the wind.

105. Sandae-togam: An official organization [the Master of Revels] in the Chosŏn court which controlled the performing arts such as mask-dance theatre during the Middle Ages. It was abolished in 1634.

106. Inwang-san Mountain: A mountain northeast Seoul.

107. *Tongji:* An official rank of the office of Chungch'u-wŏn which administered the security and military secrets of .the Chosŏn court.

108. Tolmori: This whitish mask has ink-drawn hair and eyebrows. Its lips are rouged. Its chignon style hair is decorated with a red ribbon. The player of this character wears a yellow jacket and a red skirt.

109. Sinnong-ssi: A king in Chinese legend who had the head of a cow and the body of a human. He was supposed to be the first person who taught the art of agriculture to the people.

110. Six flavors: This refers to the tastes of bitterness, sweetness, saltiness, unsaltiness, puckishness, and spiciness.

111. Eight flavors: A tonic mainly for woman.

112. *Sipchŏndaebo-t'ang:* A tonic for the lack of vigor and for exhaustion.

113. *Samch'ul-t'ang:* A medicine for nausea for a pregnant woman.

114. *Taegŭmŭmja:* A medicine for indigestion resulting from drinking.

115. *Tossidodam-t'ang:* A medicine for dizziness and phlegm.

116. *Onbaekwŏn:* It is not clear whether there is such a medicine.

117. *Sŏkkal-t'ang:* It is also not clear whether there is such a medicine.

118. *Pulyiŭm:* It is not clear whether there is such a medicine.

119. *Kŏnri-t'ang:* A medicine for sharp pains in the stomach.

120. *Ukong-san:* A medicine for problems of urination.

121. *Yuksin-hwan:* A medicine for the stomach troubles and nightmares of children.

122. *Orim-san:* A medicine for gonorrhea.

123. *Wiryŏng-t'ang:* A medicine for stomach ache and diarrhea.

124. *Yijin-t'ang:* A medicine for excessive phlegm.

125. *Pogyŏngbanha-t'ang:* A medicine for excessive phlegm.

126. *P'aedok-san:* A medicine for cold.

127. *Soch'e-hwan:* A medicine for digestional problems.

128. *Kamŏn-t'ang:* It is not clear whether there is such a medicine.

129. *Sŏgaksotokŭm:* A medicine for skin disease.

130. *Ssanghwa-t'ang:* A medicine for excessive exhaustion.

131. Namkang Noin: This mask is identical with the Yŏnngam mask. The player of this character wears a white Korean overcoat, trousers, and a horse-hair hat.

132. Shaman: The player of this character wears the Somu mask, a blue jacket, a red skirt, dark blue armour, and a felt hat. She has a fan and a bell.

133. Frequently, the play ends with Namkang Noin who performs an exorcism by himself without Shaman as he plays an hourglass-shaped drum to the tune of *kutkŏri* and sings. He also has the following dialogue: "Children. Stand up! The windows on the south and east sides are already bright."

Kkoktu Kaksi: Puppet Play

Introduction

Origins

P uppet theatre is one of the oldest forms of popular entertainment in Korea, but it is impossible to document its precise origins.

The traditional Korean puppet has generally been identified with *kkoktu* or *kkoktu kaksi,* the etymology of which cannot be determined. For half a century or more, this word's linguistic origins and interpretation have remained an enigma to many scholars. There are those who claim that it originated with a Chinese word for puppet, *kuotou,* while others insist that it can be traced further west to the Turkish word *kukla,* or even the Greek word *koulka.* These suggest that the Korean puppet may have had its origins either in China or Asia Minor. However, nowhere in the scholarship on the origins of the Korean puppet is there a theory suggesting that it was an imported art. Instead, it is invariably claimed that Korean puppetry was a creation of the Korean people.

Some scholars claim that Korean puppetry originated in the early period of the Koguryŏ dynasty [37 B.C.-668 A.D.],[1] while others have suggested that it was the product of a later period.[2] The existing evidence is fragmentary and insufficient to construct a complete history. This lack of evidence creates a great confusion, and little can be said with certainty about the history of Korean puppet theatre.

As to the purpose of puppetry in Korea, there are several explanations. First, puppets served a religious purpose. They were often worshipped as images of supernatural forces by the ancient people. It is said that shamans probably made use of a primitive puppet to invoke from the gods the favor of prosperity on their patrons.[3] A second theory is that puppets were used for ancestral worship. Tradition says that in the beginning of the Kingdom of Koguryŏ, puppets which represented the images of the founder of the nation and his mother were enshrined in the royal temple. All subsequent rulers of the kingdom followed the same pattern of ancestor worship by enshrining representational puppets in the temples.[4] A third theory is based on ceremonial purposes. During the Koryŏ period [918 A.D.-1392 A.D.], there was an important national ceremony called *yŏndŭng*. This festivity was held on such occasions as Buddha's birthday or the dedication of a new government building or a temple. The court of Koryŏ made lavish preparations for the ceremony, and puppets were included on these occasions.[5]

While none of these theories establishes the origins of Korean puppetry, they suggest that puppets were used for a variety of purposes early in the nation's history. At the same time there is no indication that the beginning of Korean puppetry was related to the same art in other nations. Judging purely from the above theories, one may surmise that the early puppet was an indigenous art of Korea. The continuing confusion over the origins of the word *kkoktu* remains to test future scholarship.

The Early Players and Performance

As in the instance of the mask-dance performers, the puppeteers generally belonged to the lowest class of society throughout history. Customarily, most of the puppeteers established no permanent domiciles because they traveled from village to village or from port to port, performing whenever possibe.

Historically, puppeteers have generally been called *namsatang*, a troup of song-and-dance people. They lived communally, entertaining their patrons with songs and dances when they were not performing puppet shows. It is said that the puppet theatre of Korea, regardless of its origins, was transmitted and preserved by these nomadic people. However, it is unknown whether these wandering performers brought puppetry along with them or took up this profession after they migrated to Korea.

The theory that they might have originated in the far western part of Asia or India and reached Korea through China during the Koryŏ period is advanced by a Korean folk scholar who asserts that the forefathers of Korean puppet theatre may have been the last of the wandering Tartars, called *muchari,* who arrived in Korea, probably during the reign of the first King of Koryŏ [918 A.D.-958 A.D.].[6] Koryŏ, heavily influenced by Buddhism, the national religion, practiced humanism and was known throughout Asia as a nation where not even criminals were treated brutally. This reputation began to attract neighboring foreigners other than various nomadic groups and it is possible that these itinerant players came to Korea along with other immigrants during this period.[7]

Traditionally, the puppeteers traveled from village to village and set up their temporary theatre in temple court yards, in squares on market days, or on the open plains—wherever there were enough people for an audience. A company of puppeteers was generally made up of six to eight people. Three or four of these were musicians, while the rest were puppeteers. Whenever all musicians were not needed to perform music, they were called upon to act as puppeteers and help with the production's preparation.

Unfortunately, not enough is known about either the history of puppeteers or their companies. Perhaps, as with other performing arts in the old society of Korea, this is due to social prejudice. This bias existed throughout history because entertainers were regarded as social outcasts, and performing artists the lowest of these professionals. Consequently, scholars made no attempt to describe or even to record these activities until the 1930s. Activities of the folk theatre came to a virtual standstill from the outbreak of World War II until its end. Today in Korea there is neither one regularly performing company nor one theatre exclusively for the performance of the traditional puppet drama.

The main reasons for this decline were economic and political. The occupying Japanese military took oppressive measures against all the nationalistic arts of Korea. However, since the end of World War II a number of attempts have been made to revive the puppet theatre of South Korea; those responsible for this are the remaining puppeteers, scholars, students, and other interested people. Reliable information about the activities of the traditional puppet theatre in North Korea is not available in the West at the present time.

In 1956 with the few remaining puppeteers, the Korean Folklore Society sponsored a performance of traditional puppet plays at Wŏnkaksa Theatre [since destroyed by fire] in Seoul. In 1962 it was reported that a few university students performed *Kkoktu Kaksi*. Also during this period a few little-noted attempts were made.

To preserve and encourage this rapidly disappearing folk theatre, another notable measure was carried out in 1964: the government of the Republic of Korea declared the traditional puppet theatre "An Important Intangible Cultural Property." Since then, infrequent performances by the Namsatang Group have been held in Seoul. None of these efforts have been sustained enough to result in a lasting revival of a regularly performing puppet theatre.

One modest effort to revive the traditional Korean puppet was made by the author in the United States in 1973. In that year he organized a performing group under the auspices of the Asian Studies Center at Michigan State University. The company presented two performances of *Kkoktu Kaksi* at Michigan State University on April 19 and 20, 1974; these were followed by a performance at Western Michigan University on May 17, 1974. The company then toured to Stratford, Canada, where they performed at the Workshop Stage of the Shakespearean Festival on September 6, 1974.

Audience, Puppets, and Stage

Traditionally, in this type of theatre the number of spectators was not large; perhaps, a few dozen or rarely a hundred. There were at least two reasons for the small audience: first, it was visually impossible for a large audience to see a puppet show traditionally performed during the evening by torch light; second, it was difficult for a large audience to hear the dialogue spoken by the puppeteers.

No record has been found which specifies an admission fee. It is assumed that the charge was different from company to company. The price could never have been too high, for most of the patrons were poor. Admission fees were probably collected by one of the performers before the performance began. There being no seats available, the audience stood or sat on the ground during the performance. They also walked freely around the undefined "auditorium," spoke to friends and neighbors, and responded to the performance openly. The audience consisted mainly of the common citizens, such people as farmers, small local merchants, apprentices, servants, and novice Buddhist monks. Probably there were no age or sex distinction; men and women, old and young, made up the audience.

The Korean puppet, in the strict sense, does not belong to any of the most familiar puppet categories. That is, it cannot be classified as either a hand puppet, a rod puppet, or a marionette. Instead, it combines aspects of all of these. The body of the Korean puppet, the main stick, is held by the hand, which is reminiscent of the hand puppet; its arms, somewhat like the marionette, are manipulated by strings from below; and the unique quality of arm movement reminds audiences of the characteristic stiff mobilization of the rod puppet. It is unknown when and how the Korean puppet attained its unique features.

Generally, there are two types of puppets: those representing human beings and Buddha; and those delineating animals such as the serpent, birds, and dog. Of these, the human images are the more important and play the major roles; the rest are supporting characters. The major puppets of all Korean puppet companies would have had the same distinct characteristics, although there would have been some variations from company to company in terms of size of a particular puppet. The height might vary anywhere from two to three feet. While the traditional Korean puppets may appear simple and somewhat crude, they have authentic national features accentuated by traditional costumes.

Because of their unembellished quality, Korean puppets are rather easy to construct. Traditionally, the materials used for their construction include dried gourds, soft wood, rabbit fur, metal springs, human hair, string, cloth, and paper. The puppet head is traditionally made from either dried gourd or wood. Lamentably, not one traditional puppet made with a dried gourd exists in any Korean museum. Most of the existing puppet heads are either carved out of wood or made from papier-mâché and painted bright colors.

Into the carved wooden or papier-mache head. the main stick of the puppet is wedged. This support is usually a one-by-two-inch piece of strong light wood. The length of this main body stick depends upon the size of the puppet. A rectangular frame of thin light wood is attached a few inches below the neck of the puppet head. The main body stick must be attached exactly at the center of this rectangular frame. The upper horizontal bar of the body frame forms the shoulders. Arm sticks made with the same quality of wood used for the body frame are loosely bolted to the shoulders. This makes it possible to manipulate the string attached to the upper portion of the arm sticks. Appropriate costumes are then fitted to the puppet.

One of the unique characteristics of the Korean puppet is that it has neither torso nor legs with the exception of Hong Tongji. In performance, the style is non-realistic and does not include life-like walking or any other important use of the lower body. The hands of Korean puppets, with few exceptions, are not shown; instead, their arm sticks are kept completely covered under the sleeves.

The movement of a Korean puppet is somewhat restricted. Because of this fact, they are not required to perform such complicated movements as changing clothes, eating, drinking, or smoking pipes. A puppeteer holds only one figure at a time. A puppet is held in one hand on the lower part of the body stick while the other hand manipulates one or both strings, depending on what movements are necessary. Perhaps the simple figures lend credence to the ritual or religious representation theories of origin; puppets were made more to stand for something rather than entertain by being flexible and dexterous.

There were no rigid rules concerning how the stage sould be set up or what its exact dimensions should be. The collapsible and portable feature of the stage's construction was its most important characteristic. This simplicity must have had a direct relationship to the players' nomadic life style which required constant traveling to secure a livelihood. Greater complexity was not only beyond their means but would have made the structure difficult to transport.

Traditionally, only four wooden sticks and several yards of muslin were essential for the construction of this stage. First, the sticks were erected on four corners to form an area approximately two and one half yards square. The sides of this area were then covered with muslin. The height of this square was high enough so that the puppeteer's manipulation from below could not be seen by the audience. Neither scenic background, proscenium arch nor curtain were required for this simple outdoor stage. The stage was usually centered in one end of the "auditorium" so that the audience could assemble on three sides only. For a special performance the host village might supply a large canopy-like tent to protect the audience from bad weather or excessive mist.

As with all traditional forms of Korean theatre, music was one of the important elements of Korean puppet theatre. The group of three or four musicians usually took their place in front of the stage. Sometimes they faced the puppets or occasionally sat with their backs to them; also they might locate themselves so as to be able to see both audience and puppets. Music was generally improvised according to the dance and movement requirements of the puppet, the mood of a particular scene, or to maintain the interest of the audience during the performance. The most popular music of this theatre could be categorized as *t'aryŏng,*[8] *yŏmbul,*[9] or *kutkŏri.*[10] Three kinds of musical instruments were commonly employed: *changgo, kkwaenggwari,* and *nalnari.*

The Play

Today Korean puppet drama is often broadly referred to by three different names that can be used interchangeably: *Kkoktu Kaksi norŭm, Pak Ch'ŏmji norŭm,* and *Hong Tongji norŭm.* All of these names are derived from central characters in one of the plays' surviving versions.

In 1939 *Kkoktu Kaksi* became the first Korean puppet play to be published; it appeared in Kim Chae-ch'ŏl's book, *Chosŏn yŏngŭksa* [History of Korean Theatre]. Prior to that time, all Korean puppet plays had been preserved orally and passed on from one generation of players to another. The performances were from memory and the skills acquired through years of experience. By the time scholars began to set down these historical works, few active players remained to assist with the transcription and preservation of the plays.

The dramatic structure of Korean puppet plays is by no means uniform. Of the existing plays, some have eight scenes as in the case of *Kkoktu Kaksi,* while others have ten scenes or eleven scenes plus a prologue and epilogue. Each scene has an independent plot and together these units make up a whole play.

The independent plot structure of each scene makes it possible for this play to be rearranged without damaging the play as a whole. For the same reason, it is also possible to perform each scene separately as a short independent play. Furthermore, it is said that, to shorten the performing time, either some lines or certain scenes were often deleted from the production.[11] For example, scene four in this play can be omitted without damaging the play whatsoever. By the same token, if it were necessary to prolong the performing time, the players could insert "tittle-tattle" as long as the dialogue did not deviate too far from the main action. Under the circumstances, most of the puppeteers could improvise lines and actions which were required on such occasions.

As in the other forms of the traditional Korean theatre, the major thematic subjects of the puppet plays are satire against the members of the privileged classes: the corrupt local government official, the pretentious Buddhist scholars, the apostate Buddhist monks, and the degenerate aristocrats.

Notes

1. Kim Chae-ch'ŏl, *Chosŏn yŏngŭksa* [Seoul: Ha'kyaesa, 1939], pp. 122-123.

2. Ch'oe Sang-su, *Han'guk inhyŏnggŭk ŭi yŏngu* [Seoul: Koryŏ Sŏjŏk, 1961], pp. 6-7.

3. Innami Takaichi, *Chosen no enggeki* [Tokyo: Hokko Shobo, 1944], p. 171.

4. Kwŏn Taek-mu, *Chosŏn mingangŭk* [P'yŏngyang: Chosŏn Munhakyaesul Tongmeng, 1966], p. 22.

5. Ch'oe Sang-su, p. 6.

6. Ch'oe Sang-su, "The Descent and the Evolution of the Korean Puppet Play," *Chosen Gakuho,* No. 22 [October 1961], p. 16.

7. Yi Byŏng-to, *Han'guksa* [Seoul: Ulyu Munhwasa, 1961], pp. 8-10.

8. See Yangju *pyŏlsandae* [play], Note 16.

9. See Yangju *pyŏlsandae* [play], Note 13.

10. See Yangju *pyŏlsandae* [play], Note 139.

11. Kim Chae-ch'ŏl, p. 145.

The Play

Characters

Pak Ch'ŏmji, the head of a village

Hong Tongji, Pak's nephew

Young Pak Ch'ŏmji, Pak's younger brother

Sorceresses, Pak's nieces

Ch'oe Yŏngno, Pak's relative by marriage

P'yo Saengwŏn, an aristocrat [*yangban*] from Haenam

Kkoktu Kaksi, P'yo's legal wife

Tolmori, P'yo's concubine

Chapt'al Monk

Tongpangsŏk

Governor of P'yŏngan

Governor's Attendant

Hunter

Villager [musician]

Monks

There are also a serpent, a hunting dog, a pheasant, and a falcon in the play.

Prelude

While music is played noisily by the musicians, Chapt'al Monk enters and dances. Then an actor, wearing a four-cornered horse-hair hat, enters and sings.

> *Worldly affairs do not last*
> *Longer than a three-foot flute.*

A human life is not worth
More than a chalice of wine.

Scene 1

Pak Ch'ŏmji[1]: *Ttelu ttelu ttelu ttelu.* [A lone musician suddenly starts playing his small gong, *kkwaenggwari.*] What sound is this?

Musician[2]: Hello! Old man.

Pak: Yeah!

Musician: Why is an old man like you making so much noise after dark?

Pak: Did you call me an old man?

Musician: Yes.

Pak: I live in the upper-class village.

Musician: You live in the upper-class village? Where's the upper-class village?

Pak: If I say I live in the upper-class village, that means I live there. I am a respectable *yangban.*[3] . . .

Musician: So. . .?

Pak: Of course, there isn't a decent place to live except Seoul.

Musician: Do you mean the whole city of Seoul is your residence?

Pak: I'll explain to you in detail where I live.

Musician: Tell me in detail.

Pak: In Seoul, there are Ilkan-dong,[4] Yikolmok,[5] Samch'ŏng-dong,[6] Sachik-kol,[7] Okung-t'ŏ,[8] Yukcho-ap,[9] Ch'ilkwan-ak,[10] P'alkak-chae,[11] Kuri-kae,[12] Sipcha-ga,[13] Kwangmyŏng-churi,[14] Manri-chae,[15] Araepyŏk-dong,[16] and Utpyŏk-dong.[17] However, I'm not concerned with these streets and places. I live on Center Street. Needless to say, if you ask about Pak, a general without portfolio, everyone in Seoul knows where I live.

Musician: If so, why are you wandering about here?

Pak: Why did I come here?

Musician: That's right.

Pak: I came here. That's true. Well, . . . The reason is that my ancestral home and family have been destroyed. As a result, life has been very uninteresting in my old age. So I've undertaken a journey to all parts of the country. But, since I was tired after the end of today's journey, I decided to stay in a country inn, where I had my supper. While I was lying down in the inn, smoking a long bamboo pipe, and spitting, I suddenly heard people making "*ttung ttung ttung ttung*" sounds. So I came out. Then I heard the grown-up people saying "turŏn, turŏn, turŏn," while younger ones were whispering "*toran, toran, toran.*" When I asked them what they were chattering about, the child said they were going to the fair to see a play by the male shamans and sorceresses. Then a young man suddenly asked me why, due to my old age, I was not sleeping after my long journey. And why was I interfering in someone else's business. So I scolded him, saying my mind was still young, although my body was old. I also told him that even an old man has eyes and ears. Then all of them suddenly disappeared.

Musician: You scolded him? How did you do that?

Pak: I did. Of course, since I am a *yangban*, I didn't use abusive language.

Musician: Then. . .?

Pak: I scolded him saying he became a double asshole like an hourglass-shaped drum just as soon as his parents' hips bumped into each other.

Musician: You old piece of useless trash! Then what did you do?

Pak: After scolding him I came here, excited by the music. I saw a big crowd. Among them, I found a handsome young boy in an armour with a bright colored belt and a pretty girl who were dancing together. As soon as I saw how they were dancing, I began to be thrilled and excited . . . even in my old age. So I checked my purse. Then I found I still had a few leftover pennies.

Musician: Then. . .?

Pak: [Closing his eyes, he begins to snooze. Then he is suddenly awakened by the loud sound of the little gong.] Ah!

Musician: Hey! Pak Ch'ŏmji. What were you doing in the middle of the story? Were you taking a nap? Or dreaming?

Pak: Oh, look! What have I done? An old man like me should be dead. I was foolish enough to fall asleep at the fair since I am old and weak.

Musician: By the way, how much money did you have in your purse when you left your home?

Pak: [He begins to talk in a *t'aryŏng* [18] tune.]

> *How much?*
> *How much?*
> *How much?*
>
> *Let's see!*

Musician: Well, . . .

Pak: I had exactly seven pennies for my capital sum.

Musician: How did you spend your seven pennies?

Pak: I always spend my money in the right way, even in my old age. I will tell you how I spent it. Listen carefully! First, I gave some money to a sorceress and allowed her to hold my hand. Second, I let a beautiful girl hold a penny between her lips. Third, I called a male shaman and gave him some money. Then I also tipped the head shaman a few pennies. After spending so much money, the purse on one end of my stick was still heavy. Then I found twenty-one pennies of my capital sum, that is, three times seven, and an extra two hundred and seven pennies in the bottom of the purse.

Musician: What? A silly old useless piece of trash like you? You spent seven pennies of your capital sum, so how can you still have so much money left in your purse? That's absurd! You must have stolen someone's purse instead of tipping people.

Pak: You scoundrel! What kind of talk is that? Don't you know how to treat an old man? If you were a decent fellow, you would treat me to a bowl of rice wine. This is a main street where law and order are maintained by the government. Contrary to custom, you're trying to have me arrested by the polilce and incarcerated in my old age. I am an innocent man. What kind of talk is that?

Musician: Well. What do you mean by saying that you still have two hundred and ten pennies left after you spent your seven pennies in so many different ways?

Pak: Don't you know the law of increment and decrement?

Musician: The law of increment and decrement? What is that?

Pak: Everything on earth prospers: the flying birds lay their eggs while the crawling animals give birth to their young. If you don't understand this logic, you must be a fool. My money has also increased according to the same logic.

Musician: I'm not a fool. Pak. You must be an old fool. By the way, what did you come here for?

Pak: What did I come here for?

Musician: Yes.

Pak: I am an old man, but my mind is still young. Because I was beginning to feel carefree, I decided to journey here to dance.

Musician: So why don't you dance?

Pak: Good! Let the musicians play music. *Ttaeng, ttaeng, ttaeng, ttaeng!* [He dances to the music played by the musicians. He stops.] Hey! You!

Musician: Yes?

Pak: I've danced for a while. Look! The young sorceresses are picking herbs in the rear garden of the temple. Since they have heard the music, they're going to come out here and dance.

Musician: Tell them to come out here.

Pak: If they do, I'd better go and hide myself.

Scene 2
In the Temple Court

[Two monks [19] enter and sit on a rock, as the two young sorceresses [20] are picking herbs on the hill. The monks look at them with lustful eyes. Soon, after a short conversation, they begin to dance merrily with the girls as music is played. Pak Ch'ŏmji, hearing that the pretty sorceresses are dancing in the temple court, enters. As soon as he sees that the girls are dancing with the monks, however, he turns pale from astonishment. He begins to scold them.]

Pak: You, beastly monks! If you were decent monks, you should devote yourselves to Buddhism in the mountain. Why are you participating in the mundane life of the world, dancing and playing with the pretty girls? That is against your priesthood. Perhaps, your priesthood is that of a corrupt monk. Get out! [Pak begins to dance for a while.] Behold! Behold! What is happening? Ha, ha, ha! I too have become a piece of old trash in my old age. I must go. [He stares at the sorceresses carefully.] Absent-mindedly, I have danced in front of my nieces. What shame in my old age! Since I have already danced I don't know what I ought to do. First, I must take care of those corrupt monks. But I am an old man. I can't do much about it. Perhaps I should send my nephew to take care of them. [While the monks are dancing and fighting for the girls, Pak Ch'ŏmji is growing angry. He calls his nephew.] Hey! Hong! Come out here! [Hong Tongji²¹ enters.] Listen! I saw these young monks dancing with my daughters in the temple court. But I can't do much about it because I am weak in my old age. You must go and beat up those corrupt monks. [The monks are standing at either end of the stage with the sorceresses. Hong goes back and forth between them.]

Hong: Where are they?

Pak: There!

Hong: [Walking in that direction.] Here?

Pak: That's right.

Hong: [As he hurries toward them, he bumps his head against a monk's head.] Look! You shameless monks! Who are you? Are you corrupt monks? The last crops of wheat in the month of July? What kind of monks are you? Your eyes are fixed on the offerings in the temple instead of praying to Buddha. You have been doing nothing but dancing with pretty girls. Well, . . . since you have danced with them, why shouldn't I play with them for a while? [All of them dance.] Play the music!

[As the music is played fast, they also begin to dance in quick tempo. Then Hong begins bumping his head against those of the monks and the sorceresses, pushing them off the stage. Finally, he also exits.]

Scene 3
The House of Ch'oe Yŏngno

[Ch'oe Yŏngno²² has been busy drying kernels of rice in his yard. Although there are many members in his family, it is a busy season for them.]

Ch'oe: *Oh-yŏ*—*!* [He chases the sparrows.] Old Pak!

Pak: Yeah—! Why are you calling me?

Ch'oe: You, old piece of trash! Why do you stay inside the house? If you chase the sparrows in the millet field while baby-sitting, you don't have to worry about having clothes lined with cotton in May and June. You have always been so eager to go everywhere—feasts, funerals, and even where dogs are having intercourse. You old piece of trash. Why are you becoming a piece of such useless old trash? By the way, none of those people who were sent to the millet field to chase the sparrows have come home yet. Can you go and see what has happened to them?

[Meanwhile, a hungry serpent from the Yong-kang River has been eating both the villagers and animals in the area. Pak Ch'ŏmji comes to the field and finds no one. At this moment, Chapt'al Monk[23] who has been chased by the serpent enters hurriedly.]

Chapt'al Monk: Everybody has been killed by the serpent from the Yong-kang River except me. I must run away from this area. But you—if you are going to go and check the situation, you'll need to have a lot of courage. You also have to take off your pants to cross the stream.

Pak: I am beginning to be absent-minded. But I don't think I need to be worried. Since you say the river is deep, I have no choice but to take off my clothes to swim. [He pantomimes walking into the stream.] Oh, the river is deep! Getting deeper. [As he swims.] Hey! *Yaeho*—*!* [He stands up.] Where is the serpent?

Chapt'al Monk: [Off-stage.] Go further!

Pak: [He looks toward the place where the serpent is hiding. Then he shouts.] What is this? I am petrified. I am sure that all the others were scared by this. I cannot tackle it by myself. I'd better tell Hong to kill it and sell its skin at the market. Hey! Hong!

Hong: [Entering.] Yes—! What are you calling me for?

Pak: Call your uncle.

Hong: Uncle—!

Young Pak [24]: [As he enters.] Why are you calling me?

Hong: The serpent from the Yong-kang River is extremely mischievous. I must kill it. First I must go inside and take off my clothes. Please wait for me. [He exits.]

Pak: Look, brother. I must go by myself. When I catch the serpent, I will shout for you. Then you must come and help me. [Young Pak follows him.] You, beast! Where are you?

Young Pak: Brother, please, be quiet. Don't talk at all. [He retreats a few steps.]

Pak: Why shouldn't I talk at all? [He approaches the serpent without noticing it. He has bad eyes. He is suddenly bitten by the serpent. Seeing that his brother has been bitten by the serpent, Young Pak runs away. At this moment, Hong enters.] Look! Hong!

Hong: What is happening?

Pak: Please save my life!

Hong: You deserve it. You old piece of trash. [Hong approaches Pak and bumps against Pak's body. The sound of knocking against dried gourd is heard.] The serpent has already sucked out his guts.

Pak: I'm still alive!

Hong: Whether you are my uncle or a piece of useless old trash, you must obey what I say even in your old age. You deserve it. You were dumb enough to cross the stream! [Looking down at the musicians.] Hey! Since I feel pity for him, I must save his life. Play some music! [The musicians play music with a quick tempo.]

Hyŏ---yae---o! [He begins to bump his head against the serpent. The serpent turns Pak loose, and jumps up and down.]

Pak: Oh, I'm saved. [He exits dancing.]

Hong: [He kills the serpent and peels off its skin. Then he reenters, wrapping the skin around his body.] Ha, ha, ha! Where can it go? It can't escape from me. It was very strong. But I finally killed it. Now I must go to the market to sell the skin. [He exits.]

Scene 4
Old Man from an Eastern Region

[Tongpangsŏk,²⁵ an old man from an eastern region, enters and coughs.]

Musician: Hello, sir! Why do you keep your eyes closed this time?

Tongpangsŏk: Ah. Don't you know why I am keeping my eyes closed? After taking an immortal tonic in The Three Divine Mountains and studying *The Complete Collection of Buddhist Scripture,* I found everything in the world to be impure. So I have decided to keep my eyes closed.

Musician: Is that so? But the ancient and present music in this world is given to us by none other than the heavenly god. Besides, the pleasure in this world is almost as good as in paradise. So please open your eyes, even for a second.

Tongpangsŏk: [He opens his eyes and looks around.] Oh, you are right. Indeed, it is nice to see the people and look around at the world. It is a nice world.

Musician: Excuse me, sir.

Tongpangsŏk: What is the matter?

Musician: Anyone who comes here must dance and sing a song.

Tongpangsŏk: Look. I am not an ordinary man. I am different from the rest of the people. Even though I came to this earthly world, I am a man who should study Buddhism in a mountain temple. Being so different from ordinary people, how can I dance and sing a song? But since I am already in this world, I will just try to blink my eyes if you will beat out a tune. If I blink my eyes gently to the tune of your music, everything will turn out as well as we wish.

Musician: That also sounds good. Then I'll play some music. [As he plays music, Tongpangsŏk begins to blink his eyes. Being enraptured, Tongpangsŏk now dances as he flaps his arms.] Ah! Look! Since coming back to the earthly world, he has turned into an earthly and mundane man.

Tongpangsŏk: [Turning pale with astonishment, he shakes his head.] Behold! What are you saying? Have I danced?

Musician: You might not have danced at all. But you made nice turns while stretching out your arms.

Tongpangsŏk: Since you are saying I have already danced, I am no longer different from an ordinary man. I look at myself from the right and left and find no difference from other people. So I must also sing a song.

Musician: That's good! I'll play some good music. Please sing a song.

Tongpangsŏk: Well, I am going to sing a song. Listen carefully. [He sings.]

> *Go! Go! Let's go!*
> *When the moonlight shining on the blossoms*
> *Casts a long single line,*
> *The white heron from the two rivers*
> *Crosses the river.*
>
> *In the autumn river under the clear sky*
> *A lonely fisherman is in his boat.*

When the hermit rides away on a whale's back
The beautiful moon is in the autumn sky.

While loading our boat with pleasures,
Let's open our fans!

When the tortoise carries the moon on its back,
Shall we return to our home?

[He burst into laughter.] Ha, ha, ha! What has happened? I have just had a revelation of the future by checking the eight signs of divination. It says that a country gentleman from Kwanmŏri in Wando Island, Chŏlla-do Province, has lost his wife. Since then he has opened a bar near the Notul-kang River with his concubine. However, he has since then set out on a journey to look for his wife as well as to see Kŭmkang-san Mountain in Kangwŏn-do Province. He is now coming this way. Since he was an aristocrat while I was a hermit scholar in the past, it would be awkward for me to meet him here. So I must retire from this place.

Scene 5
P'yo Saengwŏn

P'yo[26]: [He enters with Tolmori,[27] his concubine.] Where shall I go? Where shall I go? It has been so many years since my wife and I were separated. Now I cannot help but think often of her. Would I Meet her if I went sight-seeing to the Eight Famous Views in the East? There are many places of natural beauty in Chŏlla-do Province. Then why did she have to go somewhere else to see scenic spots? Oh, I know it is my fault: I didn't take care of her after I began living with Tolmori, my concubine. But until now I have been looking for my wife in every village, every valley, every mountain, and every seaside. I still haven't found her. How my heart aches for my dear wife. I am filled with amorous sighs.

Tolmori: Hello, my dear! What are you suddenly talking about? What's the use of searching for your wife? I thought we were taking a journey to see the scenic spots and great temples. Now I know you came here to look for your wife. Oh, my fate! What will my destiny be?

P'yo: [Angrily.] You suspicious woman! Why do you pay any attention to what a great man talks about?

Tolmori: Now I am beginning to understand the sorrow of a concubine. [She turns away from P'yo.]

P'yo: [Patting her on the back.] Are you angry? If so, it must be due to a slip of my old tongue.

Kkoktu Kaksi[28]: [At this moment, she enters. She sings.]

> *Ah!*
> *What has been happening?*
>
> *Sorrow is the separation of man and wife*
> *And life in solitude.*
>
> *It is sadder*
> *Than anything else in the world.*
>
> *When god created*
> *Human beings and the world,*
> *Why did he not forget*
> *The creation of sorrow and separation?*
>
> *Oh, my husband!*
> *Where are you?*
>
> *Oh, my husband!*
> *Where are you?*
>
> *Where have you gone?*
> *Where have you gone?*

P'yo: Ah. Whose voice is this? Is there someone who is like me? I think I have heard my wife's voice. I too must call her. Hello! Wife! Wife!

Kkoktu Kaksi: I think I have heard my husband's voice. It must be my husband. Who is calling me? Hello! Husband! Husband!

P'yo: It must be my wife's voice. I am sure she is my wife. [He sings.]

> *Who is calling me?*
> *There shouldn't be anyone calling me.*

> *Who is calling me?*
> *Is it Sopu*[29] *or Hŏyu*[30]
> *Who lives in the steep mountain*
> *With the clean water?*

> *Or is it Yi Chŏk-sŏn*
> *Who gazes at the moonlight*
> *On the river by the stone mountain?*

> *Or is it one of the four hermits*[31]
> *On Sang-san Mountain*
> *Who wants to play checkers with me?*

Kkoktu Kaksi: Oh, whose voice is it? [As she approaches P'yo.] Whose voice is it? Aren't you my husband?

P'yo: You? . . . after all. Are you my wife?

Kkoktu Kaksi: If you say you are my husband, I must check the clothes which I made for you.

P'yo: How can you tell whether I am your husband just by touching my clothes?

Kkoktu Kaksi: I attached two testicles to the sleeves when I made your clothes.

P'yo: Dear wife! You must be my wife. I remember your voice. But where have you been all these years?

Kkoktu Kaksi: I have been searching for you all over the country: in Kŭmkang-san Mountain in Kangwŏn-do Province, in Keryong-san Mountain in Ch'ungch'ŏng-do Province, in Chili-san Mountain in Chŏlla-do Province, in T'aebaek-san Mountain in Kyŏngsang-do Province, in Kuwŏl-san Mountain in Hwanghae-do Province, and in the Yongkwang Pavilion in P'yŏngyang. . . in every valley. . . every mountain. I have been searching for you as though checking every tooth of a comb. At this moment I was going to Kwanmŏri, Haenam. Then, by chance, I happened to meet you here.

P'yo: Is that so? What shame is upon me! It is beyond my description. . . But why has your face so many speckles?

Kkoktu Kaksi: Are you talking about my face?

P'yo: That's right.

Kkoktu Kaksi: Do you know why this has happened? I must tell you. To look for you, I climbed a steep mountain in Kangwŏn-do Province where I ate acorn jello. That is the reason my face has changed to its present appearance.

P'yo: What? What are you talking about? You! You harlot! Are you trying to tell me that you have so many pockmarks on your face because you ate acorn jello? I ate mounds of corn and acorns when I was coming to Sansu Kapsan from Paektu-san Mountain in Hamkyŏng-do Province. But I don't have a single pockmark on my face. My face is as smooth as if it were planed. What an absurd and hollow liar! [A pause.] However, if a dragon appears out of a small ditch, we still must call it a dragon. And even if the guardian of a temple is made of straw, we still must call it the guardian of the temple. According to this logic, I must now admonish Tolmori, my concubine, to greet my wife. Hey! Tolmori! [He brings Tolmori to his wife.] Well. Wife. Let's stop talking nonsense. We must discuss our future. You have already passed your sixtieth birthday. I am eighty years old and poor. In addition, we don't have a single child. What a great failure! Aren't you sad about this, too?

Kkoktu Kaksi: I haven't seen you for many years, but this has been the cause of my worries.

P'yo: Since it seems to me that you understand the situation very well, I must be frank with you. I now have a little house.

Kkoktu Kaksi: What pleasant news! How could I be so extravagant to demand a big house under the present situation? Since you have built a new house, you must have used good lumber. . . and the house probably has plenty of sunlight as well. You have prepared the soy sauce for next year, haven't you?

P'yo: Oh! Oh, what are you talking about? Soy sauce. . .? Lumber? You are jumping to conclusions! To tell you the truth, I meant that I have a little wife.

Kkoktu Kaksi: Ah! Ah! Husband! What are you saying? Have I been looking for you all these years only to be treated in this miserable, cruel way again?

P'yo: Don't talk nonsense! You don't have to worry about your means of living.

Kkoktu Kaksi: I don't care whether I have to worry about my means of living or not. I am still your legal wife. Regardless of how big she is, that one is still your little wife. Make your concubine bow to me.

P'yo: Hey. Tolmori! The law is the law. We must obey the law.

Tolmori: What are you talking about?

P'yo: You must bow to my big wife.

Tolmori: I have heard already. Everyone in Yongsan, Seoul, knows who Tolmori is. Even though you have a Master's degree, you should have never asked me to bow to your wife. Though I am your concubine, you must not look down upon me. Me, bow to your wife? What kind of bow? I don't like the idea of bowing to her at all. I must go. Please live happily with your wife. [She turns around.]

P'yo: Tolmori! How can you say such a thing after we have been living together for such a long time? We can't separate like this. Please change your mind. Greet my wife!

Tolmori: Since you insist, shall I greet her like this? [She is angry. She suddenly bumps her head against Kkoktu Kaksi as she bows to her.] Please receive my greeting!

Kkoktu Kaksi: [Shocked.] Ah! What is this? Husband! What is this? Is this the way of today's greeting? If I had to exchange another greeting, I wouldn't have a head left. Isn't that right? I don't care any more about whether I am greeted by her or not. Please let us divide our properties. That is all I want.

P'yo: What kind of person are you? You're too greedy! My house is in Kwanmŏri, Haenam. My temporary lodging is an inn in Seoul. What properties are you talking about? Divide the properties? A straw will be flattened with a stroke of the club. [He is angry. At this moment Pak Ch'ŏmji enters.]

Pak: Excuse me. I was just passing by. Even though the problem is confined to your personal matters, as the chief of the village, I must intervene in the situation. So please don't regard me as an outsider.

P'yo: Oh, are you the village chief? Please give us a decision. I am P'yo Saengwŏn from Haenam. Since I was separated from my wife, I have been living with my concubine. But I happened to come here today. That devil is my wife. [He points to Kkoktu Kaksi.] To tell you the truth, she is very upset because I have a concubine. She now wants to divide our properties. I am helpless. What shall I do?

Pak: Are all three of you traveling?

P'yo: Yes, that is right. I am a stranger here.

Pak: Would you be willing to divide the properties if you had them?

P'yo: Of course, I would.

Pak: [He thinks about something for a moment.] I am the village chief. Don't worry about it. I will take care of it. [He sings.]

> *Tolmori will have four acres of land*
> *Which produces two ounces of silver*
> *In Wangsim-ri.*

Kkoktu Kaksi will have five acres of land
On the peak of Nam-san Mountain
For a single day's cultivation of red peppers.

All rafts which come to Yongsan
Will be given to Tolmori.

All tree roots which float down
With the flood next year
Will be possessed by Kkoktu Kaksi.

All chests inlaid with mother of pearls
And jewelry boxes will belong to Tolmori.

Kkoktu Kaksi will have the yard
Where dogs lift their legs
And the broken jar for ashes.

Kkoktu Kaksi: [She sings.]

Ah!
I am going!
I am going as I dance!

[She exits as she dances.]

Scene 6
A Pheasant Hunt

[The new governor of P'yŏngan has just arrived from Seoul. As soon as he finishes his journey of five hundred and fifty *ri*s,[32] he calls his attendant and orders him to prepare for a pheasant hunt.]

Governor[33]: I hear that you have a first-rate hunter in the province. Have him ready for a pheasant hunt within a few days.

Attendant[34]: Yes, sir! First of all, I must dispatch an official note to him so he will wait for further orders. [He walks nervously around the stage.] Ah, I wonder why the road of my life is so rough? He is suddenly saying that he has to go hunting. Why must he give us such a hard time? I am already tired of my official post. Whether it is a Jack-in-office or a Grand Panjandrum himself, I must resign from the office. For the past fifty years I have been doing nothing but serve someone else. What an unlucky destiny! How exasperating!

Hunter[35]: [He enters.] Hey! Where are you going?

Attendant: Good! You rascal! I'm so glad to meet you here. Nothing could make me happier than to see you.

Hunter: What kind of greeting is this for a man you haven't seen for a long time? Why are you humiliating me in such a way?

Attendant: Hey! What is the use of arguing with me? We have a serious matter here.

Hunter: A serious matter? What is it? The more serious matter we have, the happier I am.

Attendant: You rascal! A serious matter doesn't always mean a wedding or someone's sixtieth birthday party. You are always dreaming about delicious food at a feast.

Hunter: If it isn't a feast, what is it?

Attendant: Upon his arrival, the new governor ordered me to prepare for a pheasant hunt. I mean, right now. He doesn't want to bother himself with studying how to rule the people in the province. . . not even in his worst nightmare.

Hunter: Whether he is a governor or a mosquito net,[36] I don't care. Every damned governor who comes here acts in the same way! None of them care about the welfare of the people, only about pheasant hunting. By the way, why do you call pheasant hunting a serious matter?

Attendant: The governor said that he would shoot your head off if you don't shoot a pheasant. Isn't that a serious matter?

Hunter: Absurd! Absurd! I am caught in a serious situation.

Attendant: [He calls Hunter and the falcons. Then he reports to the governor.] I am reporting to you, Governor. This first-rate hunter from Kanggye and all sorts of falcons—the Sanjin falcon, the Sujin falcon, the Naljin falcon, and the Haetong falcon—are all ready to serve you in the pheasant hunt.

Governor: Good! We'll go hunting early tomorrow morning. Make sure that everything is ready by that time.

[They begin to go pheasant hunting. Hunter has a falcon on his shoulder. They also have a hunting dog. As soon as the bell on the falcon's neck begins to ring, a pheasant flies away.]

Governor: Hey! Did you shoot a cock pheasant or a hen pheasant?

Attendant: Listen, Hunter! The governor wants to know whether you shot a cock pheasant or a hen pheasant.

Hunter: I shot a cock pheasant.

Governor: As I expected, he is a first-rate hunter from Kanggye. You have demonstrated your skill well. Now let's go home.

Attendant: Yes, my lord!

[They exit as a trumpet is played and drums are beaten.]

Scene 7
The Mourning by the P'yŏngan Governor

[The pallbearers carry the coffin of the governor's mother.]

Governor: [He sings *Yangsando* [37] as well as other songs.]

> *Kkolkok!*
> *Kkolkok!*
>
> *Kkolkok!*
> *Kkolkok!*

How happy I am!
Now everything is mine.
Now I can sit on the warm side of our room.

Young Pak: [Looking at the funeral.] Whose funeral is this? Is this the crying of the chief mourner? Or the sound of someone just singing a song?

[At this moment one of the pallbearers hurts his foot. They set the coffin down.]

Governor: Listen Pak! [Pak Ch'ŏmji enters.] Listen to what I am saying. One of the pallbearers has hurt his foot. They can no longer carry the coffin. Bring a laborer!

Pak: It is impossible to get a laborer so quickly. But I have a nephew who not only likes to do many different kinds of work, but is also strong like a horse. But he is an outlandish-looking fellow. I must recommend him to you.

Governor: Hey! I'm in a hurry. Bring him here at once!

Pak: Yes, sir---! [He calls Hong Tongji.] Hong! Listen! One of the pallbearers has hurt a foot on the way to the graveyard. Can you carry the coffin? We'll let you eat three or four meals, and also give you seven brand-new pennies.

Hong: What are you talking about?

Pak: Don't you hear what I say? If you are late, you will be flogged until your bones fly off. Come out quickly before it is too late.

Hong: Uncle, are you telling the truth?

Pak: Why should I tell you a lie?

Hong: Is it all right even though I am completely naked?

Pak: It doesn't matter at all.

Hong: Well. I will come and see. [He walks quietly to the governor and casts a furtive glance at him. Then he looks at the coffin and sniffs it.] Oh! What on earth is this?

Pak: What are you talking about?

Hong: It smells like a small rotten dog at the height of summer.

Pak: You rascal! What kind of talk is that? What will you do if you are heard by the governor?

Hong: If his feelings are hurt, I could tell him that it smells like a big rotten dog.

Governor: [He sings.]

> *Kkolkok!*
> *Kkolkok!*
>
> *Kkolkok!*
> *Kkolkok!*

[He walks to and fro.]

Hong: Chief mourner! Please accept my greetings.

Governor: You beast! The coffin holds a respectabe lady's body. In spite of this, you are totally naked. What kind of greeting is this?

Hong: You stupid imbecile. What does it matter whether I am naked or not? What are you talking about? Isn't it enough if I can carry the coffin?

Governor: I am glad to hear that you came to carry the coffin. But how on earth can a naked fellow carry a coffin? A naked and uncivilized fellow. What an impudent fellow! Arrest him! [He arrests Pak Ch'ŏmji angrily and starts to whip him.]

Pak: In spite of my old age, I did my best to bring a laborer. For what crime are you whipping me?

Governor: You! This is a respectable funeral, and the coffin holds a lady's body. But you brought a completely naked fellow. How can I use a naked pallbearer?

Pak: He is my nephew. He can carry the coffin by himself very well.

Governor: Since you say so, I will use him only this once. Have him take up the coffin immediately. Right now!

Hong: By the way, chief mourner, what in the world are you carrying on your shoulder?

Governor: Are you talking to me?

Hong: That's right

Governor: This is a dog. I bought a little dog for seven pennies to use for the last service at the graveyard.

Hong: Though I have heard there was a man whose brains were in his feet, I've never heard of anyone who used a lowly dog for a funeral service. Well. Anyway, shall I carry the coffin? Can I carry it this way?

Pak: You rascal! What are you trying to do? Aren't you satisfied yet with putting your uncle in such a miserable spot? Everyone knows that a coffin must be carried on the shoulder. Why are you trying to carry it with the thing under your navel [penis]?

Hong: That's right. Well. Let me carry it in a more formal way. [He starts to carry the coffin on his shoulder and begins to jiggle his body. Then he begins to sing a song in an excess of mirth.]

> *Nŏ-hwa*
> *Nŏ-hwa nŏmch'a!*
>
> *Nŏ-kori*
> *Nŏ-hwa nŏmch'a!*

Governor: [He sings.]

> *Kkolkak.*
> *Kkolkak.*
> *Kkolkak.*

I heard the lantern carrier for the funeral was saying that

Pukmang-san Mountain[38] was far away. But it is just a few steps away from the gate.

Hong: [He sings.]

Nŏ-hwa nŏmch'a!

Pak: [He sings.]

Nŏ-hwa nŏmch'a!

Hong: [He sings.]

Nŏ-hwa nŏmch'a!

Scene 8
The Erection of the Temple

Pak: Hello! I wonder what period we are living in now? It must be ancient times. Do you know why the monks are building a Buddhist temple by the great river and the famous mountain? A great temple is being built to hold the one-hundredth day Buddhist prayer for the governor's dead mother. The Buddhist monks are building a temple. I must retire now.

[Two monks enter and bow twice.]

Monks: [They sing.]

Let's build a Buddhist temple!
A Buddhist temple will be built!

[As soon as they finish the construction of the temple, they open the door of the building and bow with their hands together. They pray in a singsong tone.]

We are building a Buddhist temple!
A Buddhist temple will be built!

When we offer poetry and wine in this temple
Our dreams will come true!

*Namuamit'abul
Kwanseŭmposal!*[39]

[The monks demolish the temple.]

Notes

1. Pak Ch'ŏmji: This puppet, portraying the role of an old fallen aristocrat, *yangban*, has a whitish face, gray hair, and beard. He wears a white coat with long sleeves. Hereafter he is simply called Pak.

2. This role is played by one of the accompanying musicians, but not by a puppet.

3. See Yangju *pyŏlsandae* [play], Note 39.

4. The prefix *"il"* means first, while *"kan"* implies a block. The *"dong"* means street. The compound of these three words, thus, means first block of street.

5. The prefix *"yi"* means second, while *"kolmok"* denotes a side street. The compound of these two words, thus, means the second side street.

6. Samch'ŏng-dong: A street in Seoul. The prefix *"sam"* means third.

7. Sachik-kol: An area in Seoul. The prefix *"sa"* means four.

8. Here *Okung* appears to be *Okun* which means five armies during the Koryŏ period. The affix *"t'ŏ"* means a place or places, while the prefix *"o"* means five.

9. *Yukcho-ap:* The Six Boards of the Government of the Chosŏn dynasty. The prefix *"yuk"* means six. Also see Yangju *pyŏlsandae* [play], Note 61.

10. There is no such place in Seoul. The prefix *"ch'il"* means seven.

11. There is no such place in Seoul. The prefix *"p'al"* means eight, while the word *"kak"* is angle. The affix *"chae"* means a ridge. The compound of these three words may mean the octagonal ridge.

12. There is no such place in Seoul. The prefix *"ku"* means nine.

13. Sipcha-ka literally means a cross road. The prefix *"sip"* means ten.

14. There is no such place in Seoul.

15. The prefix *"man"* means ten thousand, while *"ri"* is a unit of distance. Ten *ri*s make approximately four kilometers. The affix *"chae"* means a pass. The compound of these words, thus, implies ten thousand *ri* pass.

16. There is no such place in Seoul. The prefix *"arae"* means under, while *"pyŏk"* is a wall. For a meaning of *"dong,"* see Note 4.

17. There is no such place. The prefix *"ut"* means above.

18. See Yangju *pyŏlsandae* [play], Note 16.

19. Monks: These puppets have whitish faces. Their eyes, eyebrows, noses, and mouth are all ink-drawn. Traditionally, the peaked cowls of the Buddhist monks and nuns are worn by them. One of them wears a monk's yellow dress with a red belt, while the other is in a red dress with a yellow belt.

20. Sorceresses: These puppets also have whitish faces with three rouge dots: one on their foreheads and one on either cheek. Their lips, too, are rouged with red. They have ink-drawn eyes and eyebrows. One of them wears a yellow jacket, *chŏkori*, and a red skirt, *ch'ima*. She has a braided hair with a red ribbon. The other one wears a red jacket with a purple skirt. She has a round chignon hair-do.

21. Hong Tongji: This muscular naked puppet is usually carved out of light wood. This is the only puppet having legs. His body is painted a reddish crimson color. The wide-open eyes, large topknot, and enlarged genitals, which are moveable, are the prominent features of this puppet. Hereafter he is simply called Hong.

22. Ch'oe Yŏngno: This puppet has a whitish face with ink-drawn eyes and eyebrows. He wears a dress with red and blue colors. On his head, he wears a scarf.

23. Chapt'al Monk: This role is played by one of the monks.

24. Young Pak Ch'ŏmji: This puppet has a whitish face with light red rouge on his cheeks. In contrast to his partially gray hair and eyebrows, the beard and mustache are brown. A white dress is worn by him.

25. Tongpangsŏk: This puppet, with a whitish face, has gray hair and a long beard. One of the unique aspects of this puppet is its moving eyes which are made to open and close. He wears a horse-hair hat worn by scholars and a white dress.

26 P'yo Saengwŏn: A country gentleman, *yangban*. This puppet has a whitish face with gray hair and beard. He wears a white coat. Hereafter he is called P'yo.

27. Tolmori: A concubine and barmaid. This puppet has a whitish face with three rouge dots: one on her forehead and one on either cheek, and a round chignon hair-do. She wears a yellow jacket and a red skirt.

28. Kkoktu Kaksi: This puppet has a brownish ugly face with many dark speckles and a slanted asymmetrical mouth. She generally wears a white jacket and a dark skirt.

29. See Pongsan *t'alch'um* [play], Note 18.

30. See Pongsan *t'alch'um* [play], Note 18.

31. He is referring to the four hermit scholars who went to the mountain in order to avoid the war during the Han dynasty in China.

32. See Note 15.

33. Governor: This puppet has a whitish face with dark mustache and beard.

34. Attendant: This puppet has an earthy brown face. He wears a simple suit of armour.

35. Hunter: This puppet has an earthy brown face. He wears a green coat with a falcon attached to the right shoulder. A few pheasant feathers are stuck to his coat.

36. The word mosquito net in Korean has a similar sound to the word for governor, although they are not the same.

37. *Yangsando*: A folk song from Kyŏnggi-do Province.

38. See Suyŏng *yayu* [play], Note 37.

39. A Buddhist invocation.

Selected Bibliography

Akiba Takshi. *Chosen minsokusi* [Korean Folkways]. Tokyo: Rokusan Shoin, 1954.

An Whak. "Sandaigeki to shoyobu to nan" [Sandaegŭk, Ch'ŏyongmu, and Nan] *Chosen* [1932], Vol. 201.

Cho Oh-kon. "The Comic Effects of Hahoe Pyŏlsin-kut: A Traditional Korean Festival Mask-dance Drama," *Korea Journal* [Seoul: Korean National Commission for UNESCO, 1980], Vol. 20, No. 7.

_____. "Ogwangdae: A Traditional Mask-dance Theatre of South Kyŏngsang Province," *Korea Journal* [Seoul: Korean National Commission for UNESCO, 1981], Vol. 21, No. 7.

_____. *Korean Puppet Theatre: Kkoktu Kaksi.* East Lansing, Mich.: Michigan State University Asian Studies Center, 1979.

_____. "The Mask Dance Theatre from Hwanghae Province," *Korea Journal* [Seoul: Korean National Commission for UNESCO, 1982], Vol. 22, No. 5.

_____. "A Mask-dance Theatre of Northeastern Korea," *Korea Journal* [Seoul: Korean National Commission for UNESCO, 1981], Vol. 21, No. 12.

_____. "A Mask-dance Theatre of Southeastern Korea," *Korea Journal* [Seoul: Korean National Commission for UNESCO, 1981], Vol. 21, No. 10.

_____. "On the Traditional Korean Puppet Theatre," *Korea Journal* [Seoul: Korean National Commission for UNESCO, 1981], Vol. 21, No. 1.

_____. "The Theatrical Presentation at the Hahoe Village Festival," *Korea Journal* [Seoul: Korean National Commission for UNESCO, 1981], Vol. 20, No. 12.

346 TRADITIONAL KOREAN THEATRE

_____. "The Traditional Korean Puppet Drama: A Mirror of Satire in the Feudal Society," *Korea Journal* [Seoul: Korean National Commission for UNESCO, 1981], Vol. 20, No. 10.

_____. "Yangju Pyŏlsandae: A Theatre of Traditional Korean Mask-dance Drama," *Korea Journal* [Seoul: Korean National Commission for UNESCO, 1981], Vol. 21, No. 4.

Cho Tong-il. *Han'guk kamyŏngŭk ŭi mi* [Aesthetics of Korean Mask-dance Drama]. Seoul: Han'guk Ilposa, 1975.

Cho Wŏn-kyŏng. "Narae wa kamyŏngŭk" [Narae and mask-dance drama], *Ha'klim* [Seoul: Yonsei University], No. 4.

Ch'oe Sang-su. "The Descent and Evolution of the Korean Puppet Play," *Chosen Gakuho* [Tenri, Japan: Tenri University, 1961].

_____. *Haesŏ kamyŏŏngŭk ŭi yŏngu* [A Study of the Mask-dance Theatre from the Western Korea]. Seoul: Taesŏng Munhwasa, 1967.

_____. *Han'guk inhyŏnggŭk ŭi yŏngu* [A Study of the Korean Puppet Plays]. Seoul: Koryŏ Sŏjŏk, 1964.

_____. "Han'guk kamyŏngŭk ŭi yŏngu" [A Study of Korean Mask-dance Drama], *Minjok munhwa yŏngu* [Seoul, 1965].

_____. "Sandae kamyŏngŭk ŭi yŏngu" [A Study of the Mask-dance Drama], *Ha'ksulji* [Seoul, 1964], Vol. 5.

Ch'ŏn Je-dong. "Tongrae yayu yŏngu" [A Study of Tongrae Mask-dance Drama], *Sŏnangdang* [Seoul, 1973], No. 4.

Han'guk munhwa yaesul jinhŭngwŏn. *Kkoktu kaksi norŭm* [Korean Puppet Drama]. Seoul: Han'guk Munhwa Yaesul Jinhŭngwŏn, 1979.

Im Tong-kwŏn. *Han'guk minsokha'k rongo* [A Study of Korean Folkways]. Seoul: Tongmyŏng Munhwasa, 1971.

Innami Takaichi. *Chosen no enggeki* [Korean Theatre]. Tokyo: Hokko Shobo, 1944.

Kang Kwŏn. "Han'guk inhyŏngŭk ŭi sogo" [A Paper on Korean Puppet Plays], *Kukŏ kukmunhak* [Seoul, 1957], No. 16.

Kardos, John. *An Outline History of Korean Drama.* New York: Long Island University Press, 1966.

Kim Chae-ch'ŏl. *Chosŏn yŏngŭksa* [History of Korean Theatre]. Seoul: Ha'kyaesa, 1939.

Kim Woo Ok. "P'ansori: An Indigenous Theatre of Korea." Unpublished Ph.D. Dissertation, New York University, 1980.

Kim Yang-gi. *Chosen no kamen* [Korean Masks], 3 volumes. Tokyo: Sinko Bijutsu Shuppan, 1967.

——. *Chosen no geino* [Korean Folk Arts]. Tokyo: Yiwazaki Bijutsu Shuppan, 1967.

Korean Center of the ITT. *The Korean Theatre: Past and Present.* Seoul: Korean Center of the International Theatre Institute, 1981.

Korean National Commission for UNESCO. *Traditional Performing Arts of Korea.* Seoul: Korean National Commission for UNESCO, 1975.

Kwŏn T'aek-mu. *Chosŏn mingangŭk* [People's Theatre of Korea]. P'yŏngyang: Chosŏn Munha'k Yaesul Ch'ongtongmeng, 1966.

Lee Meewon, "Kamyonguk: The Mask-Dance Theatre of Korea." Unpublished Ph.D. Dissertation, University of Pittsburgh, 1983.

Ministery of Culture and Information. *Masks of Korea.* Seoul: Ministery of Culture and Information, 1981.

Mitamura Senggyo. "Pak Ch'ŏmji no oshieru ninggyo seisaku kwatei" [Pak Ch'ŏmji: Puppet making], *Tabi to tensetsu* [December 1932].

Sim Wu-sŏng. *Han'guk ŭi minsokgŭk* [Korean Folk Theatre]. Seoul: Ch'angjak kwa Pip'yŏngsa , 1975.

—— and Kim Se-chung. *Introduction to Korean Folk Drama.* Trans. by Margaret M. Moore. Seoul: Korean Folk Theatre Troupe "Namsatang," 1970.

_____. *Namsatangp'ae yŏngu* [A Study of Namsatangp'ae]. Seoul: Tonghwa Ch'ulp'ansa , 1974.

Song Sŏk-ha. "Chosen no minsokugeki" [Korean Folk Theatre], *Minsokha'k* [Seoul, 1932], Vol. 4, No. 8.

_____. "Chosen no nynggyo shibai" [Korean Puppet Plays], *Minsok yaesul* [Seoul: 1929], Vol. 2, No. 4.

_____. "Ch'ŏyongmu, narae, sandaegŭk ŭi kwange rul nonham" [A Study on the Relationship among Ch'ŏyongmu, Narae, and Sandaegŭk], *Jindan ha'kpo*. [Seoul, 1934], Vol. 2.

_____. *Han'guk minsokko* [A Study of Korean Folk Arts]. Seoul: Ilsinsa, 1963.

_____. "Pak Ch'ŏmji ni daisuru susan kosatsu" [On Pak Ch'ŏmji], *Ninggyo shibai* [December 1933].

Yae Yong-hae. *In'gan munhwaje* [Human Cultural Properties]. Seoul: Omungak, 1963.

Yang Je-yŏn. "Sandaegŭkae ch'u hayu" [On Sandaegŭk], *Chungang taeha'kyo samshipjunyŏn kinyŏm nonmunjip*, 1955.

Yi Hye-gu. *Han'guk ŭmak nonch'ong* [Essays on Korean Music]. Seoul: Sumuntang, 1976.

_____. *Han'guk ŭmak yŏngu* [A Study of Korean Music]. Seoul: Han'guk Umak Yŏnguhoe , 1957.

Yi Tu-hyŏn. *Han'guk kamyŏngŭk* [Korean Mask-dance Drama]. Seoul: Munhwa Kongpobu , 1969.

_____. Chang Suggŭn, Yi Kwang-kyu. *Han'guk minsokhak gaesŏl* [An Introduction to Korean Folk Arts]. Seoul: Minjung Sŏkwan , 1975.

_____. Han'guk yŏnguksa [History of Korean Theatre]. Seoul: Minjung Sŏkwan, 1973.

_____. "Han'guk yŏngŭk kiwŏn ae daehan myŏtkaji koch'al" [A Study on the Beginning of Korean Theatre], *Yaesul nonmunjip* [Seoul, 1965], No. 4.

_____. "Sandae togamgŭk ŭi sŏngnip ae daehayo" [On the Beginning of Sandaegŭk], *Kukmunhak* [Seoul, 1969], No. 18.

Korean Dynasties

Puyŏ [roughly from the 13th century B.C. to the 3rd century A.D.]

Mahan [roughly from the 3rd century B.C. to the 3rd century A.D.]

Yae [roughly from the 3rd century B.C. to the 3rd century A.D.]

The Kingdom of Silla [57 B.C.-935 A.D.]

The Kingdom of Koguryŏ [37 B.C.-668 A.D.]

The Kingdom of Paekje [18 B.C.-660 A.D.]

The Koryŏ dynasty [918 A.D.-1392 A.D.]

The Chosŏn dynasty [1392 A.D.-1910 A.D.]

Glossary

Aeogae [or Ahyŏn] Sandae: An early group of mask-dance players.

Aigo is often used to express feelings. But *aigo,* with an exclamation mark, often means "woe is me" or "boo-hoo."

Aigu: See *aigo.*

Anaiyae or *anaya:* A kind of interjection which appears in mask-dance drama. This is often used as a cue for the next person.

The Analects of Confucius: The book which contains the characters and behaviors of Confucius and his disciples.

An Ch'o-mok: A legendary official of the local government of Pongsan who alledgedly made some changes in Pongsan *t'alch'um* such as the replacement of wooden masks with paper ones.

Bae-dance: A shamanistic dance.

Big wife: This commonly refers to a legal wife, while a little wife implies a concubine in Korean.

The Book of Ode: The book which contains the Chinese poems between the first century B.C. and the eighth century A.D.

The Canon of History: A book written by a Chinese scholar of the Sung dynasty.

Changgo: An hourglass-shaped drum.

Chara-dance: This dance is danced by Somu or Waejangnyŏ. The basic form of this dance: Bring the dancer's right hand to the front of her face, then she turns her hand upside down. Now she lifts her hand quickly and lowers it. This dance is often danced by a female to seduce a man.

Ching: A large brass gong.

Chisin-pabki: A festival for earthly deity.

Ch'ŏngun: A ceremony for heaven worship of Mahan, an ancient tribal state of Korea.

Ch'ŏnja: The Thousand Character Text, a primer of Chinese characters.

Chosŏn: Another name for Korea. This name was officially adopted in 1392 A.D.

The Chosŏn dynasty [1392 A.D.-1910 A.D.]: The most recent dynasty of Korea.

Chŏtdae: A transverse flute made of bamboo.

Ch'unhŭng-gye [the society of spring and prosperity]: An early performing group of T'ongyŏng *ogwangdae.*

Ch'un Hyang: A legendary virtuous heroine in *Ch'un Hyang Jŏn,* an ancient novel by an anonymous author.

Chusŏk: A rank of the membership in the Yangju Pyŏlsandae Group.

The eight beauties: They refer to the eight beautiful lovers of Yang So-yu, the main character, in *Kuunmong,* a novel by Kim Man-jung.

The four hermits: They refer to the four hermit scholars of the Han dynasty of China who went to the mountain to avoid the war.

Haegŭm: A two-stringed Korean fiddle.

Haetong: Another name for Korea in the old days.

Ha'k-dance: This dance which is also called Tongrae *ha'k*-dance is modeled on the walking pattern of a crane.

Hanyang: Today's Seoul, the capital of Korea.

Hato and *Naksŏ: Hato* refers to an ancient picture of China which depicts the scene of a flying horse from the Yellow River, while *Naksŏ* means the Eight Diagrams of Divination which are supposedly based on the patterns of a turtle's back.

Hojŏk: A Korean oboe. See also *nalnari* and *t'aep'yŏngso.*

Hong Tongji Norŭm: A common name for the traditional puppet play of Korea.

*Hŏrijapi-*dance: In this dance the dancer lifts his leg alternately stepping on the same spot as he keeps his hands on his waist. This dance is often danced in front of another dancer to tease him.

The Hour of the Ox: The second hour of the twelve hour day: between one and three o'clock in the morning.

The Hour of the Rat: The first hour of the twelve hour day: between eleven o'clock in the evening and one o'clock in the morning.

Hwarang: The flowers of youth in Silla dynasty. They excelled in beauty, bravery, and military arts. The word *hwarang* also often refers to shamans.

Kaepokch'ŏng: A temporary costume room for the performance of mask-dance drama.

*Kalchija-*dance: One of the basic dance forms of *kkaeki-*dance. This is generally danced by Nojang or Om. The dancer waves his sleeves this way and that way as he dances with tottering steps, moving his hips, and swaying his shoulders.

Kangnyŏng *t'alch'um:* A form of mask-dance theatre in Hwanghae-do Province.

Kilnori: A procession which usually takes place prior to the performance of Suyŏng *yayu* or Tongrae *yayu.*

Kimch'i: Pickles made of radish, cabbage, or cucumber spiced with pepper, garlic, onion, ginger, etc.

Kisaeng: Professional sing-song women.

*Kkach'igŏlŭm-*dance: A form of dance which is modeled on the walking pattern of a magpie. The dancer lifts his legs while stepping with long strides.

*Kkaeki-*dance: A basic form of dance. This dance uses every part of the dancer's body.

Kkaekkiri-dance: One of the basic dances of mask-dance drama. This dance is usually danced to the tune of a six-beat pattern. Throughout its long history the pattern of this dance has been changed a great deal. But the basic form of this dance resembles the movements of a harvesting farmer who kicks his feet while he waves his arms.

Kkoktu Kaksi: These words generally mean puppets or puppet plays, although their etymological meanings are not determined yet.

Kkoktu Kaksi norŭm: A common name for the traditional Korean puppet plays.

Kkwaenggwari: A small brass gong.

Kŏdurŭm-dance: A form of dance which requires the movements of the whole body.

Koguryŏ [37 B.C.-668 A.D.]: An early dynasty of Korea.

Kŏmmu: A sword dance based on the story of the legendary seventh son of King Tonghaeyong, Ch'ŏyong.

Kŏmun'go: A six-stringed Korean musical instrument.

Kopch'u-dance: A kind of improvisational dance to be followed when the dancer is in a state of ecstasy.

Kopsa-dance: See *Kopch'u*-dance.

Kopsawi-dance: This dance involves the dancer retreating backward from the musicians while waving his arms over his shoulders.

Koryŏ: [918 A.D.-1392 A.D.]: A dynasty of Korea.

Kubul-dance: A dance which is danced as the dancer lies down while bending his back.

Kŭmkang-san Mountain: A famous scenic mountain in Kangwŏn-do Province.

Kungdungi-dance: A dance which is danced as the dancer turns around.

Kurayae or *kuraeae:* An interjection.

Kutkŏri: A tune of music derived from the farmers' music from Kyŏnggi-do Province.

Kŭtŭrŭm-dance: The pattern of this dance is as follows. The dancer tilts his head to the left as he raises and waves his right hand. Now he raises his left hand as he tilts his head to the right. Then he bows to the deity of heaven, stooping gradually, while holding his hands together.

K'waeja: Armour.

Kwanchachaeposal: A Buddhist invocation.

Kwandŭngnori: A lantern festival in which the performance of mask-dance drama was a part of the program.

Magoja: An outer jacket.

Mahan: A tribal state which ruled the southwest of the Korean peninsula roughly from the fourth or the third century B.C. to the third century A.D.

Maiden Sim: A legendary virtuous maiden Sim Ch'ŏng in *Sim Ch'ŏng Jŏn,* an ancient novel by an anonymous author, who was sold for six hundred bushels of rice to be sacrificed in water. The rice was offered to Buddha in order to make her blind father see again.

Mal: A cylindrical wooden measuring utensil for grain. One *mal* is equal to approximately half a bushel.

Mŏngsŏkmari-dance: A dance of forward movement in which the dancer moves as though he is rolling a rug.

The Moral Rules to Govern the Five Human Relations: They include the relations between prince and minister, father and son, husband and wife, among brothers, and friends.

Muchari: The wandering Tartars who arrived in Korea probably in the tenth century A.D. They have been credited with bringing the art of puppetry to Korea.

Much'ŏn: A ceremony of heaven worship of Yae.

Mudong-dance: A dance which is danced by a boy on a man's shoulders.

Munha-sijung: A prime minister.

Muntungi-dance: An improvisational dance which appears in T'ongyŏng *ogwangdae* and Suyŏng *yayu.*

Mutdong-dance: The basic movement patterns of this dance are as follows. Bring the dancer's right hand to the front of his face. Then he turns his hand upside down. Now he lifts his hand quickly and lowers it.

Nalgaep'yŏgi-dance: This dance is done by opening and closing the dancer's arms while dancing.

Nalnari: See *hojŏk.*

Namsatang: A troup of song-and-dance people who have been credited with the preservation of the traditional Korean puppet theatre.

Namuamit'abul: A Buddhist invocation.

Narae: A ceremony which was performed to rid the palace of evil spirit.

Noryangjin Sandae: An early group of mask-dance players.

Ododogi T'aryŏng: A ballad tune which is from Cheju-do Island, a southernmost island of Korea.

Ogwangdae: A form of mask-dance drama in South Kyŏngsang-do Province, particularly in the towns of T'ongyŏng and Kosŏng.

Okkae-dance: A dance which is danced while the dancer moves his body, shaking his shoulders.

Olsigu chot'a: Very good! Excellent!

Ongdŭngi-dance: See *kungdungi*-dance.

Osang: A rank of the membership in the Yangju Pyŏlsandae Group.

Paekje [18 B.C.-660 A.D.]: An early kingdom of Korea.

Pak Ch'ŏmji norŭm: See *Kkoktu Kaksi norŭm.*

Pip'a: A loquat-shaped four-stringed musical instrument.

P'iri: A fife made with bamboo.

Ponsandae: This refers to the origial mask-dance drama from which the present-day Yangju *pyŏlsandae* [a different *sandae*] allegedly originated.

Puk: A barrel drum.

Pullim: A nonsense-syllable phrase which is often employed to cue the musicians as to what type of music is to be played for the dance.

Puyŏ: An ancient state which ruled present-day Manchuria from roughly the thirteenth century B.C. to the third century A.D.

Pyŏlsandae: A traditional form of mask-dance drama of Korea which is kept alive in the Yangju area in Kyŏnggi-do Province.

Pyŏlsin-kut: A theatrical performance which was held in Hahoe Village in North Kyŏngsang-do Province.

P'yŏnnom: A lowly person who engaged in the performance of entertainments such as mask-dance dramas in Korea.

Ransa-gye [the society of epidendrum]: An early performing group of T'ongyŏng *ogwangdae.*

A red gate: This refers to the red gate which was built in front of a house whose family was honored by an exemplary woman.

Ri: A unit of distance in Korea. Ten *ri*s make approximately four kilometers.

Rokpŏnri Sandae: An early group of mask-dance players.

Sa-daebu: A person of high rank.

Saemachi: A tune of music.

Saja-dance: A dance by lion in the traditional Korean mask-dance drama.

Sajikkol Ttakttagip'ae: An early group of mask-dance players.

Samhyŏn-yukkak: The six musical instruments which include two fifes, one transverse flute, one two-stringed Korean fiddle, one hourglass-shaped drum, and one barrel drum.

Samjin-samt'oe: Originally a form of military dance. Basically, this dance requires three steps forward and another three steps backward.

Sandaegŭk or *sandae:* A traditional Korean mask-dance drama.

Sandae-togam: The office of the Chosŏn dynasty [A Master of Revels] which controlled the performers and various entertainments. It was abolished in 1634.

Sapangch'igi-dance: A dance which requires the dancer to face all directions in turn.

Sasŏsamkyŏng: This includes *the Analects, Mencius, the Doctrines of the Means,* and *the Great Learning; the Books of Odes, the Canon of History,* and *the Book of Changes.*

The seven-stringed harp: A musical instrument which is basically the same as *kŏmun'go* except for the additional string.

Sibak: Tryouts for Suyŏng *yayu.*

Sijo: A short lyric poem developed in the late Koryŏ period.

Silla [57 B.C.-935 A.D.]: An early kingdom of Korea.

Sim Ch'ŏng: See Maiden Sim.

Sinawich'ŏng: A popular song in Cheju-do Island.

The Six Boards of the Government: These included the Civil Office Board, the Ceremonies Board, the Revenue Board, the Punishment Board, and the Public Work Board, and the War Board in the Chosŏn dynasty court.

Sŏnang-tang: The shrine of the village deity.

Sŏngjup'uli-dance: A dance for the guardian deity of the homesite.

Taegwangdae-p'ae Group: An early mask-dance group which existed in Pammŏri in Kyŏngsang-do Province.

T'aep'yŏngso: See *hojŏk.*

T'alch'um: A form of mask-dance theatre which is prevalent in the area of Hwanghae-do Province.

T'alje: A sacrificial ceremony for the masks to pray for a safe performance.

T'alnori: Mask paly.

T'alpo: A piece of cloth which is sewed along the edge of the mask. This cloth is used to cover the back of the wearer's head as well as to fasten the mask around the head.

Tano Festival: A important festival which is held on the fifth day of the fifth month according to the lunar calendar.

T'aryŏng: A popular ballad tune.

The Thousand Character Text: See *Ch'ŏnja.*

The Three Basic Human Relations: They include the relations between sovereign and subject, father and son, and husband and wife.

The Three Classics of Ancient China: They include *the Books of Odes, the Canon of History,* and *the Book of Changes.*

Three officers: They imply the three official ranks of the Koryŏ dynasty. They are *t'aeui, sato,* and *sakong.*

Todori: A musical tune.

T'oekaewŏn Sandae: An early group of mask-dance players.

Tŏgŏri: A jacket.

Tojung: The mask-dance drama guild which was comprised of three different types of membership: *yŏngwi, chusŏk,* and *osang.*

Tongji: An official rank of the Office of Chungch'uwŏn which administered the vigilance and military secrets of the Chosŏn court.

Tongmongsŏnsŭp: The book which contains the teachings of moral rules to govern the Five Human Relations and the abbreviated history of the relationship between Korea and China.

Top'o: A Korean full-dress outfit.

Tŏtpaegi-dance: A dance which is employed for the performance of T'ongyŏng *ogwangdae.* This dance was at one time characterized by brisk, vivacious qualities.

Tŭlnorŭm: See *yayu.*

T'ungsu: A Korean flute.

Turumagi: A Korean overcoat.

Uihŭng-gye [the society of justice and prosperity]: An early performing group of T'ongyŏng *ogwangdae.*

Yae: A tribal state which dominated the people on the eastern coast of the Korean peninsula approximately from the fourth or the third century B.C. to the third century A.D.

Yang: A monetary unit in the old society of Korea.

Yangban: An upper class or privileged class people in the old society of Korea. In the old society, civil officials were called *munban* and military officials, *muban.* The affix—*ban*—means "class," while *yang* implies both. *Yangban,* thus, suggests "both classes of aristocrats."

Yangsando: A popular folk song from Kyŏnggi-do Province.

Yayu or *yaryu:* A form of mask-dance drama in South Kyŏngsang-do Province, particularly in the area of Pusan.

Yŏdaji-dance: This dance requires forward movements. The dancer places both hands on the upper part of his body and, extending them forward, pantomimes the opening of his chest while his feet kick forward.

Yŏmbul: A tune of music which is like a Buddhist invocation.

Yŏndŭng: A lantern festival which was held on the eighth day of the fourth month, Buddha's birthday, according to the lunar calendar.

Yŏnggi: A rectangular banner which is carried during the procession prior to the performance of Yangju *pyŏlsandae.*

Yŏnggo: A festival which was held in the twelfth month according to the lunar calendar in Puyŏ.

Yŏngsanhoesang-gok: A music which consists of approximately ten different tunes.

Yŏngwi: A rank of the membership of the Yangju Pyŏlsandae Group.

yuhak: The study materials for the scholars without office.

Index